Women's Work, Men's Work

9801

Sex Segregation on the Job

Barbara F. Reskin and Heidi I. Hartmann, editors

Committee on Women's Employment and Related Social Issues
Commission on Behavioral and Social Sciences and Education
National Research Council

National Academy Press
Washington, D.C. 1986

NATIONAL ACADEMY PRESS   2101 CONSTITUTION AVENUE NW   WASHINGTON, DC 20418

NOTICE: The project that is the subject of this report was approved by the Governing Board of the National Research Council, whose members are drawn from the councils of the National Academy of Sciences, the National Academy of Engineering, and the Institute of Medicine. The members of the committee responsible for the report were chosen for their special competences and with regard for appropriate balance.

This report has been reviewed by a group other than the authors according to procedures approved by a Report Review Committee consisting of members of the National Academy of Sciences, the National Academy of Engineering, and the Institute of Medicine.

The National Research Council was established by the National Academy of Sciences in 1916 to associate the broad community of science and technology with the Academy's purposes of furthering knowledge and of advising the federal government. The Council operates in accordance with general policies determined by the Academy under the authority of its congressional charter of 1863, which establishes the Academy as a private, nonprofit, self-governing membership corporation. The Council has become the principal operating agency of both the National Academy of Sciences and the National Academy of Engineering in the conduct of their services to the government, the public, and the scientific and engineering communities. It is administered jointly by both Academies and the Institute of Medicine. The National Academy of Engineering and the Institute of Medicine were established in 1964 and 1970, respectively, under the charter of the National Academy of Sciences.

This project was sponsored by the Carnegie Corporation of New York, the U.S. Department of Labor, and the U.S. Department of Education.

Library of Congress Cataloging in Publication Data
Main entry under title:

Women's work, men's work.

  Bibliography: p.
  Includes index.
  1. Sex discrimination in employment—United States.
2. Women—Employment—United States.   3. Equal pay for
equal work—United States.   4. Sex discrimination—
Law and legislation—United States. I. Reskin,
Barbara F. II. Hartmann, Heidi I. III. National
Research Council (U.S.) Committee on Women's
Employment and Related Social Issues. IV. National
Research Council (U.S.) Commission on Behavioral and
Social Sciences and Education.
HD6060.5.U5W66   1985   331.1′33′0973   85-11541

ISBN 0-309-03429-9

Printed in the United States of America

Committee on Women's Employment and Related Social Issues

Contents

Tables and
Figures

FIGURES

Preface

The Committee on Women's Employment and Related Social Issues came into being at the initiative of the National Research Council. The impetus came from the Commission on Behavioral and Social Sciences and Education, whose members and staff believed that women's employment was in need of serious study. As the participation of women in the labor force has increased, indeed making it the majority experience, the continuing wage gap and other employment disparities between the sexes and the consequences of these facts for the families of female wage earners brought a sense of urgency to our mission.

The committee, 14 members representing a broad spectrum of social science disciplines and nonacademic sectors in American society, accepted the challenge to review and assess research on women's employment and related social issues; to consider how this research could be brought to bear on the policymaking process by informing relevant agencies; and to recommend and stimulate needed further research.

The first issue to engage our attention was job segregation by sex. Although women constitute a large and growing proportion of the labor force (43 percent in 1984), and their employment plays a vital role in our economy, they earn substantially less than men and typically work in a small number of occupations that predominantly employ women. The Carnegie Corporation of New York, the U.S. Department of Labor, and the U.S. Department of Education provided the resources for the committee to undertake this first phase of its work.

The committee had available to it a significant amount of work in this field, in particular the report *Women, Work, and Wages: Equal Pay for Jobs of Equal Value* on the subject of the comparable worth of jobs from the National Research Council's Committee on Occupational Classification and Analysis. Still more work was needed to pursue the issue of job segregation. The committee commissioned a number of papers—both literature reviews and original research—that were presented at a workshop in May 1982 on job segregation, involving several dozen scholars working in this field as well as the members of the committee. There was a lively and informed exchange on fundamental research questions, significantly strengthening the committee's competence in a number of areas pertinent to our inquiry. Many of the papers presented at the workshop and several others appear in *Sex Segregation in the Workplace: Trends, Explanations, Remedies,* the companion volume to this report; its table of contents appears in this volume as Appendix A.

Our report, the product of these collective labors, reviews evidence showing that employment segregation by sex has grave consequences for women, men, families, and society—but particularly for women. The dramatic increase of women in the work force and the numbers of persons dependent on their wages thus makes the issue of the negative consequences of occupational sex segregation both central and compelling. For these reasons, the committee believes that this and future studies directed toward a fuller understanding of sex segregation in employment and strategies for its amelioration are of high economic, social, and human priority.

The complexity and pervasiveness of the problem have made our report somewhat different from what some of us imagined it would be at the beginning. We have considerably extended our documentation of the extent and consequences of sex segregation on the job. Our recommendations are modest, yet that does not mean that they are easy to implement or unimportant. They represent the essential next steps for ameliorating the waste to the economy, the financial loss to women and their families, and the demeaning of the human spirit that comes from the rigidities inherent in segregating jobs by sex.

ALICE S. ILCHMAN, Chair
Committee on Women's Employment
and Related Social Issues

Acknowledgments

Several factors have made this report a difficult one to complete. First, the complexity of the subject and the variety of views by committee members about the most fruitful approaches to the topic placed burdens on both committee members and staff. Second, as the committee grew in knowledge about the subject, the members wanted to include more studies, more evidence, greater scope, more exhaustive explanations, and more far-reaching recommendations. Third, the process of distillation and refinement of all this material was a lengthy one. However, our splendid study directors, Barbara F. Reskin of the University of Illinois and subsequently Heidi I. Hartmann of the National Research Council, were more than equal to the task. As the editors of our report, they consistently added clarity and edited out confusion. They gave us what we asked for, even when they knew we would later tell them we did not want it after all. Our debt to them is boundless.

Barbara Reskin served as study director during the major part of the committee's work on this report. She ably organized our work, carried out extensive research, and prepared several drafts of the report. Marie A. Matthews served as staff assistant and aided our work in myriad administrative and substantive ways. Judith Stiehm, of the University of Southern California, was a visiting scholar during the early part of our work and participated in our discussions. In completing the report the efforts of Heidi Hartmann, now study director of the committee, Lucile A. DiGirolamo, staff assistant, and Rose S. Kaufman, administrative secretary for the Commission on Behavioral and Social Sciences and Education, were indispensable.

Many final details were attended to by Rita Conroy and Suzanne Donovan of the committee staff. Several student interns provided useful research assistance over the course of the project: Ben Warner, Oberlin College; Lori Froeling, University of Chicago Law School; Ray Nadolski, Indiana University; and June Lapidus, Uni-

xi

versity of Massachusetts, Amherst. We also owe a particular debt to the librarians at the National Academy of Sciences-National Academy of Engineering Library, who procured a multitude of materials for us through interlibrary loan and checked many references.

A report of this length and complexity requires and benefits from careful review by those not directly involved in its writing. Patricia A. Roos, of the State University of New York, Stony Brook, offered detailed comments on several drafts of the report. Andrea Beller, University of Illinois; Suzanne Bianchi, U.S. Bureau of the Census; Donna Lenhoff, Women's Legal Defense Fund; Sharon Harlan, State University of New York at Albany; and Margaret Marini, Vanderbilt University, all reviewed portions of the penultimate version for accuracy. James Smith, Rand Corporation, reviewed an earlier draft. Members of the commission and of the National Academy of Sciences' Report Review Committee carefully reviewed several drafts. Eugenia Grohman, associate director for reports, and Christine L. McShane, editor for the commission, greatly improved the clarity of our report. To all these dispassionate readers and reviewers we are extremely grateful. Their suggestions helped us to delineate and strengthen our arguments.

We thank those organizations whose financial support made this report possible: The Carnegie Corporation of New York, the U.S. Department of Education, and the U.S. Department of Labor. In addition, the program officers from these groups deserve special recognition for their substantive suggestions, their sustained interest, and their patience during the course of our work: Vivien Stewart at Carnegie, Paul Geib at the Department of Education, and Ellen Sehgal at the Department of Labor. I would also like to express deep appreciation to David A. Goslin, who as executive director of the Commission on Behavioral and Social Sciences and Education encouraged the initiative that brought us into being and consistently supported our efforts.

Throughout our work we have found our joint endeavor to be strenuous and gratifying. I believe the respect the members of the committee accorded to each other's differing concerns and contributions and their productive interaction were unusual. The tension of hard work was always alleviated by humor, genial colleagueship, and, above all, our common commitment to the importance of the task. It has been for us all a personal and professional pleasure to work together.

ALICE S. ILCHMAN, Chair
Committee on Women's Employment
and Related Social Issues

Women's Work, Men's Work

Sex Segregation on the Job

1 The Significance of Sex Segregation in the Workplace

Women are a large and growing portion of the labor force, and paid employment is clearly of growing importance in many women's lives. More women work outside the home and for longer portions of their lives than ever before. Women's employment, like men's, plays a vital role in our economy. Nearly 50 million women were in the labor force in 1984 and constituted 43 percent of the labor force. Of all women ages 18-64 in April 1984, 63 percent were in the labor force. Nearly all women work at some point in their lives, and the average woman today is expected to spend 12 more years working than did women in her mother's generation. In fact, the labor force participation patterns of women and men appear to be converging, as women's participation has increased and that of men has decreased somewhat in recent years.

Despite increasing similarities in women's and men's work lives, significant areas of difference remain—in particular, earnings and occupations. Although for most women as for most men, their earnings are crucial to their own support and to the financial support of their families, women's earnings are substantially less than those of men. For as long as data have been available for the United States, women's average earnings have been about 60 percent of men's for full-time, year-round workers. Women also often work in different kinds of jobs. The majority of women work in a small number of occupations, particularly in occupations in which the workers are predominantly women. Men work primarily in occupations that are predominantly male, although the number of occupations is larger.

The concentration of women and men in different jobs that are predominantly of a single sex has been labeled sex segregation in the labor market. The overall degree of sex segregation has been a remarkably stable phenomenon; it has not changed much since at least 1900. This stability is surprising in light of the enormous changes that have taken place in the structure of the economy: the turnover in occupations as obsolete occupations disappear and new ones develop; the narrowing of educational differentials between men and women, particularly since World War II; and, most recently, the increasing similarity in the work patterns of men and women over their lifetimes. It is this stable phenomenon—the concentration

1

of men and women in different jobs—that is the subject of our report.

In the past women have not had equal opportunity in the labor market, and they have faced discrimination in hiring, pay, and advancement. To some extent the differences in women's and men's earnings and in the occupations they hold reflect that past discrimination; to some extent they reflect current discrimination; and to some extent they reflect a host of other factors, such as differences between women and men in their preferences, attitudes, values, experience, education, training, and so on. And it is highly likely that all these factors are interrelated.

In this report we attempt to unravel the various causes of sex segregation in the workplace, to understand its extent, future direction, and remarkable persistence. To the extent that it reflects the preferences, values, and attitudes of women themselves, it may not be an appropriate object of public concern. But to the extent that it reflects restrictions on women's choices that result from discriminatory practices in the labor market or various other barriers, it is a matter of grave public concern. Women have the right to participate in the labor market, as they choose, without social or legal coercion and without unfair treatment in pay or other working conditions. Equal employment opportunity is an established goal of national policy: it contributes not only to the better utilization of the country's human resources and to economic growth, but also to the full participation of all members of society in the nation's political, social, and economic life.

In this report we seek to deepen understanding of the processes that give rise to sex segregation in the workplace, to assess the aspects of sex segregation that are harmful, and to offer guidance on how to ameliorate those aspects. Our method has been to gather and assess the available research literature on these issues. Any literature review is necessarily selective, and ours is no exception. We have tried to identify significant research from a variety of perspectives, however, and to assess the major alternative explanations that have been offered for the persistence of job segregation.

In the remainder of this chapter we provide further description of the situation of women in the labor market; discuss the concepts of segregation in general and sex segregation in the workplace; and briefly review the literature on the consequences of the latter. We find that those consequences are several and significant and we believe they warrant the committee's effort to better understand sex segregation in the workplace and the ways in which it can be affected.

In subsequent chapters, we look at the recent past and likely future of sex segregation, identify its causes, and assess a variety of interventions that have been implemented to reduce segregation. In Chapter 2, in order to better understand what it is that requires explanation, we review estimates of the current extent of segregation and identify the changes that have occurred over the past decade among certain groups of women and within certain occupations. We also present projections of the extent of segregation for the rest of this decade. In Chapter 3 we review the evidence for the most important explanations of labor market segregation, assess their relative strengths, and give our view of the most likely cause of continued segregation. In Chapter 4 we assess the evidence regarding the effectiveness of federal regulations and legislation prohibiting discrimination and mandating affirmative action in employment, employment training, vocational education, and general education. Finally, in Chapter 5 we present a summary of our findings and make recommendations for strategies to reduce job segregation by sex and increase equal opportunity in the workplace.

WOMEN IN THE LABOR MARKET

Women's Participation in the Labor Force

The majority of adult women are in the labor force, and their rate of participation has been steadily increasing throughout the century (Waite, 1981). In contrast, men's labor force participation rates have been slowly declining. In 1950, 86.4 percent of men ages 16 and over were in the labor force; by 1984 the percentage had dropped to 76.4 (U.S. Department of Labor, Bureau of Labor Statistics, 1985a). The rate of increase for women has been substantial since the 1950s and has not yet tapered off, as can be seen in Figure 1-1. Between 1950 and 1984 the labor force participation rate of women ages 16 and over increased from 33.9 to 53.6 percent. Labor force participation rates for women vary by age, marital status, and race and ethnicity. And more women work at some time during the year than are in the labor force at any one time. The 1982 Work Experience Survey of the Current Population Survey indicated that 58 percent of women ages 16 and over worked some time during 1981 (U.S. Department of Labor,

Women's Bureau, 1983). Annual averages for 1984 indicate that 53.8 percent of all women were in the labor force, with black women most likely to be in the labor force (55.5 percent), white women next most likely (53.4 percent), followed by Hispanic women (49.8 percent; U.S. Department of Labor, Bureau of Labor Statistics, 1985b:Table 2). Women's increasing rates of labor force participation are reflected in their growing work-life expectancies. In 1979-1980 a 20-year-old woman could expect to work 27.2 years, compared with 14.5 years in 1950; the comparable estimate for a 20-year-old man in 1979-1980 was 36.8 years (S. Smith, 1985).[1] Of all women in the labor force, seven-tenths hold full-time jobs.

The disparity between the labor force participation rates of married and unmarried women has declined, as the labor force participation rates of married women have increased rapidly. In 1984, 63.3 percent of never-married women age 16 and over were in the labor force, compared with 52.8 percent of married women with husbands present, 61.1 percent of married women with husbands absent, and 74.3 percent of divorced women. For younger married women the rates are quite high. Increased rates of employment by married women with children have contributed substantially to the growth in women's labor force participation. In 1950 about 12 percent of women with a child under 6 years old were in the labor force; in 1980 the ratio was 52.1 percent (Hayghe, 1984).

Figure 1-2 illustrates the historical change in the age-specific labor force participation rates for women who were born between 1926 and 1960. In 1980, for the first time, the labor force participation rate did not decline for women ages 25-29, a peak childbearing group. In fact, the job-leaving rates

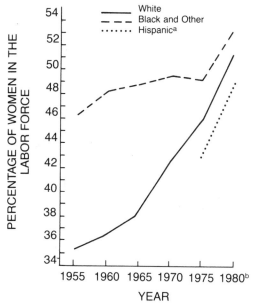

ᵃData for Hispanics were not available until 1973.
ᵇ1980 data are for civilian women age 20 and over.

FIGURE 1-1   Labor force participation rates of women ages 16 and over, based on annual averages for selected years between 1955 and 1980. SOURCES: U.S. Department of Labor, Bureau of Labor Statistics (1980: Tables 65 and 66; 1981c:Table 44).

[1] These estimates are based on age-specific probabilities of movement into and out of the labor force (S. Smith, 1982:16-17).

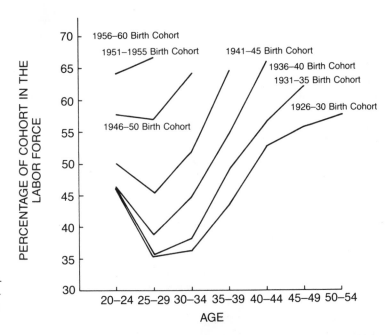

FIGURE 1-2 Women's age-specific labor force participation rates by birth cohort. SOURCE: Hartmann and Reskin (1983).

for women at all ages under 55 dropped between 1970 and 1977 (S. Smith, 1982).

Women's Earnings

In 1981 the median earnings of women who worked full time year-round were $12,001, or 59 percent of what men earned, $20,260. For workers over age 18, the earnings ratio for white women and men was 60 percent; for black women and men, 76 percent; and for Hispanic women and men, 73 percent. The ratio of black women's earnings to those of white men was 54 percent; of Hispanic women's earnings to those of white men, 52 percent (U.S. Department of Labor, Women's Bureau, 1983).

Most women who work contribute substantially to or fully support themselves and their dependents. In 1981, about one out of five women workers maintained families on their own. U.S. Department of Commerce data as of March 1984 indicate that one-sixth of all U.S. families (about 9.9 million) were maintained by women with no husband present; they were never married, separated, divorced, or widowed (U.S. Department

of Commerce, Bureau of the Census, 1984b). Most of these families depend principally on the earnings of women. The incomes of married women living with their husbands are also important for their families' economic well-being. In general, the lower a husband's income, the more likely it is that his wife works (Sweet, 1973). The earnings of women who are married are especially likely to be important to families when the husbands' earnings are low. (insert 6)

In 1981, the median percentage of family income contributed by married women (with husbands present) was 26.7. The percentage increases to 69 percent if annual family income is less than $10,000; 56 percent if it is between $10,000 and $14,999; and 46.6 percent if it is between $15,000 and $19,000 (U.S. Department of Labor, Women's Bureau, 1983). Minority women make larger economic contributions to their families than white women. In 1980, minority women's incomes represented one-third of their family income, compared with one-quarter for white women (personal communication, Harriet Harper, Women's Bureau, U.S. Department of Labor, 1982). And wives' earnings take on particular importance during periods of high unemployment.

In sum, even though women earn substantially less than men, their earnings are a significant source of support for themselves and their families. Women are more likely than ever to be in the labor force, and they can expect to spend a substantial portion of their adult lives doing paid work. For these reasons the consequences of sex segregation are significant and enduring.

SEX SEGREGATION IN
THE WORKPLACE

The term *segregation* has been used to connote many different phenomena. It has often been used to describe situations involving the physical and social separation of members of different socially identifiable groups, particularly the isolation of a minority group from the majority group. Its Latin roots are *se*, meaning apart, and *grex*, meaning flock. For example, apartheid in South Africa today—like past racial segregation in the southern United States—involves the physical separation of the races in neighborhoods, schools, and public accommodations, often by law and sometimes by social custom. Even when the races are in close proximity, as they often are in employment situations, social norms enforce social distance. When segregation is the result of this type of legal and social restriction, it usually connotes the inferiority of the minority group and can be an important means of maintaining its minority status.

Segregation can also be a voluntary matter. For example, many neighborhoods in cities and regions of the country that are ethnically identified are so primarily as a matter of choice and not compulsion, though compulsion and limited opportunities may have played some role in their initial establishment. Many people like to live among their kin or coreligionists and close to churches, stores, and schools that cater to their ethnic group. Others do not. Observed patterns of segregation may also be partly coerced and partly voluntary, brought about by a combination of social pressure, lack of knowledge of alternatives, socialization, and choice.

Sex segregation in the workplace, which takes both physical and social forms, is almost certainly the result of both restriction and choice, although we have come to the considered conclusion, based on the evidence we have reviewed (which is presented in the following chapters), that restriction plays the more important role. The measure of sex segregation in employment most commonly used in this report, and in other social science research, measures the degree of segregation against a standard of total integration. The index of dissimilarity, often called the segregation index, measures the degree to which the distributions of the groups being studied (women and men here) across a set of categories (occupations or jobs here) differ from each other.[2] Such a measure implies a goal of complete integration, with the proportions of women and men within every occupation identical to their representation in the labor force as a whole. There is no reason to believe, however, that if all barriers to the free and informed exercise of choice by women in the labor market were removed, the distributions of women and men across all occupations would be identical. They might be, but they might equally well not be. Some differences between women and men are deeply rooted in culture and may last for decades; some, though perhaps not many besides the most obvious, are rooted in biology and may last

---

[2] The index of segregation, I.S., is defined as

$$\text{I.S.} = \frac{1}{2} \sum_{i=1}^{n} | x_i - y_i |$$

where x_i = the percentage of one group (e.g., women) in the ith category of a classification (e.g., a particular occupation), and y_i = the percentage of the other group (e.g., men) in that same category (Duncan and Duncan, 1955).

TABLE 1-1 Occupational Distribution Over Major Occupational Groups by Race and Sex, 1984

	Men			Women			Percentage Female
	Total	White	Black	Total	White	Black	
Managerial and professional specialty	24.6	25.7	12.3	22.5	23.3	15.8	41.6
Executive, administrative, and managerial	13.0	13.7	6.3	8.5	8.9	5.2	33.6
Professional specialty	11.6	12.0	6.1	14.0	14.4	10.6	48.5
Technical, sales, and administrative support	19.6	20.0	15.0	45.6	46.9	36.5	64.4
Technicians and related support	2.8	2.8	1.9	3.3	3.3	3.3	48.1
Sales occupations	11.1	11.8	4.6	13.1	13.9	7.8	47.9
Administrative support, including clerical	5.7	5.4	8.5	29.1	29.8	25.3	79.9
Service occupations	9.4	8.4	18.4	18.7	17.2	30.7	60.8
Private household	.1	.1	.1	2.1	1.6	5.9	96.2
Protective service	2.5	2.3	4.1	.5	.4	.8	12.9
Service, except private household and protective	6.8	6.0	14.2	16.2	15.2	24.0	64.8
Precision production, craft, and repair	20.2	20.8	15.8	2.4	2.4	2.6	8.5
Operators, fabricators, and laborers	21.1	20.0	33.6	9.6	8.9	13.9	26.0
Machine operators, assemblers, and inspectors	8.0	7.6	11.4	7.1	6.5	11.0	41.1
Transportation and material moving occupations	6.9	6.6	11.2	.8	.8	1.0	8.3
Handlers, equipment cleaners, helpers, and laborers	6.2	5.8	11.0	1.6	1.6	1.8	16.6
Farming, forestry, and fishing	5.1	5.2	4.9	1.2	1.3	.5	15.6
Total	100.0	100.0	100.0	100.0	100.0	100.0	43.7
N (thousands)	(59,091)	(52,462)	(5,124)	(45,915)	(39,659)	(4,995)	

SOURCE: U.S. Department of Labor, Bureau of Labor Statistics (1985a:Tables 21 and 23).

even longer. The appropriate policy goal is not therefore the complete elimination of segregation as measured by the index of dissimilarity, but rather the elimination of barriers to women's full exercise of their employment rights. We have not estimated how much sex segregation would be reduced if equality of opportunity were achieved or how much would remain out of choice, but we believe, on the basis of our review of the evidence, that the reduction would be substantial.

The segregation of the sexes is a basic feature of the world of work. The strikingly different distributions of women and men across occupations can be seen in the distribution of the sexes across major occupational categories. Table 1-1 provides comparisons for black and white women and men across 13 broad occupational categories in 1984. When one looks at detailed occupational categories, sex segregation is still clearer. In 1980 among 503 occupational categories, the most detailed level at which census data is tabulated, workers in 187 categories were at least 90 percent members of one sex; 275 occupations were composed of at least 80 percent female or male workers (computed from U.S. Department of Commerce, Bureau of the Census, 1983b:Table 1). Almost half of all employed women work in occupations that are at least 80 percent female (Rytina, 1981), which include librarians, health technicians, secretaries and typists, data-entry keyers, nurses, bank tellers and bookkeepers, telephone operators, sewers and stitchers, child care workers, and dental assistants (U.S. Department of Commerce, Bureau of the Census, 1983b). The occupation of most women not in the labor force, homemaker, is one of the most segregated occupations. Slightly over half of all men work in occupations that are at least 80 percent male. Among these 229 predominantly male occupations are engineers, architects, natural scientists, physicians and dentists, lawyers, nonretail sales representatives, mail carriers, electrical and elec-

tronic equipment repairers, construction workers, machinists, motor vehicle operators, and freight, stock, and material handlers.

There is some division of labor by sex in most societies (Burton et al., 1977). Across all societies, moreover, there is a pattern to this division of labor. Women generally do those tasks that are compatible with child care—tasks that are not dangerous, do not take them far from home, do not require close attention, and are readily interrupted (J. Brown, 1970). As consistent as this pattern is, it is not unmodifiable. In societies in which women must do work incompatible with breast-feeding, for example, babies are started on breast milk substitutes earlier (Nerlove, 1974); where women's work requires them to travel distances, as they do to gather vegetable food in hunting/gathering economies, or to participate in long-distance trading networks, they leave children with substitute caretakers. The only universal with no exception seems to be that everywhere, it is primarily women who mother.

Within the limits of female-assigned child care and sexual dimorphism in strength and energy, there is a great deal of variability across societies as to which gender is expected to do what job, even in the West. For example, dentists are primarily female in Denmark, Poland, and the Soviet Union, in contrast with the United States, where dentistry is 93 percent male (computed from U.S. Department of Commerce, Bureau of the Census, 1983b:Table 1). In the Soviet Union, both physicians and street cleaners are usually female (Lapidus, 1978). Beyond industrial societies, there is yet more variability. Household servants, predominantly female in the West, are typically male in India (Blumberg, 1978), and construction labor is shared by the sexes (Boserup, 1970). West African women engage in highly organized long-distance trading that is elsewhere an exclusively male occupation (Hammond and Jablow, 1976); and, as do women in other horticultural economies, they hoe the fields. In hunting/gathering societies, women commonly do virtually all the gathering of vegetable food, which is the dominant source of subsistence in half the known ethnographic cases (Friedl, 1975:13). This degree of cross-societal variation in the sex division of labor, and even reversal of what is traditionally considered men's or women's work from society to society, suggests that most occupational sex typing is highly influenced by cultural constructions of gender. The degree of cross-national agreement that is also observed suggests that many cultural values are shared.

The division of labor and sex segregation in work changes with time. Historical evidence shows change in the sex typing of many specific occupations (Davies, 1975; Tyack and Strober, 1981; Kessler-Harris, 1982). Since World War II several occupations in the United States have changed sharply in their sex composition; for example, bank teller, insurance adjuster, and real estate agent have all changed from male to female. Sex segregation in employment, however, seems to be deeply ingrained in cultural beliefs and well established in the organization of work. Occupations change their sex typing, but segregation remains. The aggregate amount of sex segregation across occupations, as measured by the index of dissimilarity, has been virtually stable since 1900 until 1970.

Sex segregation in the workplace takes many forms. In addition to the most obvious form, occupational segregation, men and women in the same occupation often work in different industries or for different employers.[3] Establishment and industry segregation are common, and they occur even when occupations are integrated. For example, the occupation waiter includes men and women, but many restaurants hire all

men or all women. Industries have also been found to be more segregated than would be expected from their occupational mix, indicating additional segregation beyond that measured by occupational segregation alone. For example, clerical workers, a large and diverse category that is approximately two-thirds female, are more likely to be male in some industries than in others. Because the sex composition of occupations differs in different establishments and industries, aggregate measures of occupational segregation underestimate the degree of segregation in the world of work.

Aggregate measures of occupational segregation underestimate segregation for another reason as well. Occupational categories are themselves aggregates, composed of smaller categories, some of which may be even more segregated. For example, women were 59 percent of all workers in service occupations in 1980, but they made up 95 percent of all private household workers and 12 percent of all workers in protective service occupations, both of which were subcategories of service occupations (computed from U.S. Department of Commerce, Bureau of the Census, 1983b:Table 1). Calculations based on even the most detailed census occupational classification (the three-digit level) underestimate the amount of segregation because each category sometimes combines occupations with widely different sex ratios.[4] The *Dictionary of Occupational Titles* (U.S. Department of Labor, 1977) lists

---

[3] See Blau (1977) for a thorough discussion of different types of sex segregation in employment.

[4] The Census Bureau categorizes occupations at varying levels of detail. The broadest classification includes 13 major categories (see Table 1-1), recently modified from 11 (see Rytina and Bianchi, 1984, and Bianchi and Rytina, 1984, for a discussion of comparability with earlier census years). A somewhat more detailed classification, sometimes referred to as the two-digit Census Bureau categories, included 44 occupations in 1970. The classification referred to as detailed or three-digit included 441 occupations in 1970 and 503 in 1980. When we refer in the text to "detailed census occupational categories" or "three-digit census occupations" we mean this refined classification.

over 12,000 unique job titles, which represent an aggregation of perhaps 1 million jobs done by 115 million members of the labor force (Miller et al., 1980). Thus, even the 500 detailed occupations classified in the census or the Current Population Survey involve substantial aggregation.

Because measures of occupational segregation underestimate segregation in work, it would be very desirable to have data for jobs, rather than occupations, in order to be able to assess the extent of and changes in segregation accurately. A job can be defined as a particular task within a particular work group in a particular company or establishment performed by one or more individuals (Bridges and Berk, 1978). Examples are check-out clerk at the Indianapolis Speedway K-Mart store or upholsterer at the Boeing plant in Renton, Washington.

Distinguishing between job segregation and occupational segregation is critical for reasons other than the tendency of occupationally based measures to underestimate the true amount of segregation. Most important, the processes that contribute to occupational segregation may differ from those that produce job segregation. Theories that focus on workers' choices are concerned with occupational outcomes, but hiring decisions occur at the establishment level and must be explained with data on men's and women's access to jobs. In addition, focusing on occupational segregation may imply different remedies than those suggested by an emphasis on jobs. These differences and the committee's ultimate concern with the total amount of sex segregation in the workplace dictate focusing on jobs when the data permit. Often, however, constraints imposed by available data or research limit our focus to occupations.

THE CONSEQUENCES OF SEX SEGREGATION IN EMPLOYMENT

The consequences of sex segregation in the workplace extend beyond the symbolic fact of its existence. Society, the economy, and individuals all lose when workers are allocated to jobs on the basis of characteristics such as gender, race, or age rather than on their ability to perform the work. Segregation necessarily restricts individuals' chances for self-fulfillment. When jobs are classified as men's work or women's work, neither men nor women are free to do the jobs that might best suit them. Because it has made substantial investments in developing its members' abilities, society as well as its individual members lose when workers are assigned to jobs on the basis of their gender rather than their talents. To the extent that involuntary job segregation restricts employment opportunities for otherwise qualified workers, it represents the failure of the economy to make use of the available labor supply most appropriately. The misallocation of human resources in the work force necessarily depresses national productivity, and the loss in productivity that job segregation entails will increase if it persists at current levels at the same time that more women attain advanced education and their expected work life increases. To the extent that declines in the sizes of adolescent and young adult cohorts (U.S. Department of Commerce, 1981) and the numbers of high school graduates (U.S. Department of Education, 1981) reduce the traditional supply of new workers for skilled and technical jobs, labor shortages may well occur unless these jobs are open to talented individuals irrespective of their gender.

Although gender affects what jobs are available to persons of both sexes, segregation is more harmful to women primarily because the occupations held predominantly by women are less desirable on various dimensions than those held predominantly by men. In particular, segregation contributes to women's lower wages. Female-dominated occupations also provide less on-the-job training and fewer opportunities for mobility. These and other consequences of sex-segregated work careers also follow women into retirement. Because wage consequences are so important, we enumerate several ways in which wages are affected by job segregation; we then take up other consequences.

Wage Consequences

Occupational sex segregation, sex segregation across firms, and job segregation within firms all reduce women's earnings relative to men's.

Occupational Segregation and Wage Disparity

In the United States, full-time, year-round white female workers on the average earn approximately 60 percent as much as full-time, year-round white male workers, a ratio that has been almost constant for at least the last 25 years. According to the report of the National Research Council's Committee on Occupational Classification and Analysis (Treiman and Hartmann, 1981), a substantial part of this overall earnings differential can be attributed to the low wages women earn in predominantly female occupations. For 499 detailed occupational categories in the 1970 census classification, the correlation between median annual wage and salary earnings (adjusted for time spent working) and the percentage female among occupational incumbents is −.45: the higher the percentage female, the less an occupation paid. Employment in a female-dominated occupation depressed wages of workers of both sexes; each additional percentage point female in an occupation was associated with $42 less in median annual earnings. The expected median wage in an occupation filled exclusively by women was $3,946, less than half the $8,185 median in exclusively male occupations (Treiman and Hartmann, 1981). Differences in occupational characteristics (as measured by the *Dictionary of Occupational Titles*) accounted for about 35 percent of the gross association with percentage female. The report also estimated the proportion of the gross male-female earnings differential that could be attributed to sex segregation among detailed occupations. The analysis indicated that the segregation of men and women into different occupations accounts for about 35-40 percent of the sex difference in average earnings. The remainder is due to the fact that within each detailed occupation men tend to earn more than women. These and other data led that committee to the conclusion that occupational segregation has a substantial effect on women's earnings and that, in particular, the wages of female-dominated occupations are depressed relative to what they would be in the absence of segregation.

Although the 1980 census data have not yet been analyzed to assess whether the effect of occupational segregation on earnings differentials has changed since 1970 (the year to which the Committee on Occupational Classification and Analysis's estimates pertain), a crude assessment is possible through the use of published data from the Current Population Survey (CPS). The main deficiency of the CPS data is that the relatively smaller sample size requires considerable aggregation of occupational categories. From 1970 through 1974, data on the mean earnings of full-time, year-round workers by sex are presented for 24 occupational categories; in 1975 the number of categories was expanded to 51. Table 1-2 compares 1970 with 1979 data using the 24-category classification and 1975 with 1979 data using the 51-category classification. Probably because of the highly aggregated classifications, only 22 percent of the gender difference in earnings in 1970 can be attributed to occupational segregation, compared with the figure of 35-40 percent based on the 499 categories of the 1970 census. The comparison across years suggests a slight decrease in the effect of segregation between 1970 and 1979. In 1970 the average earnings of women would have been 90 percent of those of men had women earned as much as men in the same occupation; by 1979 this had increased to 92 percent. The 1975-1979 comparison based on

TABLE 1-2   Decomposition of Earnings Differentials Between Men and Women Into Within-Occupation and Between-Occupation Components, for Full-Time Year-Round Workers in Selected Years, 1970-1979

	24-Category Classification[a]		51-Category Classification[a]	
	1970	1979[b]	1975	1979
Earnings differentials				
Mean earnings of men	$9,918	$19,109	$14,029	$19,109
Expected mean earnings of women if they earned the male average in each occupation[c]	8,975	17,583	12,550	17,230
Mean earnings of women	5,675	10,876	7,930	10,876
Earnings differentials expressed as a percentage of male earnings				
Mean earnings of men	100%	100%	100%	100%
Expected mean earnings of women	90	92	89	90
Mean earnings of women	57	57	57	57
Decomposition of earnings differentials				
Percent due to occupational segregation	22	18	24	23
Percent due to within-occupation pay differences	78	82	76	77

[a] Each classification was based on the most disaggregated set of categories available.

[b] The 51-category 1979 classification was aggregated to 24 categories to match the 1970 classification by taking a weighted average of the mean earnings of men or women in each of the component categories, weighted by the number of men in each component category. The number of women in the aggregated category is just the sum of the number of women in each component category.

[c] The means for male workers had to be estimated for three categories (secretaries and stenographers, typists, and private household workers, aggregated to two in the 24-category classification) for which there were too few incumbents for the CPS to be willing to report a mean. For 1979 and for the first two categories in 1975, means were calculated directly from the published distribution by scoring the income categories at their midpoint. In the case of secretaries and stenographers in 1979, an outlier—an estimated 2000 cases with annual earnings of $60,000-$75,000—was omitted from the computation. For 1970, and for private household workers in 1975, means were estimated by assuming that the category mean to be estimated bore the same ratio to the mean earnings of the total male labor force as it did in 1979.

SOURCE: Current Population Reports, Series P-60: No. 80, Table 55; No. 105, Table 52; No. 129, Table 58.

51 occupational categories yields similar results although the changes are not as large, perhaps because of the shorter time period.

Job Segregation and Wage Disparity

Sex segregation *within* occupations further contributes to the earnings gap. As we noted above, sex segregation occurs within occupations because men and women who perform the same occupation may be segregated by firm or enterprise, and because within firms men and women in the same occupation may do different jobs. That ex- pensive restaurants almost always employ men to wait on tables, while inexpensive restaurants and coffee shops are much more likely to hire women, is an example of between-firm segregation. Since expensive establishments pay better and provide larger tips, male waiters earn more than female waiters. An example of within-firm segregation contributing to the income gap is the assignment of men to higher-paid night work.

The evidence regarding the consequences of job segregation for earnings differentials is sparse. The small number of studies must be regarded as suggestive rather than definitive, especially since none estimates the proportion of the earnings differential within occupations that can be attributed to job segregation.

Segregation Across Firms   Although no economy-wide quantitative estimates of the effect on earnings differences of the segregation of men and women in the same occupation in different firms are available, examples suggest that such segregation is an important source of the wage gap. Several studies show that within specific occupations women and men tend to be employed in different establishments, with better-paying firms disproportionately employing men. Blau (1977) has shown that within sex-integrated occupations, such as accounting clerk, men tend to earn more than women because they tend to work in higher-paying firms. She found that more of the male-female wage differential within each occupation was between rather than within firms. That is, men were overrepresented in higher-paying firms, which hired fewer women across all the occupations she studied. Buckley (1971) and McNulty (1967) found similar results for clerical jobs, as did Talbert and Bose (1977) for retail clerks, Allison (1976) for beauty salon operators, and Johnson and Stafford (1974) and Darland et al. (1974) for college and university faculty members. Other evidence of the importance of this type of segregation for earnings comes from industry data; industries provide a crude proxy for firm differences. Calculations by Malveaux (1982a) show that industrial sex segregation accounted for 13.5-27.5 percent of the wage gap within broad (one-digit) occupational categories when industrial distribution was also controlled at the one-digit level.

Segregation Within Firms   It is not possible to estimate the overall wage effect of the segregation of men and women into different jobs within the same occupation and firm, but some evidence suggests that this type of segregation also contributes to earnings

differences because men and women filling the same occupation within firms are assigned different specific jobs at different pay rates. The most direct evidence comes from the work of Bridges and Berk (1978), who found that white-collar female-dominated jobs in Chicago financial firms paid less largely because they did not compensate incumbents' qualifications and job characteristics at the same rate as did male-dominated jobs. Almost three-quarters of the $2,250 annual wage disparity was due to differential payment for qualifications and job characteristics, while differences in the mean qualifications of workers in male- and female-dominated jobs accounted for a little more than $300 of the wage gap. Similarly, Talbert and Bose (1977) found that male retail sales clerks were more likely to be assigned to "big-ticket" departments of stores (e.g., furniture, large appliances) and hence earned more on average than female clerks. (Interestingly, however, there was a strong interaction between gender and department in determining earnings; department mattered more for men than for women, so that the earnings gap between the sexes was greater in the big-ticket departments.)

Using 1960 data, Halaby (1979b) found that female managers in a large public utility firm earned on average 64 percent as much as male managers. Only 9.7 percent of the earnings gap could be explained by differences in levels of education, seniority, and previous work experience, while 75.3 percent was explained by the difference in returns to human capital for men and women. In analyzing the source of differential returns to human capital, Halaby found that men and women were largely segregated into different managerial "ranks." While more than 94 percent of women were in ranks V and VI (the lowest ranks), more than 85 percent of men were in rank IV or above. When rank was entered as an explanatory variable, the difference in distribution of men and women across ranks alone explained 65 percent of the wage gap, reducing the effect of differences in human capital levels and returns to 27.3 percent. Halaby concludes that rank segregation severely restricts women from transforming their stocks of human capital into higher salaries. Between 45 and 55 percent of the men's earnings advantage among professional employees in a large research organization that Malkiel and Malkiel (1973) studied could be attributed to the greater tendency for men to be assigned or promoted to higher rank, even if attributes thought to be related to productivity (post-high-school education, college field of study, job-related labor market experience, rate of absenteeism, and personal productivity as measured by number of publications) are controlled for. The remainder of the earnings gap stemmed from sex differences in these variables. An important mechanism in producing wage differences is the propensity of firms to assign men initially to higher ranks (Cabral et al., 1981; Newman and Wilson, 1981; Harlan and O'-Farrell, 1982) or to promote them more rapidly than similarly qualified women (Committee on the Education and Employment of Women in Science and Engineering, 1983). Judging from the available evidence, within-firm pay differences for workers in the same occupation appear mainly to reflect differences in rank.

Progress in studying the effect of job segregation on earnings differentials will depend on the availability of much more detailed data than is available from the census. Such data are nearly always limited to studies of single industries or single enterprises. Despite their limited generalizability to the labor force as a whole, studies of industries and enterprises that make use of very detailed job classifications should be encouraged because they illuminate the processes of segregation.

Other Consequences of Sex Segregation

Wages are but one aspect of the negative consequences for women of sex segregation in the labor market. Job segregation also contributes to sex differences in retirement income, susceptibility to unemployment, on-the-job training, occupational and status mobility, prestige, stress, power, and the division of labor within the household.

Retirement Income

Women are less likely than men to be covered by private pension plans—40 percent of full-time women workers are covered by such plans, compared with 55 percent of similar men (D. Beller, 1981)—partly because they are concentrated in low-wage firms and occupations and less profitable industries that are less likely to provide pension coverage (Benson, 1980). Although the sex difference in pension coverage is also partly due to women's shorter average tenure in their current jobs, it remains considerable even after controlling for years employed narrowed the coverage gap between the sexes (D. Beller, 1981). Twenty-five percent of all women (half of those employed in the private sector) work in retail and service industries, which have the lowest pension coverage (U.S. Department of Labor, Labor-Management Services Administration, 1980). Only 10.5 percent of women over 65 received money from private pensions, compared with 27.7 percent of men (Moss, 1983). Of course, because women earn less than men, both their social security and retirement benefits are lower (Moss, 1983).

Susceptibility to Unemployment

The link between occupational sex segregation and unemployment is not straightforward. Until 1981 women's unemployment rates typically exceeded men's by 1-2 percentage points (Lloyd and Niemi, 1979; U.S. Department of Labor, Bureau of Labor Statistics, 1981a, 1981b). However, in late 1981 the adult male unemployment rate surpassed that of women by 0.1-0.5 percentage points (U.S. Department of Labor, Bureau of Labor Statistics, 1982a). Their different occupational distribution exposes men to a greater risk of cyclical unemployment than women (Barrett and Morgenstern, 1974; Niemi, 1974; R. Smith, 1977; Urquhart and Hewson, 1983). Women are concentrated in clerical and service occupations and industries, which are less cyclically sensitive than the predominantly male blue-collar occupations in manufacturing and construction. Indeed, Cornfield (1981) and Blau and Kahn (1981a) found that women's occupational and industrial distributions contribute substantially to their lower layoff rates relative to those of men.

Much of the beneficial effect of women's concentration in occupations and industries that are less vulnerable to cyclical unemployment, however, is cancelled out by their greater propensity to be labor force entrants, which subjects them to high unemployment rates. Moreover, although women's concentration in certain occupations or sectors reduces their aggregate risk of unemployment, women who work in female-dominated occupations are unemployed significantly longer than are other women (Barrett and Morgenstern, 1977). In addition, women's occupation-specific unemployment rates continue to exceed men's within many occupations (Urquhart and Hewson, 1983). With the exception of the 1980 recession, women in manufacturing and blue-collar occupations have been more likely to be laid off than men during a recession (Terry, 1982).

Women who have recently entered male-dominated occupations are especially vulnerable to layoffs during economic downturns (Kelley, 1982). During the recent recessions in the United States and Europe this was true for women in certain blue-collar occupations, such as durable goods manufacturing (O'Neill and Smith, 1976; R. Smith, 1977). In recent federal "reductions in force," women in positions with ratings of GS 12 or above were laid off at a rate 2.3 times the average rate, presumably primarily because they had less seniority, although veterans' preference also protected men

(Federal Government Service Task Force, 1981). Thus, in the short run, reducing segregation would place women in more cyclically sensitive sectors or occupations, but in the long run it would probably increase their labor force attachment and thereby reduce both the male-female unemployment differential and the overall sex difference in labor force participation.

On-the-Job Training

On-the-job training offers workers the opportunity to acquire skills that facilitate occupational mobility and wage increases (Mincer, 1962b). Thurow's (1975) characterization of the labor market as a training market in which training slots are allotted to workers recognizes the importance of access to training. But women tend to receive less training than equally experienced men, their jobs involve shorter training periods (Duncan and Hoffman, 1978, 1979), and, among federal employees at least, their training costs less per hour (Taylor, 1985). Evidence that sex segregation accounts for these differences is indirect and thus only suggestive. For example, since training is usually reflected in more rapid wage gains over time, the flatter experience-wage profiles Zellner (1975) observed for female-dominated occupations is consistent with the finding of less on-the-job training.

Occupational and Status Mobility

Research on sex differences in occupational mobility suggests that, in part because of occupational segregation, women experience less career mobility than men. For example, Rosenfeld and Sorensen (1979) found that most of the difference in men's and women's chances to move between particular sets of occupations was due to differences in their distribution over occupational categories. Using Duncan's socioeconomic index (SEI)[5] to measure occupational status, Wolf and Rosenfeld (1978) found that women experienced less upward SEI mobility than men over a five-year period. Leaving the male sector increased the likelihood of a prestige loss for both sexes. Neither men nor women who shifted from one female-dominated job to another were likely to experience upward SEI mobility, although starting in a female-dominated occupation did not reduce the mobility chances of either sex, provided they moved to a non-female-dominated occupation.[6] However, 80 percent of the men and only 31 percent of the women made such moves. Researchers who assessed mobility in terms of wage changes found that men's earnings rose faster than women's (Rosenfeld, 1980; Blau and Kahn, 1981b).

Because female-dominated occupations have characteristically shorter career ladders, i.e., opportunities to advance in pay and status from entry-level positions, women often attain their maximum level within a few years. Typically female entry-level jobs, such as telephone operators or stitchers (Grinker et al., 1970) tend to be on shorter ladders than typically male entry-level jobs (Blau, 1977; Kanter, 1977; Stevenson, 1977; New York State Commission on Manage-

ment and Productivity, 1977; Peterson-Hardt and Perlman, 1979; C. Smith, 1979; Ratner, 1981; Haignere et al., 1981), and women in typically male occupations may be assigned to jobs that offer few promotion opportunities (Martin, 1980; Hochschild, 1975; Epstein 1970b).

As a result, short-term comparisons underestimate long-term differences in the probability of upward mobility. When Sewell et al. (1980) observed occupational mobility over a longer period, the women began in occupations with higher SEI scores, but 18 years later the men had surpassed them, and married women with children had actually lost ground. Even childless women gained little occupational status over the course of their working lives, and never-married women gained only one-third as much as did men (Sewell et al., 1980). Marini (1980) also found that after controlling for education and labor force experience, women showed very small gains in occupational status between their first and a subsequent job, while men's occupational status increased over time. Some of the sex difference was due to the differential ability of men and women to benefit from their education and employment experience. This difference stems from both their different concentrations in occupations that reward these personal resources differently and the tendency of some employers to hold women to higher promotion standards than men (Olson and Becker, 1983).

Occupational Prestige

Several studies (see Bose and Rossi, 1983; Jacobs and Powell, 1983, for reviews) suggest that workers in sex-atypical occupations do not have the occupational prestige accorded sex-typical incumbents of the same occupations. For example, Jacobs and Powell (1983) found that the more an occupation was dominated by one sex, the greater the discrepancy between the prestige that raters accorded to sex-typical and sex-atypical job-

---

[5] The socioeconomic index (Duncan, 1961) was constructed to measure occupational prestige. It computes occupational prestige on the basis of the salaries and the educational attainment of incumbents of occupations. England (1979), Roos (1981), and others have criticized the use of the SEI to compare the sexes because it does not take into account differences in the kinds of occupations women and men typically hold.

[6] Although Wolf and Rosenfeld (1978) found no evidence that men changing jobs within the "female sector" had more SEI mobility than similar women, men may have an advantage in some female-dominated occupations. For example, Grimm and Stern (1974) found that men were overrepresented in higher-status and administrative jobs in teaching, nursing, academic librarianship, and social work, and Fox and Hesse-Biber (1984) confirmed this finding for a larger number of professions more recently.

holders. Given the differing amounts of prestige accorded to male and female incumbents in the same occupation, a move that would represent upward prestige mobility for men might mean downward mobility for women. According to the prestige ratings their respondents assigned sex-typical and sex-atypical workers, florist to plumber and typist to electrician represent such moves (Powell and Jacobs, 1984).

Job Stress

Across-the-board comparisons indicate that women and men find their jobs equally satisfying (U.S. Department of Labor, Employment and Training Administration, 1979c). But sketchy evidence suggests that some female-dominated occupations may be more stressful. Secretaries, for example, had the second-highest incidence of stress-related diseases among workers in 130 occupations studied by the National Institute of Occupational Safety and Health (NIOSH) in 1975. A 1980 study revealed that data-entry clerks who operated video display terminals full time exhibited the highest stress levels of any occupational group NIOSH had ever studied, including air traffic controllers (cited in Working Women Education Fund, 1981). Haynes and Feinleib (1980) found that coronary heart disease among participants in the longitudinal Framingham Heart Study was about twice as common among female clerical workers who had children as among other women workers or housewives. Suppressed hostility, a nonsupportive boss, little job mobility, and a blue-collar husband were all associated with coronary heart disease among clerical workers, presumably because they contributed to increased stress. However, knowledge of the effects of occupational segregation on workers' levels of psychological stress is very sketchy at this time.

Power and Work Within the Family

Job segregation and the resulting differences in earnings may influence women's home lives by affecting the distribution of power between marriage partners and the division of household labor. No studies have tested these suppositions directly, however. McDonald's (1980) review of studies of family power notes that resource theory provides the principle framework for such studies. Most posit a material base for marital power, supplemented by ideology or psychological factors.

Some evidence supports a connection between wives' employment and material power within the family; Rainwater (1979) suggests that wives' employment influences family consumption patterns, away from "male" goods such as sporting equipment and toward "female goods" such as home appliances. In contrast, time use studies based on data from the late 1960s (Meissner et al., 1975; Walker and Woods, 1976; Vanek, 1980) show little if any increase in husbands' contribution to household work when their wives are employed. More recent time budget studies based on data from the mid-1970s (Pleck with Rustad, 1981; Berk, 1979; Stafford and Duncan, 1979) reveal a slight convergence in the amount of time husbands and wives spent in family roles and in total work time (both paid and family). But the slight increase in husband's family time is not linked to wives' employment, since husbands' time in family roles does not vary with their wives' work time. Although working wives have reduced their family time, particularly housework, substantially in recent years, women still do the vast majority of housework. As Moore and Sawhill (1978), Hartmann (1981), and others have noted, women have taken on a new set of activities without forgoing their traditional responsibilities.

The household division of labor appears to share with job segregation a resistance to change, and the two are likely to be mutually reinforcing. The failure of husbands' household time to respond to their wives' paid work may contribute to their wives' choices regarding paid work. Women's choices both contribute to and result from occupational segregation, and segregation reduces the resources women bring to the marital unit and thus, potentially, their power in the household.

CONCLUSION

We have reviewed evidence that shows that sex segregation in employment has significant consequences for women, men, families, and society—but particularly for women. It contributes to women's low wages and lesser employment-related benefits of all kinds, and some have argued that it contributes to a household division of labor that also seems to disadvantage women. The negative consequences of sex segregation in employment are likely to increase, if sex segregation does not decline as more women work for wages and families come to increasingly rely on their earnings. Sex segregation in employment, as we use it in this report, generally refers to any observed difference in the distributions of women and men across job categories. Some of the difference observed may not be problematic for women or society, because it results from a voluntary sorting out of people and jobs. To the extent that the difference is voluntary, it may not be an appropriate object of public policy.

Sex segregation is only one manifestation of unequal opportunity in the workplace. Women's lower earnings and such phenomena as sexual harassment and unequal fringe benefits are others. In our view, job segregation is among the most significant. And perhaps most important, to the extent that sex segregation in the workplace connotes the inferiority of women or contributes to maintaining women as men's inferiors, it has great symbolic importance. We believe that sex segregation is fundamentally at odds with the established goals of equal opportunity and equality under the law in American society. Therefore we focus on the factors affecting the occupational outcomes of women. Our emphasis is on why women end up in a small number of less remunerative occupations and how to alter these outcomes in order to improve women's occupational opportunities.

2 Sex Segregation: Extent and Recent Trends

The most common method of assessing the extent of sex segregation compares the distributions of women and men across a set of occupational categories. The difference in the distributions of the sexes across occupational categories can be summarized by the index of segregation (see note 2, Chapter 1, for the formula), which was developed by Duncan and Duncan (1955). Its value represents the minimum proportion of persons of either sex who would have to change to an occupation in which their sex is underrepresented in order for the occupational distributions of the two groups to be identical. Its value is 0 in the case of complete integration, in which the occupational distributions of men and women are identical, and 100 when every occupation is either entirely female or entirely male. For example, in 1981 the index of sex segregation computed over 11 major occupational categories was 41 among whites and 39 among nonwhites (see Table 2-1), indicating that at least 40 percent of all women or men would have to change to an occupational category dominated by the other sex for their broad distributions to be identical (and for the proportion female or male in each category to be equal to the proportion female or male in the total labor force).

In interpreting the value of the index of segregation, one must bear in mind that its magnitude is unaffected by the type of occupational shifts workers would need to make. Shifts from a sex-typical occupation to a closely related sex-atypical occupation—for example, from elementary school teacher, which is 84 percent female, to school administrator, which is predominantly male (U.S. Department of Labor, Bureau of Labor Statistics, 1981c)—are considerably more probable in the short run than shifts to occupations requiring vastly different skills that are performed under different working conditions. Given the occupational structure, however, to achieve total integration both women and men would have to move to occupations that are atypical for their sex. As we noted in the previous chapter, our use of this measure of segregation does not imply that we believe complete integration of all occupations is an appropriate policy goal. We do, however, believe that job segregation should be substantially reduced.

The index of segregation is influenced by the sizes of more and less segregated oc-

TABLE 2-1 Occupational Segregation Indices Across Major Census Categories for Sex and Race, 1940-1981

	1940	1950	1960	1970	1981
Occupational segregation by sex among:					
Whites	46	43	44	44	41
Blacks and others	58	50	52	49	39
Occupational segregation by race among:					
Men	43	36	35	30	24
Women	62	52	45	30	17

NOTE: Indices are calculated for occupational distributions across 11 major census categories. The data from 1940 to 1960 are classified according to the 1940 census detailed occupational classification; the 1970 data are classified according to the 1960 census detailed occupational classification; and the 1981 data are classified according to the 1970 census detailed occupational classification.

SOURCES: For data from 1940 to 1970, Treiman and Terrell (1975b:167), Copyright ©, Russell Sage Foundation, 1975. Reprinted by permission of the publisher, Russell Sage Foundation. The indices for 1981 were computed from data published in U.S. Department of Labor, Bureau of Labor Statistics (1982a).

cupations. If the most sex-typed occupations employed relatively few workers and the most integrated occupations employed most of the work force, the index would be fairly low. Alternatively, a few large, highly segregated occupations could dominate a large number of small, integrated occupations to yield a large index. This feature of the index is desirable because it represents the actual occupational structure workers encounter. When one compares segregation levels over time or across populations with differing occupational structures, however, differences in the values of the index will confound differences in the amount of segregation within occupations with differences in the sizes of occupations. (Blau and Hendricks, 1979, and Bianchi and Rytina, 1984, decompose the total index into components representing these aspects; we discuss their findings below.)

To get a feeling for how much segregation is associated with a particular value of the index, it is helpful to compare different types of segregation. In Table 2-1 segregation indices are computed for 11 major census occupational categories by both race and sex for each decade since 1940. Although the amounts of race and sex segregation across these broad occupational categories were similar in 1940, by 1981 the drop in the race segregation index was substantial (from 43 to 24 among men and from 62 to 17 among women), while the index of sex segregation decreased much less (from 46 to 41 among whites and from 58 to 39 among blacks and other races). One can also evaluate the magnitude of the index in the context of typical levels for other industrial countries. Using 14 broad occupational categories, Roos (1985) computed indices for 12 societies. The value for the United States, 47, fell toward the high end of the distribution, which ranged from a low of 27 for Japan to a high of 60 for Sweden. Of course, these values are a function of the number of occupational categories (which differed slightly across the countries), and we present these results only as a gauge for assessing the magnitude of a single index.

The magnitude of the index changes as the number of occupational categories increases. Using 1981 Current Population Survey data, Jacobs (1983) calculates the index as 40 on the basis of the 10 major census occupational categories and as 62.7 on the basis of 426 three-digit census occupations. The magnitude of the latter index is comparable to the values shown in Table 2-4, also based on detailed census occupations.

The index of segregation can also be calculated for subsets of occupations, to investigate how subsets compare with each other or to the whole. A. Beller (1984) computed the index for 1981 data for 262 occupations as well as for the subset of 59 professional occupations classified at the same level of detail. As we would expect, the index for the professional occupations was smaller than that for the full range of occupations (51 and 62, respectively), indicating less segregation across professional occupations than across all occupations.

CURRENT EXTENT OF SEX SEGREGATION

In 1980, 48 percent of all women worked in occupations that were at least 80 percent female (Rytina and Bianchi, 1984). These include many clerical occupations (bank tellers, bookkeepers, cashiers, data-entry clerks, receptionists, secretaries, typists, and telephone operators) and service occupations (chambermaids, waitresses, practical nurses, child care workers, hairdressers, and private household workers) as well as operatives in apparel manufacturing. Men were even more likely to work in occupations dominated by members of their own sex: 71 percent were employed in occupations that were at least 80 percent male, such as scientific, technical, and professional occupations (engineers, chemists, dentists, pharmacists, and physicians), skilled crafts (carpenters, electricians, painters, plumbers, machinists, and auto and heavy equipment mechanics), operatives (meat cutters, grinding machine operators, forklift operators, welders, deliverymen, and truck drivers), and laborers (construction laborers, freight handlers, and gardeners). These proportions are slightly lower for black women and men (Malveaux, 1982b).

Based on data for 312 detailed occupations, Table 2-2 shows employment in the 10 largest occupations for women and men, and their percentage female in 1980. Of the largest 10 occupations for women, 9 were more than 70 percent and 7 were more than 80 percent female, compared with the total civilian experienced labor force, which was 42.5 percent female. Of the 10 largest occupations for men, all were at least 70 percent male and 7 were more than 80 percent male. Only one occupation—managers, not elsewhere classified—was common to both lists.

As we noted in Chapter 1, even measures of segregation based on detailed occupational categories underestimate actual levels of segregation in employment because they do not measure the segregation of the sexes at the level of the establishment. As we noted further, sex segregation can occur within occupations when the sexes have the same occupation, but at different ranks, within an establishment. For example, Halaby (1979b) provides evidence of rank segregation among managerial employees in a utility firm, and Norwood (1982) notes that among assemblers and machine tool operators in the motor vehicle parts industry, women were disproportionately concentrated in class C, the lowest-paid class. Occupations can also be more segregated across establishments than they are in the aggregate.

Blau's (1977) investigation of office workers in three northeastern standard metropolitan statistical areas documented intraoccupational sex segregation across firms (i.e., the segregation of female and male workers in the same occupations in different firms). She assessed the amount of segregation for several occupations that were relatively sex-integrated in each city by comparing the actual index of segregation for an occupation with the expected index given the size of the pool of qualified female and male workers and the percentage of women in the occupation in each firm. In most occupations, the difference between the expected and actual was considerable. Interestingly, it was smallest among computer programmers, an occupation that had grown twentyfold during the 1960s. Blau also found

TABLE 2-2 Employment in the 10 Largest Occupations for Men and Women, 1980

Ten Largest Occupations for Men				1970-1980 Change in Percentage Female
Detailed 1980 Occupational Title and Code	Number of Men	Percentage Female		
		1980	1970	
1. Managers, N.E.C. (019)	3,824,609	26.9	15.3	11.6
2. Truckdrivers, heavy (804)	1,852,443	2.3	1.5	0.8
3. Janitors and cleaners (453)	1,631,534	23.4	13.1	10.3
4. Supervisors, production (633)	1,605,489	15.0	9.9	5.1
5. Carpenters (567)	1,275,666	1.6	1.1	0.5
6. Supervisor, sales (243)	1,137,045	28.2	17.0	11.2
7. Laborers (889)	1,128,789	19.4	16.5	2.9
8. Sales representatives (259)	1,070,206	14.9	7.0	7.9
9. Farmers (473)	1,032,759	9.8	4.7	5.1
10. Auto mechanics (505)	948,358	1.3	1.4	−0.1

Ten Largest Occupations for Women				1970-1980 Change in Percentage Female
Detailed 1980 Occupational Title and Code	Number of Women	Percentage Female		
		1980	1970	
1. Secretaries (313)	3,949,973	98.8	97.8	1.0
2. Teachers, elementary school (156)	1,749,547	75.4	83.9	−8.5
3. Bookkeepers (337)	1,700,843	89.7	80.9	8.8
4. Cashiers (276)	1,565,502	83.5	84.2	−0.7
5. Office clerks (379)	1,425,083	82.1	75.3	6.8
6. Managers, N.E.C. (019)	1,407,898	26.9	15.3	11.6
7. Waitresses and waiters (435)	1,325,928	88.0	90.8	−2.8
8. Salesworkers (274)	1,234,929	72.7	70.4	2.3
9. Registered nurses (095)	1,232,544	95.9	97.3	−1.4
10. Nursing aides (447)	1,209,757	87.8	87.0	0.8

SOURCE: Rytina and Bianchi (1984).

that firms tended to have consistent patterns of sex segregation across occupations. If a firm employed more men than expected in one occupation, it was likely to do so in other occupations, and such firms tended to pay workers of both sexes higher wages.

In another study of segregation at the establishment level, Bielby and Baron (1984) found an astonishing amount of job segregation. Using data for 393 firms that the California State Employment Service collected between 1959 and 1979, they found that 30 firms employed workers of only one sex. In an additional 201 firms, women and men shared none of the same job titles. Thus, 231 of 393 firms were totally segregated (indices of 100). Only 16 establishments had segregation indices below 60, and closer ex-amination of these relatively integrated firms revealed that in very few did women and men work side by side at the same jobs. For example, one integrated establishment employed apartment house managers, each of whom resided in the building he or she managed. In another, women worked during the day shift, while men in the same job worked at night. Studies of specific occupations (travel agents by Mennerick, 1975; retail clerks by Talbert and Bose, 1977) or establishments (Harlan and O'Farrell, 1982) confirm patterns of considerable segregation by sex at the firm or job level.

Industries, too, differ both in their propensity to employ women and in their levels of occupational sex segregation. The distributions of the sexes across eight broad industrial categories, shown in Table 2-3, differ considerably. In general, women are concentrated in personal and professional services; finance, insurance, and real estate; communications; and retail trade. In contrast, they make up less than 10 percent of workers in logging, fisheries, horticulture, construction, metals and mining, and railroads (U.S. Department of Labor, Bureau of Labor Statistics, 1981c:Table 30). This is not surprising given that industries have different propensities to employ workers in particular occupations that we know to be sex-segregated. For example, financial firms employ many clerical workers, most of whom are women, and construction firms employ many laborers, most of whom are men. Sex segregation across industries occurs, however, in amounts greater than would be expected from their occupational distributions alone (Blau, 1977; Stolzenberg, 1982). For example, in 1970, 49.4 percent of all assemblers, who usually work in manufacturing, were women. In electrical machinery manufacture, women constituted 74.2 percent of assemblers; in motor vehicle manufacture, they constituted only 17.2 percent (U.S. Department of Commerce, Bureau of the Census, 1972). Several researchers have concluded that women tend to be concentrated in economically peripheral industries (Kohen, 1975; Bridges, 1980), while men work disproportionately in the "core" sector of the economy (Beck et al., 1980), but there is disagreement regarding this finding and the definition of core and peripheral sectors.

We stress that sex segregation at both the firm and the industry level limits the employment opportunities of women. Some firms consistently exhibit more segregation than would be expected from the occupational mix they hire, and more firms do this than would be expected by chance. It is hard to escape the conclusion that discriminatory practices of one sort or another are probably occurring. Such segregation appears, from the few studies available, to be quite extensive, and it is not measured by occupational segregation alone. Clearly we need more data and more studies at the establishment level. The next section examines trends in segregation by sex and necessarily relies on occupational-level data.

RECENT TRENDS IN OCCUPATIONAL SEX SEGREGATION

Summary measures indicating current levels of segregation are primarily of interest as data points that reveal trends over time.

TABLE 2-3   Sex Distribution Over Major Industrial Categories for Nonagricultural Industries, October 1984

Industry Division	Women		Percentage Female	Men	
	Number (in thousands)	Percentage distribution		Number (in thousands)	Percentage distribution
Mining	123	.3	12.2	889	1.7
Construction	439	1.0	9.5	4,206	7.9
Manufacturing	6,461	15.1	32.4	13,396	25.2
Transportation and public utilities	1,434	3.4	27.2	3,838	7.2
Wholesale trade	1,605	3.8	28.5	4,032	7.6
Retail trade	8,573	20.1	51.9	7,961	15.0
Finance, insurance, and real estate	3,462	8.1	60.7	2,240	4.2
Services	12,587	29.4	59.9	8,440	15.9
Government	8,061	18.9	49.7	8,152	15.3
Total	42,745	100.0	44.6	53,154	100.0

SOURCE: U.S. Department of Labor, Bureau of Labor Statistics (1985a:Tables B-2 and B-3).

After decades of considerable stability, there has been some reduction in segregation over the past 10-20 years. Whether the overwhelming impression is one of change or stability, however, depends partly on whether one looks at the overall picture, which reflects the experiences of more than 100 million workers, or at certain occupations or subgroups in the labor force. Among the latter, increased integration has taken place. We begin by examining two summary measures that necessarily mask change within specific occupations; we then turn to data on the experience of young people; we conclude by examining changes within selected occupations.

The concentration of workers in occupations that are at least 80 percent male or female has increased slightly over the last three decades (Blau, 1977; Waite, 1981). The trend, however, is sensitive to the definition of a sex-dominated occupation and may be an artifact of the growing number of occupations that the census distinguishes. Using as a criterion the overrepresentation of either sex by at least 5 percentage points relative to its representation in the labor force, A. Beller (1984) observed a decline during the 1970s in men's concentration in some traditionally male occupations.

Beller's finding of a decrease in the proportion of men in male-dominated occupations for the 1970s is corroborated by Rytina and Bianchi (1984). They also found a decrease in the proportion of women in female-dominated occupations. The occupational data from the 1980 census and all earlier censuses are especially difficult to compare because of sweeping changes made in the 1980 census occupational classification scheme. Using data for a sample of 120,000 individuals in the experienced civilian labor force whose occupations were "double coded" with both the 1970 and the 1980 detailed occupational codes, Bianchi and Rytina (1984) were able to recode 1970 data into 1980 categories and then compare the sex composition of occupations in the two census years.

This procedure allowed them to use virtually all occupations representing the entire 1970 and 1980 labor force. Using a 20 percentage point spread around the proportion female in the labor force (taken as 40 percent), they defined male-intensive occupations as those that were no more than 20 percent female and female-intensive occupations as those that were at least 60 percent female. The proportion of men who were in male-intensive occupations fell from 72.3 percent in 1970 to 52.9 percent in 1980, and the proportion of women who were in female-intensive occupations fell from 73.6 percent in 1970 to 63.3 percent in 1980. The proportion of men employed in female-intensive occupations did not change, while the proportion of women employed in male-intensive occupations actually fell, from 9.4 to 6.1 percent, but the proportion of both men and women working in the sex-neutral occupations rose substantially (Bianchi and Rytina, unpublished data, 1984).

Indices of occupational sex segregation for the labor force as a whole show remarkable stability over most of this century[1] as well as a decline during the 1970s. The index of segregation computed for three-digit occupational classifications for each decennial census has fluctuated between 65 and 69 between 1900 and 1970 (Gross, 1968; Blau and Hendricks, 1979) and declined to about 60 in 1980 (A. Beller, 1984; Bianchi and Rytina, 1984).

The index increased slightly between 1950 and 1960 and then dropped slightly between 1960 and 1970. According to Blau and Hendricks (1979), the increase during the 1950s stemmed primarily from the growth of predominantly female clerical and professional

---

[1] Attempts to determine the extent of occupational segregation in the nineteenth century (Oppenheimer, 1970; Sorkin, 1973; Williams, 1979), although plagued by problems of the comparability of data, suggest some movement toward desegregation between 1870 and 1920, probably due to the emergence of new occupations that had not yet been sex-typed.

occupations, while the decline during the 1960s was due largely to increased integration of occupations, which was the consequence of men's movement into traditionally female professions such as elementary school teacher, librarian, nurse, and social worker, rather than to an increase in women's representation in male-dominated occupations. Since the number of job openings generated by occupational growth and turnover sets limits on the amount of desegregation, Blau and Hendricks compared the observed decline in the index with the amount that would have occurred had all positions that became available during the period been filled randomly with respect to sex.[2] This simulation, summarized in Table 2-4, indicates that sex segregation would have dropped by almost 25 percent during each of the two decades had the allocation of workers to new jobs been sex neutral. In light of this, the actual decline of 3 points (4.5 percent) between 1960 and 1970 is extremely modest.

Recent research (A. Beller, 1984; Jacobs, 1983; Bianchi and Rytina, 1984) suggests that more rapid change has occurred during the 1970s. The segregation indices that Beller computed for 262 detailed census occupations[3] declined by 6.6 points between 1972

and 1981, from 68.3 to 61.7. To put these values in some context, Beller computed indices for the same 262 occupations in 1960 and 1970 using census data. During that decade the index declined from 68.7 to 65.9, a decline of only 2.8 points.[4] Between 1972 and 1981 the index of segregation declined at an annual rate nearly three times that for the 1960s (Beller, 1984). Of the decline of 6.6 points between 1972 and 1981, 18 percent was due to changes in the sizes of more and less segregated occupations; the remaining 82 percent represents changes in the sex composition of the occupations and reflects increased integration of occupations. Using data from the 1970 and 1980 censuses for virtually all occupations, Bianchi and Rytina (1984) obtained similar results. The indices of segregation they calculated declined by 8.4 points (from 67.7 to 59.3) between 1970 and 1980, with 76 percent of the decline due uniquely to shifts in sex composition within occupations. Jacobs (1983) used Current Population Survey data to compare sex segregation for 1971 and 1981 across both broad and narrow occupational categories as well as for over 10,000 occupation-by-industry categories. Jacobs's results for 426 detailed occupations closely resemble those of Beller for 262 occupations and those of Bianchi and Rytina for the complete set of occupations. Of particular interest is the decline during the 1970s of over 13 percent (from 80.3 to 69.6) in the seg-

---

[2] Blau and Hendricks (1979) operationalized sex-random hiring to mean that new positions are filled according to the sex ratio that prevailed in the pool of new labor force entrants and individuals released from declining occupations. Lacking data on the magnitude of replacement, they assumed no change in occupational sex composition due to turnover, thereby ignoring the potential contribution to integration that sex-blind replacements of job turnover would produce and thus underestimating the amount of integration possible. They also note, however, that failing to consider occupational entry requirements may yield an overestimate of the amount of integration that could occur in filling new positions.

[3] In order to construct a consistent data series for the period 1972-1981, Beller included only those occupations that had at least 25 respondents—representing occupations with at least 40,000 incumbents—

in both the 1974 and 1977 Current Population Surveys (CPS) (Annual Demographic Files). Beller used CPS data for 1971-1974 and 1977. In addition, the 1972, 1977, and 1981 indices were based on Bureau of Labor Statistics annual averages of monthly Current Population Surveys. The Current Population Survey and the Bureau of Labor Statistics annual averages yield slightly different results. Their comparability is discussed in A. Beller (1984).

[4] The values Beller obtained differ from those of Blau and Hendricks and Bianchi and Rytina (shown in Table 2-4) because each used different data and occupational categories. Only comparisons within the individual studies are appropriate.

TABLE 2-4   Actual and Predicted Segregation Indices, 1950-1980, and Percentage Decline

Year	Actual			Predicted If Hiring During Previous Decade Were Sex-Neutral[a]		
	Index	Decadal Change	Percentage Decline	Index	Decadal Change	Percentage Decline
1950	73[b]					
1960	74[b]	+1	0.0	56	-17	23.4
1970	71[b]	-3	4.2	56	-18	24.0
1970	67.7[c]					
1980	59.3[c]	-8.4	12.4	47.8	-19.9	29.4

[a]Each value reflects the amount of change that would have occurred over the previous decade, relative to the actual level of segregation at the decade's beginning. Thus, had hiring been sex-neutral between 1960 and 1970, the segregation index in 1970 would have declined by 18 points from 74 to 56.

[b]Indices are computed for 183 detailed occupational categories in all three decennial censuses. Large residual categories such as "other operatives," which are necessary to account for the entire labor force, were eliminated. The occupations included employed 66-70 percent of the labor force in the three census years.

[c]Indices are computed for all occupational categories in the 1980 census, with 1970 census data recoded to the 1980 categories.

SOURCE: 1950-1970: computed from Blau and Hendricks (1979:Table 3 and text). 1970-1980: computed from Bianchi and Rytina (1984:Table 7).

regation index computed for over 10,000 detailed occupation-by-industry categories.[5]

These three major studies of sex segregation in the 1970s (A. Beller, 1984; Jacobs, 1983; Bianchi and Rytina, 1984) all agree that sex segregation declined substantially during the decade, although earlier studies (e.g., Lloyd and Niemi, 1979) failed to find a substantial decline. Most of the decline, furthermore, was found to be due to the greater integration of occupations, not to changes in the size of the predominantly male or predominantly female occupations. Nevertheless, change was less rapid than it would have been had all hiring during the decade been sex-neutral. Bianchi and Rytina (1984) replicated for the 1970s the exercise Blau and Hendricks (1979) carried out for the 1950s and 1960s, comparing actual and potential declines in occupational segrega-

tion. The 12.4 percent decline in the segregation index actually observed represented less than half of the 29.4 percent decline that would have occurred had all new hires been independent of sex (see Table 2-4).

Changes in Sex Segregation Among Population Subgroups

Given the large amount of stability built into the occupational structure (Blau and Hendricks, 1979; Tolbert, 1982; Treiman and Hartmann, 1981), the potential for change in sex segregation should be greatest for new entrants into the labor force and among those who are young enough to train for or shift to sex-atypical occupations. Bureau of Labor Statistics data for 1981 support this expectation. Younger workers showed slightly less segregation across 44 two-digit occupations. The index of segregation for all workers was 53.5, but for workers ages 20-24, it was 51.1. Women ages 20-24 were more likely than women of other ages to work as engineers, engineering and science technicians, other salaried professionals, managers, and administrators; and they were underrepresented among retail salespersons, operatives

---

[5] The decline was greatest in the New England and Pacific and Mountain states, which showed the lowest values in 1981, and smallest in the Mid-Atlantic and South Central states, the latter of which showed the highest level of occupational segregation of any of the regions in 1981.

(especially in nondurable goods, a predominantly female occupation), and in most service occupations (see Table 2-5). The occupational distribution of women ages 25-34 was closer to that for older women. Jacobs's (1983) results for 426 detailed occupations, while also revealing slightly less segregation among younger workers, differ in showing the greatest decline in the segregation index and the least segregation among women ages 25-34; those ages 16-24 were slightly more segregated.

A. Beller (1984) also found that workers who had been in the labor force no more than 10 years were less segregated than the remainder of the labor force in both 1971 and 1977, and that the gap has been widening. She identified two sources of change: the 1971 entry cohort became less segregated as it aged and the cohort entering in 1977 was less segregated than the 1971 cohort had been at entry. An earlier study by Beller (1982a) may explain some of this change. She found that equal opportunity legislation enhanced the likelihood of getting into a sex-atypical occupation more for new entrants into the labor market than for any other group.

According to Jacobs (1983), the segregation index declined by about the same amount among whites and blacks, but other groups (primarily Hispanics and Asian Americans) showed the most decline. Their sex segregation index dropped from 75.6 to 64.6 between 1971 and 1981. Beller (1984), who distinguished only whites and nonwhites, observed larger declines among the latter, although the index for professional occupations dropped more for whites than nonwhites, indicating that much of the increase in integration by sex for nonwhites occurred at the lower end of the occupational distribution.

Changes in Sex Segregation Among Occupational Subgroups

Of course, the decline in segregation was far from uniform across occupational cate-gories, much less within detailed occupations. For example, using census data through 1970, Scott and Semyonov (1983) report that three major occupational categories—operatives, farm managers, and managers—became more male-dominated, while clerical occupations became more female-dominated; occupations that moved toward parity were professional and sales, and, since 1960, domestic service, crafts, and labor. Rytina and Bianchi (1984) report that managers have become much more integrated since 1970; in 1980, managers were 31 percent female, a very substantial increase of 12 percentage points since 1970. Jacobs (1983) and A. Beller (1984) examine patterns of change within detailed occupations since 1970. Jacobs's analysis of the 1971 and 1981 Current Population Survey data showed that among nonfarm occupational categories the index of segregation declined most for professional occupations (by almost 27 percent: 16.5 points).

Beller (1984) concluded that the decline observed in the index of sex segregation during the 1970s was due, in addition to increased integration of some occupations, to declines in the sizes of two heavily female occupations—private household maids and servants and sewers and stitchers; each accounted for more than a one-point decline in the segregation index. Three other occupations dominated by one sex (telephone operator, private household child care worker, and delivery and route worker) also contributed to the dropping index because they declined in size. A smaller proportion of the female labor force worked as retail sales clerks, typists, and cooks, while women entered three rapidly growing male occupations: accountant, bank officer and financial manager, and janitor. Beller also showed that the observed decline in the index masked some changes in the occupational structure that actually contributed to greater segregation. Several female-dominated occupations have grown rapidly (i.e., registered nurse and office manager), and some have simultaneously become more female (com-

TABLE 2-5   Percentage Female in Detailed Occupational Groups by Age, Twelve-Month Annual Averages, December 1981

Occupation	All Workers	Ages 20-24	Ages 25-34
Total	43 (100,397)	47 (14,122)	42 (28,180)
Professional, technical, and kindred workers	45 (16,419)	53 (1,687)	47 (5,906)
Engineers	4 (1,537)	13 (132)	6 (447)
Physicians, dentists, and related practitioners	14 (828)	52 (23)	21 (240)
Other health professions	86 (2,297)	83 (336)	84 (911)
Teachers, except college and university	70 (3,197)	78 (226)	71 (1,176)
Engineering and science technicians	18 (1,141)	23 (226)	18 (427)
Other salaried professionals	36 (6,668)	47 (713)	39 (2,482)
Other professional and self-employed workers	27 (751)	40 (32)	27 (223)
Managers and administrators, except farm	27 (11,540)	42 (754)	29 (3,051)
Manufacturing, salaried	15 (1,566)	36 (58)	20 (374)
Other industries, salaried	30 (8,011)	44 (640)	32 (2,292)
Retail, self-employed	35 (870)	29 (24)	31 (154)
Other independently self-employed	16 (1,093)	15 (32)	15 (231)
Sales	45 (6,425)	51 (854)	39 (1,626)
Retail	63 (3,262)	57 (583)	56 (667)
Other	26 (3,162)	39 (271)	27 (958)
Clerical	80 (18,564)	82 (3,352)	80 (5,212)
Bookkeepers	91 (1,961)	89 (251)	92 (515)
Office machine operators	73 (966)	74 (231)	73 (349)
Stenographers, typists, secretaries	98 (5,022)	98 (928)	99 (1,463)
Other clerical	70 (10,615)	74 (1,942)	70 (2,885)
Craft and kindred workers	6 (12,662)	6 (1,656)	6 (3,879)
Carpenters	1 (1,122)	3 (177)	2 (395)
Other construction crafts	1 (2,593)	2 (376)	2 (808)
Foremen, not elsewhere classified	11 (1,816)	15 (115)	11 (471)
Machinists and job setters	4 (668)	4 (97)	5 (199)
Other metal	4 (626)	4 (65)	6 (180)
Mechanics, auto	0.6 (1,249)	0.4 (243)	0.7 (408)
Other mechanic	3 (2,159)	3 (266)	3 (692)
Other craft	17 (2,430)	20 (317)	17 (726)
Operatives, except transport	40 (10,540)	33 (1,841)	35 (3,002)
Mine workers	2 (357)	2 (90)	2 (134)
Motor vehicle equipment	19 (452)	17 (52)	19 (148)
Other durable goods	36 (4,153)	30 (736)	33 (1,233)
Nondurable goods	58 (3,339)	52 (543)	52 (928)
All other	30 (2,240)	22 (419)	26 (560)
Transport equipment operatives	9 (3,476)	6 (480)	9 (1,029)
Drivers, delivery	10 (2,966)	7 (382)	10 (862)
All others	5 (511)	5 (98)	4 (166)
Nonfarm laborers	11 (4,583)	10 (1,037)	12 (1,035)
Construction	2 (797)	1 (203)	3 (203)
Manufacturing	15 (986)	13 (230)	13 (254)
All other	13 (2,800)	12 (605)	15 (577)
Private household workers	96 (1,047)	93 (87)	97 (152)
Service workers, except private household	59 (12,391)	59 (2,054)	60 (2,776)
Cleaning	39 (2,489)	30 (320)	37 (441)
Food	66 (4,682)	62 (926)	68 (840)
Health	89 (1,995)	86 (385)	86 (561)
Personal	76 (1,766)	78 (252)	81 (476)
Protective	10 (1,459)	13 (171)	10 (459)
Farmers, farm manager	11 (1,485)	7 (81)	11 (252)
Farm laborers, foremen	25 (1,264)	15 (239)	25 (261)
Paid labor	16 (1,010)	14 (211)	16 (223)
Unpaid family members	65 (254)	29 (28)	84 (38)

NOTE: Numbers in parentheses are numbers of workers; they represent actual sample sizes and include both men and women.

SOURCE: Unpublished data, U.S. Department of Labor, Bureau of Labor Statistics (1981).

TABLE 2-6   Sources of Employment Growth for Women, 1970-1980

Panel A   Occupations in Which the Percentage Female Increased 20 Points or More, 1970-1980

Occupation	Number of New Female Jobs	Percentage Female 1970	Percentage Female 1980
Executive, administrative, and managerial occupations			
Management-related occupations, N.E.C.	12,006	20.1	53.5
Professional and specialty occupations			
Inhalation therapists	24,963	28.6	56.5
Foreign language teachers	2,432	34.2	59.4
Recreation workers	6,308	45.4	67.6
Public relations specialists	37,199	26.6	48.8
Technicians and related support occupations			
Broadcast equipment operators	24,040	22.1	44.0
Sales occupations			
Advertising and related sales occupations	33,526	20.5	41.6
Sales occupations, other business services	126,439	8.4	37.4
Administrative support occupations, including clerical			
Computer operators	192,037	33.9	59.1
Production coordinators	85,479	20.2	44.4
Samplers	449	20.4	44.8
Insurance adjusters, examiners, and investigators	70,483	29.6	60.0
Protective service occupations	12,238	22.2	42.3
Service occupations, except protective and household			
Bartenders	95,480	21.2	44.3
Food counter, fountain, and related occupations	88,063	56.8	81.1
Guides	13,676	32.9	57.2
Farming, forestry, and fishing occupations			
Animal caretakers, except farm	26,781	30.7	59.0
Graders and sorters, agricultural products	3,246	52.0	78.6
Precision production, craft, and repair occupations			
Engravers, metal	4,074	15.7	38.1
Machine operators, assemblers, and inspectors			
Typesetters and compositors	24,779	16.8	55.7
Miscellaneous printing machine operators	17,903	23.8	52.9
Total, experienced civilian labor force 16 years and over	13,957,618	38.0	42.6

puter and peripheral equipment operator and miscellaneous clerical worker). According to Rytina and Bianchi (1984), women's participation increased most between 1970 and 1980 in those occupations that were between 20 and 60 percent female in 1970. Some of these occupations became more female-intensive (those more than 40 percent female), while others became more integrated (those less than 40 percent female). Women's participation also increased to a lesser degree in some occupations that were

80-90 percent male but failed to grow in those that were 90-100 percent male.

Among all male-dominated occupations, women's representation increased more rapidly between 1972 and 1981 than during the 1960s (A. Beller, 1984). Prior to 1970, their representation increased in only one-fourth of the occupations in which men were overrepresented by at least 5 percentage points. However, between 1972 and 1981, their representation increased in more than half of those occupations as well as in most

TABLE 2-6   Sources of Employment Growth for Women, 1970-1980 (continued)

Panel B   Ten Detailed Occupations Providing Largest Number of New Jobs for Women, 1970-1980

Occupation	Number of New Female Jobs	Percentage Female 1970	Percentage Female 1980
Secretaries	1,145,033	97.8	98.8
Managers and administrators, N.E.C., salaried	900,308	15.6	26.9
General office clerks	800,124	75.3	82.1
Cashiers	756,132	84.2	83.5
Registered nurses	491,031	97.3	95.9
Teachers, elementary school	482,892	83.9	75.4
Assemblers	418,955	45.7	49.5
Child care workers, except private household	405,284	92.5	93.2
Nursing aides	382,383	87.0	87.8
Machine operators, not specified	332,929	35.6	33.5

SOURCE: U.S. Department of Commerce, Bureau of the Census (1984a).

male white-collar occupations. According to Beller, in managerial and administrative occupations, the increases in the proportion female were large. More than 90 percent of these occupations became more female by 1981, although only 10 percent became more female during the 1960s. As noted above, Rytina and Bianchi (1984) corroborate the increased representation of women in management. Male craft, operative, and laborer occupations remained highly segregated (Beller, 1984); women's representation did not increase significantly in these occupations through 1981.

Women's increased representation in a wider range of occupations is displayed in Panel A of Table 2-6, which presents the proportions of women workers in all detailed occupations in which women's representation increased by 20 percentage points or more between 1970 and 1980. Fifteen of the 21 occupations listed in Panel A shifted from predominantly (over 60 percent) male to well-integrated occupations (less than 60 percent of either gender). Among these are managers, public relations specialists, broadcast equipment operators, protective service occupations, bartenders, animal caretakers, and typesetters and compositors. Two of the 21 occupations that experienced substantial

growth in their proportion female had only a slight majority female in 1970 but became heavily female-dominated by 1980: food counter, fountain, and related occupations, and graders and sorters of agricultural products.

Table 2-7 shows the 26 female-dominated occupations in which the representation of men increased 1 percentage point or more. In several occupations where few men have ventured, slow change is occurring, including registered nurses, prekindergarten and kindergarten teachers, cooks in private households, and textile and sewing machine operators. More dramatic shifts have occurred in the categories of chief communications operators, and hand engraving and printing occupations.

The movement of men into female-dominated occupations and women into male-dominated occupations has contributed to the decline in sex segregation during the 1970s. As noted above, the decline was slowed by the growing numbers of women in large, heavily female-dominated occupations. All the occupations listed in Panel A of Table 2-6 accounted for only 6.5 percent of the growth in female employment between 1970 and 1980. Panel B of Table 2-6 lists the 10 occupations that provided

TABLE 2-7   Female-Dominated Occupations in Which the Percentage Male Increased One Point or More, 1970-1980

Occupation	Percentage Male 1970	Percentage Male 1980	Occupation	Percentage Male 1970	Percentage Male 1980
Professional specialty occupations			Cooks, private household	5.7	13.5
			Private household cleaners and servants	4.1	5.4
Registered nurses	2.7	4.1			
Dieticians	8.0	10.1	Service occupations, except		
Speech therapists	7.4	10.9	protective and household		
Teachers, prekindergarten and kingergarten	2.1	3.6	Waiters and waitresses	9.2	12.0
Dancers	8.7	25.4	Kitchen workers, food		
Administrative support occupations			preparation	8.2	21.8
Chief communications			Maids and housemen	5.7	24.2
operators	18.2	65.6	Hairdressers and cosmetologists	10.0	12.2
Stenographers	6.3	9.1	Public transportation		
Interviewers	18.6	22.6	attendants	18.7	21.9
Order clerks	22.6	32.6	Precision production, craft,		
File clerks			and repair occupations		
Billing, posting, and	18.6	20.0	Electrical and electronic		
calculating machine			equipment assemblers	22.3	24.2
operators	9.9	13.0	Textile sewing machine		
Mail preparing and			operators	3.1	5.9
paper handling			Solderers and brazers	18.3	22.0
machine operators	21.8	37.5	Hand engraving and		
Telephone operators	6.0	9.0	printing operations	18.4	68.3
Data entry keyers	6.3	7.6	Total, experienced civilian		
Private household occupations			labor force, 16 years		
			and over	62.0	57.4
Launderers and ironers	4.6	23.8			

SOURCE: U.S. Department of Commerce, Bureau of the Census (1984a).

the largest number of new jobs for women during the same period, accounting for approximately 44 percent of the net increase in female employment. Seven of these occupations are heavily female-dominated (over 75 percent female). The occupational category "secretaries," which is 98.8 percent female, alone created more new jobs than all occupations in Panel A combined. Some female-dominated occupations have become more so; bookkeepers were 77.7 percent female in 1950 and 93 percent female 30 years later. Other clerical occupations that have become even more female-intensive since 1970 include billing clerks, cashiers, file clerks, keypunch operators, receptionists, legal secretaries, typists, and teacher's aides (U.S. Department of Labor, Bureau of Labor Statistics, 1981c; U.S. Department of Commerce, Bureau of the Census, 1973b, 1984a).

While the general tendency for white women was to move out of female-dominated occupations, black women were less likely than white women to have done the same. Nevertheless their occupational status improved substantially as they moved to white-collar jobs from lower-paid service and laborer jobs. Many black women moved from lower-paying female-dominated occupations, particularly private household worker and to a smaller degree laborer (A. Beller, 1984), to clerical and other service occupations that were also female-dominated. In 1940, 70 percent of black women workers were private household workers; by 1981, just 6 percent worked in this occupational category, and fewer than 2 percent between the ages of 18 and 34 held such jobs (Malveaux, 1982b). Between 1973 and 1981, the proportion of black women in clerical occupations increased from under 25 percent to almost 30 percent (U.S. Department of Labor, Women's Bureau, 1983; U.S. Department of Labor, Bureau of Labor Statistics, 1982b); in 1940 only 1 percent had held clerical jobs (Treiman and Terrell, 1975b). Occupations in which black women are today overrepresented include postal clerk, cashier, telephone operator, and duplicating machine operator. In contrast, black women are underrepresented among receptionists, bank tellers, and secretaries. Malveaux (1982b) notes that the clerical jobs in which black women are overrepresented have a behind-the-scenes character. While these changes among black women do not contribute to a reduction in the total amount of sex segregation, they represent an improvement in their position in the labor market and help to explain the sharp drop in the index of occupational race segregation among women shown in Table 2-1. Between 1977 and 1981, Hispanic women increased their representation in female-dominated white-collar (primarily clerical) occupations, while their representation in female-dominated blue-collar jobs declined (Malveaux, 1982b).

Is Resegregation Occurring?

The relative stability of the aggregate level of sex segregation over time, coupled with several examples of large sex shifts in occupations, has led some observers to speculate that integration of occupations is a temporary, unstable phenomenon. Perhaps, after reaching some "tipping point," inte-

grated occupations become resegregated, with members of one sex replaced by members of the other.[6] Bank tellers and secretaries exemplify originally male jobs in which women replaced men (Davies, 1975, 1982). Men have been hypothesized to leave formerly male occupations when large numbers of women are hired because of the accompanying prestige loss (Touhey, 1974) or declining real wages (Nieva and Gutek, 1981; Strober, 1984). As with secretaries and bank tellers, the shift from men to women may occur as the occupation is being restructured to provide, for example, less advancement to higher-level management, and becoming less attractive to men.

Evidence regarding the prevalence of resegregation is limited. Strober and her colleagues (Strober and Lanford, 1981; Tyack and Strober, 1981) have traced the changing sex composition of the teaching profession, but do not attribute it to tipping. Panel A of Table 2-6 includes a few occupations that shifted from being predominantly male to predominantly female. Insurance adjusters, examiners, and investigators, for example, were 29.6 percent female in 1970 and 60.0 percent female in 1980. Animal caretakers, except farm, changed from 30.7 percent female in 1970 to 59.0 percent female in 1980. Shaeffer and Axel (1978) point out that machine operators in banks and technical employees in insurance companies are both becoming predominantly female, and Nieva and Gutek (1981) have suggested that computer programming may follow the pattern of bank tellers. When the occupation emerged 20 years ago, it was male-dominated; in 1970, computer and peripheral machine operators were 29.1 percent female. Ten years later, women's representation had

---

[6] The process is similar to residential "succession," in which segregated neighborhoods that are becoming integrated are eventually abandoned by the original residents to new residents of a different race or ethnicity.

increased to 59.8 percent (although the duties have also changed), and Beller and Han (1984) conclude that the projected growth of this occupation will contribute to increased segregation. Greenbaum (1976, 1979) has argued, however, that that occupation was only briefly integrated, and, rather than tipping, it has split into two sex-segregated specialties: the computer operator and some computer programming jobs are female-dominated, while higher-level programming and systems analyst jobs are male-dominated.

Affirmative action needs to be thorough to counteract a potential tendency to resegregation. O'Farrell and Harlan (1982) point out that pressures to hire women may result in their concentration in and ultimately replacement of men in formerly male-dominated entry-level jobs. Unless these jobs are on ladders that lead to positions that men continue to occupy, resegregation is likely. Resegregation can go in either direction. In one case, Kelley (1982) found that affirmative-action hiring in a manufacturing plant between 1972 and 1976 in general meant that white men supplanted white women in job classifications previously dominated by women.

Some empirical evidence exists regarding a related issue: whether employers hire women in occupations that are declining in size or importance, usually because of technological change. In at least half of the 53 nontraditional occupations in which women had made substantial gains between 1960 and 1970, their progress was due to the slow or negative growth of male employment (Reubens and Reubens, 1979). It has been alleged, for example, that AT&T hired women for formerly male positions they planned to eliminate. As central office work was simplified by computers in that organization, women were moved into these jobs and encountered little male resistance. Two studies of AT&T (Hacker, 1979; Northrup and Larson, 1979) concluded that without careful planning, technological change could lead

to a smaller number of newly segregated jobs. Feldberg and Glenn (1980) note several examples, in addition to the AT&T case, which suggest that women are hired expressly as a transitional labor force in some instances associated with the introduction of electronic data processing.

Whether some of the newly integrated occupations will remain integrated or whether substantial resegregation will occur cannot, of course, be predicted with any certainty. The next section presents scenarios of a variety of changes and their possible effect on the aggregate index of segregation.

OCCUPATIONAL SEX SEGREGATION PROJECTED THROUGH 1990

The index of occupational segregation by sex declined by approximately 10 percent during the 1970s, but in 1981 it was still about 60. Can the changes that occurred during the 1970s be expected to continue, and, if so, at what rate? Are changes in the occupational structure likely to retard or accelerate further desegregation? As Table 2-8 shows, the Bureau of Labor Statistics (BLS) (Carey, 1981) projects substantial growth in many heavily and historically female occupational categories, such as professional and practical nurses, nurse's aides, secretaries, bookkeepers, typists, and waitresses and waiters. These occupations are included in the 20 occupations in which employment growth, in absolute numbers, is expected to be greatest until 1990. If the proportions of these occupations that are female remain approximately constant, their growth will represent a demand for an additional 3.3 million female workers. Three of the occupations of largest predicted growth are currently predominantly male but have experienced recent growth in the participation of women: janitors and sextons, accountants and auditors, and guards and doorkeepers. Several other predominantly male occupations that have not experienced substantial

TABLE 2-8   Twenty Occupations With the Largest Projected Absolute Growth, 1978-1990

Occupation	Percentage Female 1980[a]	Growth in Employment 1978-1990 (in thousands)	Percentage Growth 1978-1990
Janitors and sextons	17.3	671.2	26.0
Nurses' aides and orderlies	87.5	594.0	54.6
Sales clerks	71.1	590.7	21.3
Cashiers	86.6	545.5	36.4
Waiters/waitresses	89.1	531.9	34.6
General clerks, office	80.1	529.8	23.4
Professional nurses	96.5	515.8	50.3
Food preparation and service workers, fast food restaurants	66.9	491.9	68.8
Secretaries	99.1	487.8	21.0
Truck drivers	2.2	437.6	26.2
Kitchen helpers	66.9	300.6	39.0
Elementary school teachers	83.7	272.8	21.4
Typists	96.9	262.1	26.4
Accountants and auditors	36.2	254.2	32.7
Helpers, trades	NA	232.5	25.0
Blue-collar workers, supervisors	10.8	222.1	17.4
Bookkeepers, hand	90.5	219.7	23.7
Licensed practical nurses	97.3	215.6	43.9
Guards and doorkeepers	12.4	209.9	35.5
Automotive mechanics	.6	205.3	24.3

NA = not available.

[a]Approximate, due to the use of different occupational classifications in sources.

SOURCES: Carey (1981:48) and U.S. Department of Labor, Bureau of Labor Statistics (1981c:Table 23).

growth in their proportion female (truck drivers, automotive mechanics, and helpers in the trades) are also expected to grow during the 1980s.

Although the occupations projected to grow the most in absolute terms are nearly all predominantly male or female, several of the occupations that are expected to grow at the most rapid rate, shown in Table 2-9, are somewhat more integrated, particularly those that reflect advances in technology, such as computer programmers and computer systems analysts. Several others associated with new technology, such as data processing machine repairers and office machine and cash register servicers, are now more than 90 percent male, but they may provide likely opportunities for women. Many of the other rapidly growing occupations reflect the continued tendency for

the service and health sectors to grow; some of those occupations are fairly well integrated, while others are not. Some observers suggest that as the United States economy continues to restructure itself toward services of various kinds, sex-neutral occupations can be expected to grow in importance. Others believe the growth of occupations associated with high technology may be overestimated by the Bureau of Labor Statistics. And recently its projections of substantial growth in the female-intensive clerical occupations have been questioned for underestimating the extent to which clerical work may be affected by automation. While there are several reasons for hypothesizing continued reduction in sex segregation associated with this predicted occupational growth, available data do not yet support them.

TABLE 2-9   Twenty Occupations With the Largest Projected Growth Rates, 1978-1990

Occupation	Percentage Female 1980[a]	Growth in Employment 1978-1990 (in thousands)	Percentage Growth 1978-1990
Data processing machine mechanics	7.4	93	147.6
Paralegal personnel	NA	38	132.4
Computer systems analysts	25.1	199	107.8
Computer operators	63.2	148	87.9
Office machine and cash register services	5.6	40	80.8
Computer programmers	28.4	150	73.6
Aero-astronautic engineers	1.2	41	70.4
Food preparation and service workers, fast food restaurants	66.9	492	68.8
Employment interviewers	48.7	35	66.6
Tax preparers	NA	18	64.5
Corrections officials and jailers	5.7	57	60.3
Architects	5.0	40	60.2
Dental hygienists	NA	31	57.9
Physical therapists	67.3	18	57.6
Dental assistants	97.9	70	57.5
Peripheral electronic data processing equipment operators	63.2	26	57.3
Child care attendants	86.7	20	56.3
Veterinarians	NA	17	56.1
Travel agents and accommodations appraisers	NA	25	55.6
Nurses' aides and orderlies	84.3	594	54.6

NA = not available.

[a]Approximate, due to the use of different occupational classifications in sources.

SOURCES: Carey (1981:Table 2); Rytina (1982:Table 1).

At issue in projecting the extent of occupational sex segregation are questions of the number of new jobs created and the relative rates of growth in sex-neutral as opposed to sex-segregated occupations, as well as the rate of change of the sex composition within these occupations.

Using the Bureau of Labor Statistics occupational employment projections for 1990, Beller and Han (1984) project the index of sex segregation under various assumptions. The first set of projections, for the labor force as a whole, assumes first that the occupational desegregation of the 1970s will continue throughout the 1980s at a linear rate; the model is then permitted to take a logistic form. The rationale for the assumption of linearity is that since it is easier for women to enter growing occupations than stagnant

or declining ones, the proportion of men in an occupation is a function of the initial proportion of men and the growth rate of the occupation. The logistic model is employed for greater accuracy at the extremes, i.e., for occupations with very high degrees of sex segregation. The results based on the linear model project a decline in the index of sex segregation of 1.7 points, from 61.7 in 1981 to 60.0 in 1990, if it is assumed that the change in sex composition over time is the same for all occupations; and a decline of 1.3 points, to 60.4, assuming that the sex composition of each occupation is a function of time. Using the logistic model for individual occupations, Beller and Han project a decline in the segregation index from 61.7 in 1981 to 56.1 in 1990. Standardized to the 1981 occupational distribution (rather than that projected for 1990 by the BLS), the drop in the index is slightly greater, indicating that the direction of the projected change in occupational distribution is toward more sex segregation, although the magnitude is small. In other words, the logistically projected decline in the sex segregation index is likely to be partially offset by changes in the sizes of occupations.

To project the index of sex segregation under varying assumptions, Beller and Han examine occupational segregation by work experience cohort for four different scenarios. Their most conservative projection assumes that there will be no further changes in the sex composition within each occupation as it ages, although as the labor force ages, less segregated cohorts replace older, more segregated ones. On the basis of these assumptions only a slight decline in the index of sex segregation is projected: from 64.2 in 1977 to 62.1 in 1990. The latter figure is slightly above the actual 1981 index, reflecting the trend toward a more sex-segregated occupational distribution projected by the BLS. Beller and Han argue that the decline of 2.1 points in the index of sex segregation can be taken as a lower bound; they expect a decline by 1990 of at least that much. On the basis of the assumption that the rate of change in the sex composition of occupations for the entering cohort will be the same between 1977 and 1990 as it was between 1971 and 1977 (a period of considerable change) they project an index of 57.3 in 1990. This decline of 6.9 percentage points comes closest to the logistic projection. In what they term their most optimistic scenario, they assume that affirmative action, attitudes, and other factors will continue to change at the same rate as during the 1970s, so that all cohorts experience declining sex segregation between 1977 and 1990. The index declines 11.7 points to 50.0 on the basis of this assumption, if the rate of change between 1977 and 1990 is half that between 1971 and 1977; it declines nearly 20 points to 42.2 if the rate of change between 1977 and 1990

is double what it was from 1971 to 1977, figures they consider to be an upper bound.

Beller and Han argue that the rate of occupational desegregation during the 1970s is too great to be maintained during the 1980s because the female labor force is unlikely to grow rapidly enough; all their projections imply higher female labor force participation rates and higher growth in the female share of the labor force than the BLS projects. Hence, they do not believe that the lower levels of occupational segregation they project for 1990 are likely to occur. Despite these limitations, their results are instructive in that they set upper limits on the amount of desegregation likely to occur during the 1980s. They point out that the direction of public policy can affect the amount of future change.

SUMMARY AND CONCLUSION

The amount of occupational segregation by sex continues to be substantial. In 1981, the index of occupational segregation by sex was 62, indicating that more than 60 percent of all women or men would have to move to occupations dominated by the opposite sex for segregation across occupations to be entirely eliminated. Additional segregation occurs across industries and firms. Men and women are disproportionally distributed across firms and industries even when the occupational mix they employ is taken into account. For example, even in integrated occupations, like payroll accounting clerk or assembler, some firms and industries tend to hire more women and others more men. In one study (Bielby and Baron, 1984), 231 of 391 California firms were totally sex-segregated; men and women worked in none of the same job categories.

The current situation is of greatest interest in the context of recent trends. Decennial census data since 1940 show a small decline in the total amount of occupational sex segregation among whites and a larger decline among other races. These two trends have produced a convergence in levels of occupational sex segregation between whites and nonwhites. Since World War II occupational segregation by race has declined much more rapidly than by sex. One component of this improvement has been black women's movement out of service occupations into clerical occupations. But within a sex-segregated occupational structure, race segregation persists. For example, black women are now overrepresented among postal clerks and telephone operators relative to their proportion in the labor force.

The sex segregation index dropped more during the 1970s than during previous decades, and the decline was most pronounced among younger workers. During the past decade men became slightly more likely to work in a few heavily female occupations, such as office machine operator or telephone operator, and women's representation has increased in several predominantly male occupations, including attorney, bank official, computer programmer, baker, bus driver, and bartender. Their numbers remain small in some of the occupations that women entered or increased their representation in during the 1970s (for example, coal miner, engineer), but their participation rate has increased markedly. Women's representation also increased among several predominantly female occupations that grew during

the 1970s, including bookkeepers, billing clerks, cashiers, and keypunch operators.

Although relatively substantial change occurred in the index of occupational sex segregation in the 1970s, the most likely projections for 1990 suggest that the rate of change throughout the 1980s will be much slower. The index fell by approximately 10 percent in the 1970s, from 68.3 in 1972 to 61.7 in 1981, according to Beller (1984), and from 67.7 in 1970 to 59.3 in 1980, according to Bianchi and Rytina (1984). In contrast, various likely projections of the job segregation index range from 56.0 to 60.0 in 1990. Only slight further declines are anticipated, primarily because occupations that are predominantly male or female are expected to grow more than those that are relatively integrated. And, of course, we do not have information that would permit us to estimate probable changes in job segregation at the establishment level.

The next two chapters provide a basis for assessing the likelihood of additional change. Chapter 3 examines the evidence for several explanations that have been offered for sex segregation in employment and consequently offers some guidance for developing policies for reducing segregation. Chapter 4 reviews a variety of attempts to reduce segregation in employment, education, and training, assesses their effectiveness, and provides further policy guidance.

3 Explaining Sex Segregation in the Workplace

In the committee's judgment, the causes of job segregation are multiple, interlocking, and deep-seated—yet, as we show in Chapter 4, they are also amenable to policy intervention. In this chapter we discuss the factors we feel to be the most important in accounting for the extreme degree of sex segregation of work observed in the United States. Intertwined with the social processes that contribute to job segregation are widely shared cultural assumptions about the sexes and their appropriate activities. For example, the belief of many people, including many women, that women should place the care of their families first in their lives affects the way women are treated on the job when they do work. And such beliefs also interact with reality: many women today do indeed bear the greater share of the day-to-day work involved in family care. Similarly, it is often assumed that physical differences between the sexes make them suited or unsuited for certain types of work, and there are average sex differences in size and stature that may be significant in some occupations.

In this chapter we first examine the cultural beliefs that govern common attitudes about gender and work. We next examine barriers to employment, tracing how some beliefs became embodied in laws and judicial decisions that permitted or demanded that employers treat the sexes differently, and how they continue to provide rationalizations for both intentional and unintentional labor market discrimination against women (and, less frequently, men). Third, we investigate the roles that women's own choices and preferences play in their work careers and examine the effects of socialization and training. Assumptions about what kinds of work are appropriate for each gender, communicated through various socialization and training processes, contribute to the development of sex-typed occupational preferences in individuals. Evidence suggests, however, that such sex-typed preferences are neither fixed for life nor fully deterministic of the sex type of workers' jobs. Fourth, we examine the role that family responsibilities, actual or anticipated, play in shaping both women's choices and their opportunities. Finally, we examine the thesis that the occupational opportunity structure plays a major role in perpetuating the concentration of the sexes in different jobs. By the occupational opportunity structure we mean the distribution of occupations that are available to members of each sex (and often certain racial and ethnic groups within each sex), a distribution that is seen to be limited by institutionalized and informal barriers that restrict workers' opportunities.

Regarding the relative importance of these various factors, it is our judgment that women's free occupational choices made in an open market explain only very incompletely their concentration in a small number of female-dominated occupations. While workers' choices undoubtedly contribute to the observed occupational distributions of the sexes, their labor market outcomes depend heavily on the occupational opportunity structure, on various barriers, including employers' and coworkers' preferences, and on institutionalized personnel procedures. In this chapter we look at the evidence in more detail.

CULTURAL BELIEFS ABOUT GENDER AND WORK

Beliefs about differences between the sexes, many of them taken as axiomatic, play an important role in the organization of social life. These assumptions are often so much a part of our world view that we do not consciously think about them. As one anthropologist put it, they are "referentially transparent" to us (Hutchins, 1980). It is their transparency that gives them their force: because they are invisible, the underlying assumptions go unquestioned, and the beliefs they entail seem natural to us. Even when we do question and revise certain of these beliefs—for instance, when we realize that they are prejudicial to women—the implicit assumptions that engendered them remain intact and can serve as the foundation for future, perhaps somewhat altered, sex stereotypes. The cultural axioms that have been used to exclude women from the workplace, to restrict them to certain occupations, or to condition their wage labor fall into three broad categories: those related to

women's role in the home, those related to male-female relationships, and those related to innate differences between the sexes.[1]

Women's Role in the Home

The first category consists of those assumptions that hold that women's "natural" place is in the home. This group of assumptions underlies many specific attitudes about women and work held by employers, male workers, lawmakers, parents, husbands, and women themselves. It seeks to legitimate women's exclusion from the public sphere and hence the workplace and implies that a woman who is committed to her job is unwomanly. This axiom is neither universal nor timeless. It is an expression of cultural beliefs elaborated especially over the last two centuries and perhaps most fully developed and widely disseminated, through the popular media, in the contemporary United States. The assumption that women's place is in the home follows from the premise that men support women, so women do not need to do wage work to earn a living. By implication, if women are employed, it must be for extras or diversion from domestic life, so their concentration in low-paying, dead-end jobs is of little importance. The corollary to this set of assumptions, that men do not belong in the home during working hours, also accounts for the almost totally segregated occupation of housewife and may help to explain the resilience of the traditional sexual division of domestic work among couples in which both partners are employed full time.

Historically as well as today, the notion that women's place is in the home has not reflected the actual behavior of large sectors of the population; hence it has been in fundamental conflict with the reality of many women's lives. Women have worked to sup-

---

[1] This section on cultural beliefs relies heavily on di Leonardo (1982).

port themselves and their families; they have worked because their labor was needed. Women have replaced men gone to war. They have done heavy labor on family farms when necessary. They have sought wage work when there was no means of support for them on the farm. They have taken in boarders and devised other ways to earn money at home. Women who are urban and minority, recent immigrants, and poor in general have done menial work for low wages, without the primacy of women's domestic role being invoked. And highly educated women, earning better salaries, have also worked as nurses, teachers, social workers, office workers, and businesswomen since late in the last century. As women from all parts of the social and economic spectrum have increased their labor force participation, the contradiction between the underlying belief about women's place and reality has become more visible.

We can now see ways in which the belief system has been modified with changing circumstances and ways in which reality has been reconciled to the belief system (di Leonardo, 1982). For example, those who insist that women should not work claim the incompatibility of paid employment with women's domestic roles, in that paid work interferes with proper child care. Those who wish to justify women's employment outside the home, by contrast, try to show that it is compatible with, even complements, their home roles. The latter justification permits or even promotes jobs for women that minimize interference with child care through flexible scheduling (e.g., school teaching or part-time work), low demands on incumbents (e.g., retail sales), or work that can be done at home (e.g., data processing, typing, sewing). Certain occupations (e.g., teaching home economics) that are believed to enhance women's ability to carry out domestic duties later in their lives may be considered more acceptable than others. Other occupations (e.g., nursing, social work) have been acceptable because they have been defined

as an extension of women's domestic roles, a rationale that has been used to justify paying workers in these jobs low wages (Kessler-Harris, 1982).

Thus, despite the strong contradiction between the notion of women's place and reality, the former continues to provide the foundation for beliefs about the conditions under which women should and should not do wage work. Most important for the present endeavor are beliefs as to which occupations are appropriate for them.

Male-Female Relationships

A second category of beliefs includes those about gender differences that are relevant in male-female relationships. For example, an ancient and pervasive belief in Western thought is that women lack reason and are governed by emotion (N. Davis, 1975; Jordanova, 1980). This line of thought offers a logical basis for assuming "natural" male dominance and underlies social values that men should not be subordinate to women. Whenever the two sexes interact outside the family, women are viewed as subordinate, and when they enter the workplace, they are expected to fill subordinate occupational roles. Caplow (1954) elaborates this point, arguing that attitudes governing interpersonal relationships in our culture sanction only a few working relationships between men and women and prohibit all others. He contends that according to these values, "intimate groups, except those based on family or sexual ties, should be composed of either sex but not both" (p. 238). Intimate work groups in which men and women have unequal roles are sometimes allowed. These norms of sexual segregation and male dominance have frequently guided employers' hiring decisions. Women are rarely hired in positions of authority (Wolf and Fligstein, 1979a, 1979b). Some employers explain that they defer to workers' preferences. Male managers surveyed one and two decades ago indicated that they felt both women and men would be uncomfortable working under a woman supervisor (Grinder, 1961; Bass et al., 1971). They also thought that women in supervisory roles have difficulty dealing with men in subordinate positions.

In several recent studies, it is clear that attitudes about female supervisors have changed. Two-thirds of the respondents in a 1980 Roper survey said it made no difference to them whether they worked for a man or a woman, and only 28 percent preferred a male supervisor (Barron and Yankelovich, 1980:Table 5). A survey of 1,402 university employees revealed a preference for male bosses and professionals providing personal services (accountants, dentists, lawyers, physicians, realtors, and veterinarians), but it was weaker among women, the more educated, and those who had had positive experiences with female bosses or professionals (Ferber et al., 1979). A study of women in several traditionally male jobs in public utilities found that most subordinates of both sexes held positive attitudes toward women managers (U.S. Department of Labor, Employment and Training Administration, 1978). Of particular interest is the admission by several men that they had been initially concerned but that their apprehensions disappeared when they found that their supervisors performed effectively. More generally, this study revealed that attitudes changed quite rapidly with experience with female bosses, even when those bosses held jobs that traditional values label "very masculine" (p. 10). The effects of education and experience suggest that we may expect continued change in employee attitudes toward women supervisors. For women's occupational opportunities to increase, however, the behavior of those making employment decisions must also change.

Sexual relations, as well as power relations, are also relevant in the workplace, and fears of sexual relations particularly may contribute to occupational segregation. The folk theory that women unwittingly tempt men and that men, vulnerable to their provocation, may be prompted to seduction has been used to justify excluding women from certain occupations or work settings that are thought to heighten men's vulnerability to female sexuality. Examples include shipboard duty or jobs that involve travel with coworkers. Women have been denied certain jobs because their presence may suggest the appearance of impropriety. MacKinnon (1979) cites the example of the South Carolina Senate, which refused to hire women as pages in order to foster public confidence in the Senate by protecting its members from appearing in a possibly damaging way. Not only men but women themselves may be depicted as the victims of their unwitting sexual provocation. Reformers around the turn of the century argued that permitting the sexes to work side by side would lead women to stray, either because their presence tempts men or because corrupt men will exploit innocent and vulnerable women who have left the protection of their homes. This concern reflects the belief in women's sexuality as an autonomous force over which neither they nor the men with whom they work have control. And it also reveals, once again, the assumption that women's primary place is in the home: for the consequence of women's employment alongside men feared by reformers was that these women, once having strayed sexually, would be forever disqualified from their domestic roles as wife and mother. Kessler-Harris quotes Robert McClelland, Secretary of the Interior, in the middle of the last century: "There is such an obvious impropriety in the mixing of the sexes within the walls of a public office that I am determined to arrest the practice" (1982:100-101). Such reasoning ultimately led several states to pass laws making it illegal for women to hold a variety of occupations, including bartender, messenger, meter reader, and elevator operator, but it did not prevent women from entering offices in large numbers (J. Smith, 1974; Kessler-Harris, 1982).

More recently, the stereotype of woman as sexual temptress has been invoked to account for women's sexual harassment: simply by entering the workplace, women subject men to their sexuality and invite harassment. Sexual harassment is pervasive in male-dominated occupations that women have recently entered (Enarson, 1980; Martin, 1980; Walshok, 1981a; Westley, 1982). Gruber and Bjorn (1982) suggest that men may use it to gain the upper hand in situations in which men and women have similar jobs and earn equal wages, especially in unskilled jobs in which male coworkers cannot punish entering women by denying them work-related information. The important point here is that the unquestioned assumptions about the sexuality of both men and women underlie the limiting of women's occupational choices.

Innate Differences Between the Sexes

A third category of beliefs that shape women's occupational outcomes are those that assume innate differences between the sexes. We have already seen that women are regarded as innately less rational and more emotional, a view that has been used to justify excluding them from positions of authority. In addition, women have variously been thought to lack aggressiveness, strength, endurance, and a capacity for abstract thought and to possess greater dexterity, tolerance for tedium, and natural morality than men. A body of research reviewed in Lueptow (1980) indicates that the public continues to hold many of these stereotypes about female and male "personalities." Some of these differences further justify women's greater responsibility for family care. For example, women's supposed natural sense of morality suits them for raising children and bringing a civilizing influence to family life.

Other stereotypes contribute directly to occupational segregation by asserting sex differences in what are alleged to be occupationally relevant traits. Women's dexterity is offered to explain their employment as clericals and sometimes as operatives; their supposed passivity and compliance have been

seen as uniquely fitting them for clerical work (Grinder, 1961; Davies, 1975; Kessler-Harris, 1982) as well as other jobs involving boring, repetitive tasks. One employer's explanation, offered in the 1960s, for preferring women illustrates both points: "We feel that jobs requiring manual dexterity call for women. Also this work is particularly tedious and painstaking—definitely a women's job" (G. Smith, 1964:24). Construction firms cite women's alleged weakness and intolerance of harsh working conditions as reasons for denying them jobs (U.S. Department of Labor, Employment Standards Administration, 1981; Westley, 1982). The social expectations that women should uphold moral standards and care about the needy, perhaps because of their innate nurturance, limit their occupational opportunities. As Epstein (1981) noted, women have been encouraged to perform good works in service-oriented occupations such as social work and nursing, which, coincidentally, have often had poor career potential. And women have been believed to be "too good" for politics. They are also thought to be too sentimental and timid to enforce the law or serve in combat (Epstein, 1981). Women's alleged emotionality may disqualify them in many employers' minds for higher-level positions, especially those in law, medicine, or science that require rationality and tough-mindedness (for a brief review, see Miller and Garrison, 1982).

Sex Stereotypes and Occupational Segregation

Many of these beliefs about women's innate traits and their natural social roles persist, despite women's increasing participation in a large number of formerly male occupations, even among students training for professions (Quadagno, 1976; Beattie and Diehl, 1979). A single woman worker who violates the stereotype can be explained as exceptional; when the behavior of many women clearly belies a particular stereotype, a different one may emerge to maintain the gender homogeneity with which members of an occupation have become comfortable. For example, women lawyers were dismissed in the 1960s as "too soft" for the courtroom. When they showed themselves to be competent in court, they were restereotyped by male lawyers as tough and unfeminine—and hence implicitly unsuited to their proper role as wife and mother (Epstein, 1981).

Stereotypes about appropriate and inappropriate occupations for women and men encourage sex-typical occupational choices by affecting workers' aspirations, self-image, identity, and commitment. The stereotyped views that masculine men would not pursue certain occupations, nor feminine women others, for instance, is deterrent enough for most people. Their misgivings are realistic: the femininity or masculinity of individuals who are not so deterred is questioned (Bourne and Wikler, 1978), and they may experience disapproval, especially from males (Nilson, 1976; Jacobs and Powell, 1983). The prospects of sexual harassment or of being prejudged as incompetent at one's work may also discourage those who might otherwise opt for sex-atypical occupations.

Another way that assumed sex differences affect the jobs women and men fill is that employers' beliefs that members of one sex do not want to do certain kinds of work influence their personnel decisions. For example, individuals who made hiring decisions for entry-level semiskilled jobs in several firms in one city commented to the researcher, "Women wouldn't like this," and "Men wouldn't like to see women (coworkers) this way." Another employer who hired primarily women said, "The work is clean and women like that" (Harkess, 1980).

Statistical Discrimination

Economists (Arrow, 1972; Phelps, 1972) have termed one form of employers' reluctance to hire certain persons "statistical discrimination," a concept that refers to decision making about an individual on the basis of characteristics believed to be typical of the group to which he or she belongs. The wide acceptance of assumptions of sex differences in characteristics related to productivity provides the basis for statistical discrimination by employers (e.g., Bass et al., 1971). According to this model, employers do not hire anyone who is a member of a group thought to have lower productivity; statistical discrimination serves for them as a cheap screening device. Statistical discrimination often rests on unquestioned assumptions about women's domestic roles. For example, employers may refuse to hire a woman in the childbearing years for certain jobs—especially those that require on-the-job training—because they assume that many young women will leave the labor force to have children, irrespective of any individual applicant's childbearing or labor market intentions. In a study of book publishing, Caplette (1981) discovered that women were automatically excluded from the primary route to upward mobility, the college traveler job, on the assumption that extensive traveling would conflict with their domestic responsibilities. According to this explanation of discrimination, employers practice statistical discrimination against women solely on economic grounds and presumably would ignore gender if they came to recognize that their cheap screening device was too costly in terms of misapplied human resources. Employers might, for example, become convinced that young men were equally likely to quit their jobs or take time off to share childbearing responsibilities or that many qualified women will not quit because of family responsibilities.

Statistical discrimination contributes to sex segregation in two ways. First, employers' beliefs that the sexes differ on work-related traits may bias them to favor one or the other sex for particular occupations. Second, if they expect that women are more likely than men to drop out of the labor force, they will hire women only for jobs that require little or no on-the-job training (e.g., retail sales) or involve skills whose training costs workers themselves assume (e.g., typing, hairdressing). Using data for 290 California establishments, Bielby and Baron (1986) examined whether employers seemed to reserve some jobs for men and others for women in a manner consistent with their perceptions of sex differences in skills, turnover, costs, and work orientations. They found that employers assigned jobs involving nonrepetitive tasks, spatial skills, eye-hand-foot coordination, and physical strength to men and those requiring finger dexterity to women. The concept of statistical discrimination also encompasses employers' favoring members of a group whose performance they believe they can predict more reliably. Even if the sexes were equally productive and performed equally well on some valid employment test, if the test predicted women's performance less reliably, employers would make fewer errors by hiring men (Aigner and Cain, 1977; Osterman, 1978). For this type of statistical discrimination to help explain sex segregation, employers must believe that women's performance is less reliably predicted than that of men, and so exclude them from some occupations.[2]

Sex Labeling and Sex Typing

In an influential 1968 study, Oppenheimer argued that the individual decisions of workers and employers are reinforced by a historical process through which most occupations have come to be labeled as women's work or men's work, and hence reserved for members of the appropriate sex. Op-penheimer contended that sex labeling reflected employers' beliefs that certain occupations required attributes that were characteristic of one sex or the other or, for women, represented an extension of domestic nonwage work. To job seekers, occupations take on the characteristics of current incumbents; custom then tends to make the sex labels stick.

The related concept of sex typing implies both that an occupation employs a disproportionate number of workers of one sex and the normative expectation that this is as it should be (Merton, in Epstein, 1970a:152). Manifest in language and the mass media, sex labels and the associated norms are learned through childhood and adult socialization by current and future workers and employers. An obvious example of sex typing in the mass media is classified advertisements stipulating a particular sex or segregated by sex, now not permissible under Title VII of the Civil Rights Act of 1964. Some sex-specific occupational titles (e.g., "lineman," "stewardess") are still common, although most were eliminated in the newest revision of the *Dictionary of Occupational Titles* (U.S. Department of Labor, 1977) and other government publications. Job descriptions often use sex-specific pronouns. Television, movies, magazines, and billboards consistently depict occupational incumbents in stereotyped ways (Marini and Brinton, 1984). As we show below, these labels influence the occupations to which people aspire, for which they prepare, and ultimately in which they seek employment. Influenced also are gatekeepers—parents, educators, employers, friends, and neighbors—who guide or control decisions regarding training and hiring. The widespread acceptance of these cultural labels may affect even those who reject them. Applicants who ignore the labels are likely to encounter prospective employers who accept them implicitly. Nondiscriminating employers may at least initially have trouble finding applicants for sex-atypical jobs. Even if labels

---

[2] One study offers evidence that this is the case. Although Osterman (1979) rejected less reliable predictions of women's absenteeism as a basis for wage differentials, Kahn (1981) showed that he used the wrong indicator of predictability. Using the appropriate one, Kahn found that female absenteeism was predicted less reliably, a finding that could support statistical discrimination in wages.

deter neither employer nor prospective employee, their acceptance by other employees or by a prospective employee's family may deter her or him from taking and keeping a sex-atypical job (Walshok, 1981a).

Contingent Stereotypes

Despite the prevalence and force of sex stereotyping of occupations, it is clear that these stereotypes do change over time, often in response to changing economic conditions. As noted above, secretaries were once typically male and women thought to be unsuitable, yet the preponderance of women in clerical jobs was later rationalized by their supposed feminine virtues. Economic and technological factors often vary over time and space, and stereotypes of the same jobs often differ according to how these factors vary. Studies of the age and sex characteristics of workers in the textile industries of Japan and the southern United States (Saxonhouse and Wright, 1982) and France (Tilly, 1979, 1982) in the first quarter of this century illustrate this point. In Japan, agriculture was a family enterprise in which girls and young women were the least valuable workers, so their families permitted them to work temporarily in the textile industry, as young women did in New England in an earlier period (Dublin, 1979). Single young women filled textile jobs, even in occupations that were held elsewhere by men. In contrast, in the American South entire families who lacked land tenure and access to well-developed labor markets worked in the textile industry, where jobs were assigned on the basis of sex and age. Only adult men had access to the most skilled jobs. The situation in France was similar: mills hired entire impoverished rural families, but only boys and men could move up the job ladder to better-paying, more skilled jobs. These varied employment practices, a product of structured economic opportunity interacting with male and parental power and household patterns of labor allocation, produced

different patterns of sex segregation that persisted for some time.

The effects on sex segregation of economic factors, cultural beliefs, and the law are cumulative and reciprocal, but, as we have seen, this reciprocity can contribute positively to change. Bumpass (1982) found that the mothers of young children who worked between 1970 and 1975 were substantially less likely to agree that young children suffer if their mothers work than they had been in 1970. American cultural values about the sexes have changed since World War II (Mason et al., 1976; Cherlin and Walters, 1981; Thornton et al., 1983), at least partly in response to the women's movement. During this period women have entered occupations that were formerly closed to them. New laws and administrative regulations, such as the interpretation of Title VII of the 1964 Civil Rights Act to proscribe sexual harassment as discriminatory, help to weaken the link between traditional cultural stereotypes and employment practices. As these changes become apparent and are supported by changes in social values—especially those embodied in statutes outlawing discrimination—they transmit to future workers and employers the message that society gives women "permission" to pursue a broader range of jobs. Women's movement into occupations from which they once were excluded will also contribute to exposing the discrepancy between reality and many of our cultural assumptions about the sexes. With growing awareness that these beliefs are dubious and the traits to which they apply alterable, women's occupational aspirations and opportunities should expand accordingly.

BARRIERS TO EMPLOYMENT

A variety of barriers make it difficult for women to hold certain jobs or exclude them altogether, thus contributing to their preponderance in traditionally female occupations. Evidence suggests that employers sometimes deny women certain jobs because of their sex, by discriminating intentionally, by doing so unintentionally, or by deferring to the discriminatory preferences of employees or customers. Studies of employment practices before the passage of the Civil Rights Act reveal extensive sex segregation and the payment of lower wages to women; often these practices were explicitly codified in rules (Newman, 1976). Until recently, many state laws prohibited employers from hiring women for certain occupations or prescribed the conditions under which they could work. Some occupations (positions on combat ships in the U.S. Navy and on combat planes in the U.S. Air Force, for example) are still closed to women by law. Practices that have the effect of restricting women's access to some jobs, such as certain kinds of seniority systems or veterans' preference, are often institutionalized in formal personnel procedures. Others reside in informal aspects of the organization of work. Although it is impossible to assess the relative importance of these barriers in preventing women from entering and progressing in traditionally male-dominated jobs, it is essential to examine how they operate in order to propose and assess remedies.

Legal Barriers

Legal barriers that limit women's free occupational choice are of two types: those imposed by law or public regulation and those instituted by employers that the law encourages, permits, or does not effectively prevent.[3] As Clauss (1982) points out, prior to the late 1800s tradition and prejudice were usually sufficient to keep women in the few occupations deemed appropriate for them, but when necessary the authority of the law was invoked to contain women's nontradi-

tional aspirations. For example, Justice Bradley's opinion in *Bradwell* v. *Illinois* (83 U.S., 16 Wall., 130, 141-42, 1872), in which the U.S. Supreme Court rejected a challenge to an Illinois law prohibiting women's admission to the bar, reflects the contemporary view of women:

The natural and proper timidity and delicacy which belongs to the female sex unfits it for many of the occupations of civil life. The constitution of the family organization, which is founded in the divine ordinance, as well as in the nature of things, indicates the domestic sphere as that which properly belongs to the domain and functions of womanhood.

The first protective labor law was enacted in 1874. Although a large literature debates the motivations of the working men and women, reformers (many of them feminists), and union leaders who supported protective labor legislation for women (Freeman, 1971; Hartmann, 1976; Steinberg, 1982), their long-run effect unquestionably was to restrict women's occupational opportunities (Baer, 1978). They prohibited women from doing tasks required by many occupations such as lifting more than a maximum weight, working more than a certain number of hours, or working at night. Some states specifically prohibited women from holding certain occupations, including some that supposedly could corrupt women morally (e.g., bartending) and others (mining, smelting, meter reading, pin setting in bowling alleys, crossing watchmen, jitney driving, freight handling or trucking) for which the rationale is less clear (Clauss, 1982). The legacy of such laws cannot be overemphasized. Railroads, for example, used the California hour and weight-lifting restrictions to justify not hiring women as telegraphers (Clauss, 1982). An Illinois company used an 8-hour law for women to justify paying women operatives for only 8 hours when they were working 8½ hours. Not until the 1964 Civil Rights Act was passed and litigation occurred were these laws invalidated. Those that remain

---

[3] This section draws heavily on Clauss (1982) and Roos and Reskin (1984).

on the books are unenforceable. But even in the 1960s and 1970s, manufacturers surveyed by the California State Employment Service often cited weight-lifting restrictions to justify not hiring women (Bielby and Baron, 1984).

In *Griggs* v. *Duke Power Company*, 401 U.S. 424 (1971) the Supreme Court interpreted Title VII of the 1964 Civil Rights Act to prohibit non-job-related requirements that disproportionately exclude members of protected groups. This ruling opened some occupations to women. For example, it invalidated requirements of height and physical agility that largely barred women from being officers in the San Francisco Police Department (Gates, 1976). Yet many police departments still maintain such requirements, preventing women from becoming police officers (Martin, 1980:47).

The prohibition against using sex as an employment criterion under Title VII is not absolute. Employers may refuse to hire applicants of one sex if they can show that sex is a bona fide occupational qualification (BFOQ) reasonably necessary to their normal operation (Section 703[e]). Although the occupations in which sex is a bona fide qualification typically cited are wet nurse and sperm donor, employers have succeeded in using the BFOQ provision to justify excluding women from such jobs as prison chaplains or guards (*Long* v. *California State Personnel Board*, 41 Cal. App. 3d 1000, 116 Cal. Rptr. 562, 1974; *Dothard* v. *Rawlinson*, 433 U.S. 321, 1977) because their sexuality might provoke the passions of violent male inmates and as international oil executives because that job involves dealing with allegedly sex-prejudiced Latin Americans (*Fernandez* v. *Wynn Oil*, 20 FEP 1162 [C.D. Cal.], 1979).

Laws and regulations stipulating that preference be given to veterans—legal under the Supreme Court's decision in *Personnel Administrators of Massachusetts* v. *Feeny*, 99 S.C. 2282 (1979)—reduce women's access to certain jobs. For example, 65 percent of all government agencies and 57 percent of municipal agencies preferred veterans when selecting police officers (Eisenberg et al., cited in Martin, 1980:47). Veterans' preference rules also apply to layoffs and contributed to the higher layoff rates that female federal government employees in grades above GS 12 (in which women are underrepresented) experienced in the federal personnel cuts of 1981 (Federal Government Service Task Force, 1981). The policy of giving veterans an advantage was formally incorporated into criteria for the Comprehensive Employment and Training Act (CETA) trainees in 1978, contributing to women's underrepresentation in certain programs relative to their proportion in the eligible population (Wolf, 1981).

The policy by some employers of excluding women in their childbearing years from jobs that might expose them to substances that are potentially toxic to fetuses has demonstrable segregative consequences. Federal officials have estimated that such policies close at least 100,000 jobs to women.[4] These jobs are concentrated in industries that have historically excluded women (Clauss, 1982), and some observers (Bell, 1979; Wright, 1979) have pointed out that employers use this policy to exclude women from better-paying male jobs, while ignoring hazards in predominantly female occupations.[5] In two Title VII challenges, the courts recently ruled that employers may not penalize women employees under the guise of protecting them from reproductive hazards (*Wright* v. *Olin Corporation*, 697 F.2d 1192 [4th Cir. 1982]; *Zuniga* v. *Klebert County Hospital*, 692 F.2d 986 [5th Cir. 1982]). Until 1978

---

[4] This estimate does not include the number of military jobs closed to women because of policies that do not permit women to occupy jobs that are related to combat (Roos and Reskin, 1984).

[5] Such hazards include the exposure of operating room nurses to waste anesthetic gases, of beauticians to hydrocarbon hair spray propellants, and of clerical workers to photoduplicating fluid.

employers could exclude pregnant women from certain jobs, even when it meant that they lost accumulated seniority. Then, in response to extensive lobbying by women's groups following the Supreme Court's decision in *General Electric* v. *Gilbert*, 429 U.S. 125 (1976), which held that discrimination against the condition of pregnancy in employment benefits such as disability insurance is not illegal sex discrimination, Congress amended Title VII to prohibit discrimination against pregnant women.

Title VII, provisions of Title IX of the Educational Amendment Act, and other laws provide recourse for women who are discriminated against in various conditions of employment. Yet, private litigation, which is expensive and lengthy, is seldom a viable option for many women, and enforcement agencies and legal rights organizations must limit the number of cases they pursue through the courts. Satisfactory redress of many of these cases, even of relatively overt discrimination, is not therefore easily attained.

Discriminatory Acts and Behavior

Most economic theories of labor market discrimination were constructed to explain wage discrimination rather than restrictions on access to jobs. Nevertheless, we review them briefly, concentrating on their implications for segregation in labor markets (for more extensive discussions, see Treiman and Hartmann, 1981; Blau, 1984a, 1984b). Gary Becker's (1957) theory of race discrimination presumes a "taste" for distance from blacks, on the part of employers, employees, or customers. If employers discriminate, they pay for that taste by bidding up the wage for white workers above what would be necessary if they hired blacks. A discriminating employer would hire blacks only if they were willing to work at a wage low enough to compensate the employer for the "distaste." Economic considerations could motivate even unprejudiced employers to discriminate, however. If white employees have a taste for distance from blacks, they will work in an integrated workplace only if they are paid a premium for doing so. Employers will then lower the wage of blacks in order to compensate for the higher wage that they must pay whites when blacks are hired. Likewise, if customers have discriminatory tastes, prices will have to be lowered in order to prevent the loss of those customers to firms employing only whites. Again, the employer will hire blacks only at a lower wage in order to compensate for the loss in revenue from the lower sale price. Very few efforts have been made to test empirically any of Becker's hypotheses (Cain, 1984). However, customer discrimination has been suggested by Allison (1976) with respect to the higher wages earned by male than female beauticians, and Epstein (1981) found that many law firms attributed their reluctance to hire female attorneys to an anticipated loss of clients who they believed prefer males.[6]

Indulging discriminatory tastes could produce segregation across occupations or establishments (Blau, 1984b). Assuming that employers differ in their taste for discrimination or in their willingness to pay to indulge that taste, the victims of discrimination, blacks or women, would be totally absent from some establishments and concentrated in others—at lower wages (Bergmann, 1971, 1974). If employers were more adverse to hiring women for some jobs than others (or if male workers in different occupations expressed different amounts of opposition), then occupational segregation would result.

Understanding the reasons for discriminatory tastes might explain why employers' aversion to hiring women varies across occupations and why they prefer women for

---

[6] They also cited other reasons, ranging from problems in providing separate rest rooms to their own wives' opposition (Epstein, 1981).

some. Hiring decisions in prestigious professional and managerial occupations often involve subjective appraisals of whether an
applicant will "fit in," since the potential
consequences of an error are greater given
the higher levels of uncertainty and individual control over the work process in those
occupations (Kanter, 1977). For some occupations, employers prefer female workers. A 1961 survey by the National Office
Management Association (Grinder, 1961) of
1,900 commercial and service organizations
found that 28 percent indicated that sex appeal was a qualification for some office jobs.
Since most men live intimately with women
and men often work closely with women in
lower-status jobs, clearly any taste for avoid-
ing associating with women is situation-spe-
cific.

Theories that focus on patriarchy (Hartmann, 1976; Strober, 1984) contend that
men's desire to keep women socially and
economically dependent contributes to sex
segregation and other limitations of equal
employment opportunity for women. This
would explain men balking at working with
women as equals, while accepting female
coworkers in subordinate jobs. Bergmann
and Darity (1981) have argued that a few
prejudiced workers can disrupt the workplace; they suggest that employers may defer to a few prejudiced employees in order
to maintain harmony on the job. An alternative explanation for exclusionary behavior
rests on the social perception of status. If
the evaluation of some group as lower in
social status is in general currency, then establishments or occupations that fail to hon-
or it by including more than a token number
of members of the lower-status group taint
themselves (Touhey, 1974) and jeopardize
the claim for deference they can make on
others. Thus, a law firm with more than one
or two blacks or women risks being labeled
a "black" or "women's" firm and a concomitant loss of prestige.

Another explanation of the segregation of
women and blacks into low-paying occupations rests on the potential profitability of

that arrangement. While many economists
have argued that the inefficient use of labor
resources on the part of discriminating employers will diminish employer profits (Arrow, 1972; Becker, 1957; Bergmann, 1971),
others have pointed to the circumstances
under which segregation actually increases
profitability. In neoclassical economic theory, if an employer holds some monopsony
power (either because the employer hires a
large portion of the available workers in a
particular area or because employees in a
firm have low levels of mobility) *and* if the
supply of labor is more elastic for women
and blacks, then segregating those groups
from white men and paying them a lower
wage will increase profitability (Madden,
1975; Robinson, 1936). The extent to which
these conditions persist in the labor market
is a matter of some dispute, however (Cain,
1984), and one preliminary study that looks
at the relationship between the propensity
to hire women and profitability concludes
that discrimination does impose a cost,
though relatively small, on employers (Stolzenberg, 1982).

A class analysis of discrimination posits
that employers segregate workers into groups
that are then paid differentially in order to
prevent the development of a cohesive
working class. Since a unified work force is
seen as holding more power to bargain over
wages, segregation lowers the wage of all
subgroups of labor (though some more than
others), thus enhancing employer profitability. This hypothesis has been tested with
respect to race but not to sex (Reich, 1981).

Until the late 1960s or early 1970s sex
discrimination by unions contributed to occupational segregation in several ways. Some
unions openly excluded women by policy or
maintained sex-segregated bargaining units;
others pursued practices that effectively kept
women out (Simmons et al., 1975; Kessler-
Harris, 1975; Hartmann, 1976).[7] Nepotism

_____

[7] Union behavior has been seen as largely protec-
tionist, but Hartmann (1976) argues that patriarchal

and sexism in the distribution of apprenticeships ensured women's virtual exclusion from the crafts; opportunities to learn a trade typically went to members' male relatives (Simmons et al., 1975). Collective bargaining agreements between unions and management were often openly discriminatory. For example, they frequently identified jobs as "male" or "female" and specified sex-segregated promotion and transfer ladders and separate lines of layoff and rehiring priorities for the sexes. On occasion women and men were even assigned to different locals, but this practice was ultimately found to be a violation of Title VII (Simmons et al., 1975).

Because Title VII of the 1964 Civil Rights Acts and other laws and regulations prohibit many forms of sex discrimination in employment, obtaining evidence of discrimination is now often difficult. Employers are unlikely to admit discriminatory hiring practices that they might have admitted in the past. Survey data, case studies, and experiments suggest, however, that discrimination has been an important factor in excluding women from a variety of occupations. Throughout most of this century women have faced open discrimination in employment or wages in many occupations. For example, one-third of the business and service organizations that responded to a 1961 survey by the National Office Management Association admitted a double standard of pay for female and male office employees, and two-thirds were admittedly reluctant to appoint women to supervisory jobs (Grinder, 1961).

Until quite recently, law firms openly discriminated in hiring and job assignment. Epstein (1981) recounts incidents of women lawyers being offered jobs as legal secretaries, and Rossiter (1982) tells of women scientists with advanced degrees employed as chemical librarians and scientific secretaries. Female physicians (Walsh, 1977) were commonly denied jobs for which they were qualified. Prior to 1964, employers were often candid regarding the preferred sex and race of their employees (see, for example, Grinder, 1961). A survey published by the *Harvard Law Record* in 1963 indicated that in evaluating applicants law firms rated being female more negatively than all other characteristics, including being at the bottom of one's class (Epstein, 1981). Nonprofessional occupations have been subject to less investigation, but the firing of women from craft jobs at the end of World War II to provide jobs for returning male veterans is well documented (Milkman, 1980). A comment by a female worker in a large industrial plant illustrates what is believed by many (Newman and Wilson, 1981) to be extensive discrimination in job assignments (O'Farrell, 1980:35):

I do the same work on the bench lathes as the men who do work on the big lathes. . . . We do the *same thing* to the pieces. . . . We have the *same equipment* and the *same training*. All the women welders went to welding school [run by the company] the same as the men. We passed the same tests to be certified as welders. . . . The only difference is that when we got through training, they sent all the women to be welders at a rate 14, while all the men went to a rate of 18. The women work on smaller pieces than the men, but we have to have the same skill and do the same welding work. . . . In fact, our work used to be part of the men's welding job, but the men didn't like it. . . . So [management] broke that part of the job off and put women on it, at a lower rate.

Employment practices in the Bell Telephone System prior to the 1973 consent decree illustrate the importance of occupational assignment: all formal recruiting was sex-

---

considerations have also been a factor. If the unions' only goal was simply to limit competition, sex need not have been the significant factor. Why were young men but not young women encouraged to enter trades? Why were male workers organized by unions, but not female workers? Hartmann argues that men had self-interest in maintaining women's subordinate position in the labor market so that women would continue to be economically dependent on men and perform household services. Many statements by union leaders during the nineteenth and early twentieth centuries indicate their strong support for keeping women at home.

specific, and it was impossible for applicants to pursue jobs that the company had decided were sex-inappropriate (Laws, 1976).

Cassell and Doctors (1972) used personnel records and interviews with managers and employees to examine the job grades for 2,300 workers in three manufacturing firms. They found that two of the firms discriminated in assigning job grades to women when they were hired and that this assignment tended to affect both grade and wage progression as long as the women remained with the firm.[8] They also found that firms were less likely to promote women to higher grades. Company representatives claimed that women did not want promotions because it would entail more responsibility and mean leaving their friends. Generally none of the workers, male or female, was well informed about promotion opportunities (in one of the companies, openings were posted for only two days), making it difficult for anyone to pursue them independently without official encouragement. A recent study of 3,500 employees at three large fiduciary institutions revealed similar results (Cabral et al., 1981). The researchers found that men tended to be placed in higher job categories than women with comparable education and were more likely to be promoted compared with women in similar entry positions, when seniority and previous experience were controlled. Malkiel and Malkiel (1973) found that female professionals in a large organization were assigned to lower-level jobs than similarly qualified men. Halaby (1979a) arrived at similar conclusions for managerial employees in a California public utility: while differences in experience and education translated into promotion to higher ranks for men, women remained concentrated in lower managerial ranks in which returns to increases in human capital were restricted.

A recent study of how several manufacturing firms in a southern city filled vacancies (Harkess, 1980) suggests that most of the employers explicitly considered gender in deciding whether to hire applicants for entry-level semiskilled positions, although they too explained that women would not want certain jobs. Recent field studies of the construction industry in which hiring quotas are in effect (U.S. Department of Labor, Employment Standards Administration, 1981; Westley, 1982) confirmed contractors' resistance to hiring women, even though they admitted that women were competent and indeed more dependable than men. Some cited objections by other employees as motivating their refusal to hire women.

A growing body of experimental research, some on employers or persons in training for managerial positions, also shows that employers favor men over equally or sometimes more qualified women (Fidell, 1970; Lewin and Duchan, 1971; Levinson, 1975; Dubeck, 1979). Although, taken singly, the generalizability of some of these studies is questionable, as a group they confirm the findings of surveys and statistical studies, case studies, and the accounts of women workers.

The unexpectedly large number of complaints of sex discrimination in hiring, job assignment, and promotion decisions that have been filed with federal antidiscrimination regulatory agencies since the passage of Title VII and other legislation provides evidence that women workers believe that they have been discriminated against. The number of charges filed with the Equal Employment Opportunity Commission (EEOC) increased from 2,053 in 1966 to almost 55,000 in 1983 (Equal Employment Opportunity Commission, 1984) or about one complaint for every 900 women in the labor force.

Institutionalized Barriers in the Workplace

Some of the barriers that exclude women from certain male occupations are embed-

---

[8] The data for the third firm were not adequate to draw conclusions about discrimination.

ded in the formal structure of establishments: their personnel practices, job descriptions, mobility ladders, and the organization of tasks. These institutionalized barriers may have had their origin in prejudice or may be the by-products of administrative rules and procedures that were established for other reasons (such as seniority systems). However, once they are incorporated in an organization's structure they persist regardless of the lack of any discriminatory intent, unless they are altered.[9] Most individuals looking for work approach an employer within a broad and vaguely defined category (Blau and Jusenius, 1976). Employers play an active role in the labor market; they decide whether to hire applicants as well as for what job. The set of occupations to which any worker has access is generally quite small. Once workers get jobs, the job ladders that comprise their employers' internal labor markets (Doeringer and Piore, 1971) govern the occupations open to them. Of course, management decides who among alternative candidates should be promoted to fill vacancies and how quickly (see, for an example, Harlan and O'Farrell, 1982). As a result, sex differences in the allocation of workers to entry-level jobs greatly narrow the number of jobs available to women workers and perpetuate sex segregation throughout all jobs in an establishment (Blau and Jusenius, 1976).

Most large employers have internal labor markets with highly structured recruiting practices. Depending on the characteristics they seek in workers, employers use employment services, advertise directly to particular labor pools, or use employee referrals. The common practice of relying on informal referrals reflects employers' assumptions that a homogeneous work force will facilitate on-the-job training (Stevenson, 1977) and reduce the uncertainty inherent in hiring decisions (Kanter, 1977). For example, none of the employers Harkess (1980) surveyed used classified advertisements. Even if they did not actively discriminate in hiring, their reliance on employee referrals and walk-ins was likely to discourage applications from people unlike those already working there. The people to whom employees pass on job possibilities are part of their personal networks. Not only are such networks sex-segregated as a rule, but women are less likely than men to find their jobs through such informal methods (Leon and Rones, 1980; Granovetter, 1981; Roos and Reskin, 1984). Even if asked, workers might hesitate to recommend persons of the "wrong" sex or race, in the belief that they are less likely to satisfy their employer (Harkess, 1980).

Antinepotism rules provide one example of an employment policy that, while sex-neutral in theory, in practice works against women more often than men. By precluding spouses from working in the same department or company, they have tended to exclude wives who have similar background and training as their husbands but may be slightly behind in their careers. Although such rules are no longer the impediment they were for female academics prior to the 1970s (Simon et al., 1966; Dolan and Davis, 1960), many large companies continue to have policies against employing spouses.[10]

---

[9] This section draws heavily on Roos and Reskin (1984).

---

[10] Recent evidence regarding nepotism rules comes from the popular media and is unsystematic. It does indicate, however, that nepotism rules persist in some firms. A 1978 *New York Times* article (May 8) on nepotism referred to a policy that was only two years old at the University of New Orleans. A similar article that appeared in the *Louisville Courier Journal* (May 14, 1978) mentioned a recent unsuccessful suit challenging the nepotism rule at Libbey-Owens-Ford. In fall 1982 *Newsweek* (October 11, 1982:94) quoted a statement by Edward Hennessy, chairman of the board at Allied Corporation: "We have a policy at this company that we don't hire wives," which he later amended in a letter to the editor (November 29, 1982:6) to say that Allied's policy is not to hire the spouses of corporate officers

Most institutional barriers to promotion within firms reside in rules about seniority, job bidding, eligibility for promotion, and so forth that govern the operation of their internal labor markets. Because these practices are often codified (in collective bargaining agreements or civil service rules, for example), they are more visible than the barriers to being hired that women face. Best documented, perhaps, are the segregative effects of seniority systems that link workers' promotion prospects to their length of employment, particularly when they are not plantwide (Kelley, 1982; Roos and Reskin, 1984). In large firms, seniority to determine eligibility for promotion is often accrued only within a department or job group, and having substantial seniority in one group does not help one attain promotion opportunities in a new group. In effect, one loses seniority by transferring. Since many entry-level positions and their associated job ladders are sex-segregated, narrowly constituted seniority units hamper women's opportunity to transfer to jobs held by men that may have greater promotional opportunities. Even women with considerable experience are effectively limited in their access to male-dominated jobs in other units (Kelley, 1982). When legal action opens such jobs to women, many have been reluctant to sacrifice their seniority and risk future layoffs by transferring to male jobs (O'Farrell, 1982). Seniority is consequential even when jobs are secure, since it often determines shift, overtime, and vacation assignments (Steinberg and Cook, 1981).

Plantwide seniority systems that provide bumping rights in case of layoffs (in which more senior employees "bump" less senior ones, moving into their jobs, while the junior employees are laid off) may facilitate women's movement into sex-atypical employment. Some courts have addressed this

problem (e.g., *Quarles* v. *Phillip Morris*, 279 F Supp. 505, 516, E.D. Va., 1968) by invalidating departmentwide seniority systems in firms in which departments were segregated (in this case, by race). However, a subsequent decision (*Teamsters* v. *United States et al.*, 45 LW 4514, 1977) denied remedies unless employees could show that the disparate impact of a bona fide seniority system was the result of intentional discrimination. In a recent decision (*Firefighters Local Union No. 1784* v. *Stotts*, 104 S. Ct. 2576 [1984]) the Supreme Court held that the city of Memphis could apply its bona fide seniority system rather than lay off more senior white workers while retaining minority workers with less seniority to preserve the minority percentage of the work force. The Court, in striking down a lower court's injunction against the city's use of its seniority system, reasoned that the minorities who were protected from layoff were not the actual victims of previous discrimination by the city. Redressing problems of seniority can be difficult, since altering seniority systems, which generally have the force of tradition behind them, can generate opposition from those whose effective seniority is reduced by the remedy. For example, Northrup and Larson (1979) found that the seniority overrides required in the AT&T-EEOC consent decree engendered male hostility.

Practices of job posting (O'Farrell, 1980) have also impaired women's access to sex-atypical jobs in their plants. Job posting is seldom plantwide, so women do not learn of openings in other divisions (Shaeffer and Lynton, 1979; O'Farrell, 1980). A survey of corporations revealed that improved job posting facilitated women's movement into sex-atypical blue-collar jobs in nonunionized firms in which seniority was not binding (Shaeffer and Lynton, 1979). Information about openings is not sufficient, however. Many establishments have rules about who can apply for a transfer or a promotion, and in some firms bidding rights do not extend

---

nor to permit married couples to work in the same department or supervise each other.

across all units. In one such company that O'Farrell (1980) studied, regulations against cross-plant bidding served to keep women segregated in predominantly female jobs in the smaller of two plants.

A body of research on the New York State Civil Service system documents the segregative effect of formal promotion systems within structured job sequences (New York State Commission on Management and Productivity in the Public Sector, 1977; Peterson-Hardt and Perlman, 1979; C. Smith, 1979; Ratner, 1981; Haignere et al., 1981). Job ladders were typically sex-segregated with women concentrated in the lowest-level jobs within ladders. The "female" ladders were both shorter and more difficult to climb because of more stringent educational and experience requirements (Peterson-Hardt and Perlman, 1979). Given the stipulated limits on the number of candidates who could compete for a vacancy and women's underrepresentation in the eligible pools, women's chances for promotion were necessarily lower than those of men (Haignere et al., 1981; Ratner, 1981). Using supervisors' recommendations to identify candidates for promotion can also undermine the promotion opportunities of women in supportive roles. Although supervisors may be reluctant to recommend able assistants of either sex for promotion (Kanter, 1977; Shaeffer and Lynton, 1979), women suffer more because they are more apt to hold such jobs.

Design aspects of the work or the tools used can influence women's performance and hence their retention in historically male blue-collar jobs. Although women can learn to use unfamiliar tools, most machinery has been designed to accommodate men, so small women may not be able to operate existing machinery as efficiently or as safely as men (Walshok, 1981a). AT&T's experience is illustrative: women in outdoor jobs had higher accident rates than men until lighterweight and more mobile equipment was introduced. Although it is unlikely that the intent to exclude women consciously influ-

enced decisions about machine design or equipment, the decisions may nonetheless be exclusionary in effect. Women's lack of familiarity with tools and techniques may also restrict their interest in or access to a variety of blue-collar occupations, but remedial programs have also been effective in bringing women's skill level to a par with that of male job entrants (Walshok, 1981b).

Informal Barriers in the Workplace

Exclusion also occurs subtly through a variety of processes that steer people away from work that has been culturally defined as inappropriate for their sex. Here we examine how informal processes in the workplace contribute to sex segregation either because an uncomfortable work climate leads women to withdraw from customarily male occupations or because it interferes with their ability to learn and perform their job.

Occupations that have been defined as male often provide an inhospitable context for women.[11] Women who enter them in violation of their sex labels are regarded as deviant and may face suspicion regarding their motives, hostility, or other sanctions (Aga, 1984). Men who are unaccustomed to working with women simply may be uncertain about how to behave. When work groups are integrated, gender becomes salient for the male occupants, who may subject the women to remarks calculated to put them in their place by emphasizing their deviant gender status (Kanter, 1977). These may take the form of profanity, off-color jokes, anecdotes about their own sexual prowess, gossip about the women's personal lives, and unwarranted intimacy toward them (Kanter, 1977; Martin, 1980). Kanter's analysis sug-

---

[11] Of course, the same has been true among men of different racial groups, and Kessler-Harris (1982) describes how prejudice by white female coworkers kept black women out of certain occupations and relegated them to others.

gests that male coworkers also assign women one of a small set of stereotyped nonprofessional personalities (mom, kid sister), which tend to prevent the women from participating in the group as full members. Women may respond to male hostility—whether direct or masked—with aloofness or defensiveness, which in turn makes interaction more difficult. Reskin (1978) has shown how role stereotyping limits the integration of women into the scientific community and impairs their performance.

These processes are especially likely in occupations that have a strong subculture, such as the police force (Martin, 1980) or occupations in which workers spend many hours together during slack periods. Firefighters represent such a group, as do crews that travel together (oil crews, merchant marines) or construction workers who may sit around the job site waiting out bad weather. To the extent that the work group resembles a social group, newcomers of a different sex (or race) may be viewed as intruders. Such occupations, too, may require a high degree of interdependence. The amount of interdependence in the work process can affect women's chance of success in sex-atypical jobs (Epstein, 1970a). When women are an unwelcome minority, whether they work autonomously or depend on others to accomplish their job makes a big difference in their performance. Several women pioneers in blue-collar occupations indicated that male coworkers' refusal to help them in the same way they would assist similar male workers hampered their ability to do their jobs (Walshok, 1981a; U.S. Department of Labor, Employment and Training Administration, 1978). Hostility sometimes takes the form of men sabotaging women's performance (Walshok, 1981a). In contrast, when work is organized so that women can work alone or with female partners, their retention in jobs dominated by men increases (Shaeffer and Lynton, 1979; Walshok, 1981a). It is probably not coincidental that several male-dominated occupations in which women's participation has increased do not involve working closely with others, e.g., bus drivers, real estate agents, dispatchers, mail carriers, office machine repairers (Remick, 1982).

At the extreme, women in male-dominated jobs face overt harassment (Nieva and Gutek, 1981; Walshok, 1981a). Sexual harassment is now recognized to be pervasive (Farley, 1978; MacKinnon, 1979; U.S. Systems Protection Board, 1981) and has been documented in construction (U.S. Department of Labor, Employment Standards Administration, 1981; Westley, 1982), craft jobs (Walshok 1981a), the automobile industry (Gruber and Bjorn, 1982), and forestry (Enarson, 1980). There is, however, no evidence that women entering occupations defined as male are more likely to be sexually harassed than those who work in traditionally female jobs.

Some women find superficial acceptance in predominantly male occupations but are excluded in subtle ways that impair their ability to do their jobs. Often their exclusion is not deliberate; men may be unaware of or indifferent to the process, and women reluctant to speak up (Epstein, 1970a). Since male domination of top positions is a structural phenomenon, however, the same processes that tend to strengthen the fraternity of men reinforce the exclusion of women. In the past many professional associations and unions barred women from membership (Epstein, 1970b; Simmons et al., 1975). Even today, some elite professional clubs in which important contacts are nurtured do not accept women as members, and women attending meetings there must literally use the back stairs (Schafran, 1981). More problematic because it is a daily affair is women's exclusion from informal networks. Kanter (1976:415) points out that "organizations . . . comprise a network of power relations outside of the authority vested in formal positions. . . ." Although some have observed that women lack access to these networks (Campbell, 1973; Welch and Lewis, 1980;

McPherson and Smith-Lovin, 1982), the actual processes through which access is limited are difficult to pinpoint, because of the subtle ways that discrimination occurs in network systems and the difficulty of quantifying the kinds of resources being distributed (Miller et al., 1981).

Women's exclusion from informal networks in which information is shared and alliances develop has implications for their learning and performing their jobs and their chances for advancement (for an example, see U.S. Department of Labor, Employment and Training Administration, 1978). Women are particularly apt to be excluded from activities that occur outside work hours (Kanter, 1977; Epstein, 1981), and, unsure of their reception, they may be reluctant to intrude (Martin, 1980). Martin (1978), for example, describes women police officers' exclusion from off-hours activities in which opportunities for desirable work assignments were discussed. In some occupations in which practitioners are self-employed (for example, physicians), collegial networks are indispensable for getting business. Yet women seem to be stuck in sex-segregated networks (Kaufman, 1977; Epstein, 1981) that put them at a professional disadvantage. Successful occupational performance is not always sufficient to gain admission to informal networks. In a case study of female school administrators, Ortiz and Covel (1978) found that even women who used formal networks effectively were barred from informal networks. Determining the consequences of women's exclusion from networks is difficult, but some findings are suggestive of deleterious effects. Kaufman's (1977) study of sex differences in faculty use of networks found that female faculty participated in less beneficial networks: they included fewer colleagues of higher rank and were judged to be less important than men judged their networks. Miller et al. (1981) found that belonging to a network enhanced the access of social service personnel to resources.

It is frequently argued that in order to advance, one must have active support from an individual who is established in one's field (Hochschild, 1975; Shapiro et al., 1978; Speizer, 1981). Sponsorship is common in the upper echelons of almost all professions (Epstein, 1970a; White, 1970; Zuckerman, 1977) as well as in some blue-collar occupations (Walshok, 1981a). Sponsors provide introductions through which an individual becomes established in the profession (Epstein, 1970a; Lorber, 1981), socialize their protégés to the values and behavior that are appropriate to the work culture (Caplow, 1954), and often provide vital instruction in the technical aspects of the job. As outsiders, women may need male endorsement to be taken seriously (Walsh, 1977) and thus may rely more than men on having a sponsor for advancement (Ortiz and Covel, 1978; Speizer, 1981). Because men hold a disproportionate number of positions of influence and few women in male-dominated fields hold high enough status to be effective as sponsors, most available potential sponsors are men. But men may hesitate to take on female protégés because they question their commitment, fear adverse reactions from wives and colleagues, or are unaware of their promise (Epstein, 1970a).

The evidence regarding the access of men and women to sponsors is scanty (Speizer, 1981), but what there is suggests that both professional and blue-collar women experience difficulty in finding sponsors (Roe, 1966; Epstein, 1970a; Walshok, 1981a). For example, most female truck drivers who said they had sponsors named their husbands or boyfriends (Lembright and Riemer, 1982). Only a few studies compared women and men. Women physicians were less likely than men to have had a sponsor in setting up practice (Lorber, 1981). Martin (1980) observed the expected sex difference in sponsorship among patrol officers, but her sample was small and unsystematic. Strober's (1982) survey of graduates of Stanford University's School of Business revealed that women were slightly more likely to have a mentor in their current job, but the sexes did not differ according to type of mentoring. Research on sex differences in the effectiveness of sponsorship is also limited. For Strober's business graduates, having a mentor was not correlated with salary and was negatively related to job satisfaction for both sexes. A study of elementary school teachers concluded that sponsorship was necessary for advancement into male-dominated school administration but was more beneficial to men than women (Poll, 1978). Lorber (1981) compared the impact of sponsorship on the careers of female and male physicians in academic, institutional, and clinical settings. She found that women benefited from sponsorship in their postgraduate training but were less often sponsored for leadership positions. In contrast, 1,250 senior executives (of whom fewer than 1 percent were female) reportedly had mentors but denied that their mentors were important for their own success (Roche, 1979).

The journeyman-apprenticeship relationship can resemble the mentor-protégé relationship, except that apprentices may be assigned to journeymen who are indifferent or hostile (Walshok, 1981a). For this reason, women are particularly vulnerable in apprenticeship programs that lack classroom instruction, in which their training depends entirely on a single journeyman. One source of journeymen's hostility may be their perception that standards were reduced for female apprentices. Walshok (1981b) reports that a competency-based testing program at General Motors alleviated this problem by reassuring the journeymen while providing the apprentices with feedback on expectations and their performance.

Doing a good job does not necessarily mean getting credit, and what counts in a career is getting credit for doing good work (Hochschild, 1975). In some male-dominated work settings, women succeed only if their work is visible and can be assessed by an objective standard such as quantity of sales. Women's concentration in less visible positions (e.g., library work in law; Epstein, 1970b) or in jobs that deal with lower-status clients or customers may contribute to their invisibility and the underevaluation of their work. Women sell cheaper goods (or serve cheaper meals) than men do and their customers are often other women (Talbert and Bose, 1977). Ironically, when women hold male jobs, it is their gender and not their performance that is highly visible (Kanter, 1977). Kanter has outlined other ways in which women's minority status interferes with their performance and hence their evaluation, and evidence for female law students supports her thesis (Spangler et al., 1978). Any propensity to ignore or undervalue women's contributions not only reduces their personal chances for career advancement but also may justify not hiring additional women.

Conclusion

In sum, women are excluded from many occupations because of the effects of past practices, remaining legal barriers, discrimination by employers and sometimes by unions and coworkers, institutionalized personnel practices, and informal barriers in the workplace that make many jobs uncomfortable for them or impair their performance. These barriers demonstrably contribute to the persistence of sex segregation in the workplace. Next we consider how and to what extent workers' occupational choices, socialization, education, and training also help to maintain a segregated work force.

SOCIALIZATION AND EDUCATION

Many approach sex segregation in the workplace with the assumption that it results from women's and men's choices. If women choose to work with other women and men with other men, the consequences of segregation, even though often negative for women, might not be seen as an appropriate matter for policy intervention. In considering why women might choose different occupations than men choose, several reasons have been noted (Treiman and Hartmann, 1981). Sex-specific socialization can influence women's and men's occupational choices in a variety of ways. First, sex-specific socialization may lead women to prefer occupations that are generally viewed as appropriate for them. Second, women's premarket education and training may restrict the jobs for which they qualify. Third, women's beliefs that certain jobs are unavailable may deter them from trying to pursue them. Fourth, women's choices may reflect their ignorance of available options. A fifth significant factor, that women's anticipated family obligations may affect their choice of occupations, is discussed in the next section.

One view of occupational choice focuses on the differential socialization of the sexes to different personality characteristics, skills, and preferences. In brief, it holds that sex-role socialization contributes to sex segregation by creating in each sex preferences for occupations that have been defined as appropriate to that sex, at the same time leaving them disinclined, ignorant of, or pessimistic regarding their chances to pursue most other occupations. Some also point to the role of socialization in limiting the kinds of occupationally relevant training that women acquire. In recent years, sex-role socialization theory has become widely regarded as incomplete and is in the process of being reconceptualized. Socialization is now more commonly regarded as an ongoing process, rather than something that occurs in early childhood with results that remain fixed for life. Resocialization can and does occur, and adults also experience socialization in various contexts.

In the following discussion of how socialization shapes preferences, several caveats about occupational choice and sex-role socialization should be kept in mind. First, the notion of a chosen career may be misleading for many workers, at least early in their work histories. Young workers of both sexes display considerable movement within the labor force. For example, about 6 percent of the young men in the National Longitudinal Survey changed jobs every month (Hall and Kasten, 1976), and a considerable number changed occupations (Spilerman, 1977), even broadly defined occupational categories (Rosenfeld and Sorenson, 1979). Second, there are a large number of unlabeled occupations, and occasionally men and women perform the same occupation in different parts of the country, so that sex-role socialization could never provide a complete explanation of occupational choice. Third, the effect of workers' perceptions of available occupational options and the extent to which women may settle for sex-typical occupations only after being discouraged from pursuing sex-atypical occupations are often underestimated by those who regard choice as the major determining factor in one's work life. Finally, it should be kept in mind that sex-role socialization also contributes to sex segregation by influencing the preferences and behavior of people who make decisions about training or hiring workers or who occupy positions that can affect women's prospects for success in sex-atypical jobs. As we noted above, employers' and other gatekeepers' normative expectations regarding the sex-typing of jobs as well as attitudes about the sexes contribute to sex segregation.

Sex-Role Socialization

Sex-role socialization refers to the lifelong process through which expectations about how each gender should behave are transmitted through the family, the educational system, and the mass media.[12] While strongly influenced by cultural standards, these expectations vary by race, ethnicity, and class. Sex-role socialization can generate sex-

_____

[12] This discussion relies heavily on Marini and Brinton (1984).

typical occupational outcomes directly by creating sex-typed occupational aspirations or indirectly by developing in males and females tastes and characteristics that are compatible with occupations that have been labeled appropriate for their sex. Socialization occurs in two ways. Socialization agents can convey the impression that different attributes and behaviors are appropriate for females and males. They can also expose boys and girls to different experiences that produce different adult attributes. Both occur in most families. Children observe that adult men and women typically do different work inside and outside the home and that their interests and personal-social characteristics differ; they then infer what are expected behaviors for adult women and men. In addition, parents treat their male and female children differently in ways that may produce sex differences in certain characteristics (Huston, 1983). This has been demonstrated in recent research on activities and interests. Experimental studies that observe adults' reactions to the same behavior when only the adults' belief of the child's gender was varied have shown that the latter influenced their judgments about and behavior toward the child (e.g., Meyer and Sobiezek, 1972; Gurwitz and Dodge, 1975; Condry and Condry, 1976). In experimental studies adults made sex-typed toy choices for children and encouraged physical play for male children and interpersonal play activity and dependent, affectionate behavior for females. Because parents typically limit their daughters' freedom more than that of their sons, girls are exposed to fewer sources of socialization outside the family and may experience greater pressure to conform to parental values (Newson and Newson, 1976; Huston, 1983).

Regarding parental behavior that may be more closely linked to children's occupational attainment, parents harbor higher expectations for their sons' than their daughters' adult achievements (Maccoby and Jacklin, 1974; Hoffman, 1977; Marini, 1978).

This is especially true with respect to mathematics (Fennema and Sherman, 1977; Fox et al., 1979; Marini and Brinton, 1984, provide a detailed review). The sex-typicality of their parents' occupations influences the typicality of the occupation to which children aspire, with the same-sex parent exercising a stronger effect (Hofferth, 1980a). Children of employed mothers hold less traditional sex-role attitudes (Huston, 1983), and, among daughters, their mother's employment is important to their career choice (Beardslee and O'Dowd, 1962; Hartley, 1966; White, 1967; Almquist and Angrist, 1971; D. Bielby, 1978b). The research is inconclusive, however, on whether these daughters are more likely to enter typically male occupations (D. Bielby, 1978a; Brito and Jusenius, 1978; but see also Almquist and Angrist, 1970; Tangri, 1972; Klemmack and Edwards, 1973; Almquist, 1974).

Researchers have documented the existence of sex-typing in the occupational aspirations of children and young people. At relatively young ages, boys and girls are aware that adult sex roles differ and express interests in and prefer activities that the culture defines as appropriate to their sex (Blakemore et al., 1979; Carter and Patterson, 1979; Edelbrock and Sugawara, 1978; Faulkender, 1980; Schau et al., 1980). Preschool and elementary schoolchildren know the more obvious sex-typed adult occupations (Tibbetts, 1975; Garrett et al., 1977; Nemerowicz, 1979; see Ruble and Ruble, 1980, for a full review), and their knowledge of these stereotypes increases through adolescence (Stein, 1971).

In keeping with this knowledge, preschool children express sex-typed occupational preferences and expectations, although some (e.g., ballerina, cowboy) are not realistic possibilities. By mid- to late adolescence occupational aspirations are almost as sex-typed as the workplace itself. The index of segregation computed for the occupations that 14- to 22-year-olds wanted to hold at age 35 was 61, only 8 percent less than the index measuring the actual level of segregation for the same occupational categories (Marini and Brinton, 1984). The young women aspired to fewer occupations, but the young men's aspirations were substantially more sex-typed. These patterns are quite stable from ages 14 to 22 (Gottfredson, 1978; Hofferth, 1980a; Marini and Brinton, 1984), although some evidence from the 1960s indicates that some women's occupational choices became more sex-stereotyped during college (J. Davis, 1965; Astin and Panos, 1969; Hind and Wirth, 1969).

Along with a general liberalization of sex-role attitudes and increasing support for women's equality of opportunity spurred on by the women's movement (Mason et al., 1976; Spitze and Huber, 1980; Cherlin and Walters, 1981; Thornton et al., 1983), the extent of sex-typing of young women's occupational aspirations has declined (Garrison, 1979; Herzog, 1982).[13] In 1968 only one in eight of the young women questioned in the National Longitudinal Survey expected to be employed in professional, technical, or managerial occupations when they were 35; by 1979 this proportion had increased to two in five (National Commission for Employment Policy, 1980:60). Lueptow (1981) also observed a marked drop in women's preferences for several traditionally female occupations, although males showed no commensurate increase in their preference for occupations defined as female. Among black female college students who expected to be employed at age 35, between 1968 and 1973 the proportion who thought they would work in sex-atypical occupations jumped from 14 to 21 percent; for whites the gain was only 2 percentage points, to 25 percent (Bri-

to and Jusenius, 1978:70). For both races, one component of the change was the declining proportion who expected to be teachers. Douglas (1980) also reported that during approximately the same period the proportion of women entering college who expected to become elementary or secondary school teachers dropped from 35 to 10 percent. Interest among college women in professional careers in fields defined as male has increased sharply. For example, in 1968 only 3.3 percent of women surveyed by the American Council on Education planned to become businesswomen, compared with 20.4 percent in 1978 (Hornig, 1980). (During this period the proportion of men expecting to go into business increased from 17.5 to 23.3 percent.)

Sex-role socialization also may lead to sex differences in skills and knowledge that may affect occupational access. After the onset of adolescence, males tend to do better at mathematical reasoning and spatial skills, and women at verbal skills (Terman and Tyler, 1954; Dwyer, 1973; Maccoby and Jacklin, 1974; Sherman and Fennema, 1977; Brush, 1979; Richmond, 1980; Liben, 1978; Thomas and Jamison, 1975), but these differences are very small relative to within-gender differences (Huston, 1983).

Limited evidence shows sex differences in some personality characteristics that may be relevant for some occupations. There is some evidence that boys are more physically active, aggressive, competitive, and dominant in their peer groups than girls; and that girls are more anxious, timid, and compliant with adults (Maccoby and Jacklin, 1974; Block, 1976; and Frieze et al., 1978, present relevant reviews).

The evidence as to whether males and females differ in the value they place on dimensions of work is mixed. Boys are more likely to value financial rewards, status, and freedom from supervision; girls are more likely to value working with people, helping others, using their abilities, and being creative (Witty and Lehman, 1930; Singer and

---

[13] A concomitant change is the decline in the number of young women who aspire to be exclusively homemakers. In the 1979 National Longitudinal Survey of young women, only one-fourth expected to devote themselves exclusively to homemaking at age 35, compared with more than 60 percent of the respondents in 1968.

Stefflre, 1954; O'Hara, 1962; Lueptow, 1980; Herzog, 1982). These differences may not hold for black high school students (Brief and Aldag, 1975). Nieva and Gutek (1981) cite several studies that failed to find sex differences in orientation toward specific extrinsic and intrinsic rewards to working. They suggest that other investigators' failure to control for workers' occupation may account for some of the sex differences observed among employed persons. Miller and Garrison (1982) also found consensus among women and men on the importance of various working conditions, although they observed differences in some of the criteria women and men use for judging work. It is not clear whether these differences in attitudes and orientation have declined in keeping with changing occupational aspirations. Several recent studies (Brenner and Tomkiewicz, 1979; Lueptow, 1980; Peng et al., 1981; Tittle, 1981; Herzog, 1982) found no change, but national surveys of college freshmen show considerable convergence in several occupationally related attitudes (*Chronicle of Higher Education*, January 28, 1980; February 17, 1982).

The evidence taken together suggests that many young women and men enter the work force with attributes and aspirations consistent with the segregation of the sexes in different jobs. Recent changes, however, suggest a trend toward convergence in attitudes and aspirations. Moreover, the question of causation is complex. We can illuminate it by attempting to answer several questions. First, does socialization produce observed pre-employment sex differences in occupational aspirations, attitudes, and expectations? Second, to what extent do pre-employment sex differences contribute to occupational segregation? Third, can and should we try to reduce occupational segregation by intervening in socialization practices?

Although several researchers have observed a link between individuals' sex role orientations and women's employment aspirations (reviewed in Miller and Garrison, 1982), the extent to which sex-role socialization produces pre-employment sex differences is not established. We have seen that young women and men do differ on several attitudes and on a few abilities and personality traits (Marini and Brinton, 1984) and that young people's expressed occupational preferences are definitely sex-typed, although females' preferences have become less so over the past several years. The evidence reviewed indicates that parents treat children differently, depending on their gender, and below we review evidence that teachers also do so. It seems likely, then, that socialization contributes to the observed differences in abilities and values. With respect to occupational aspirations, however, our understanding of their formation is still quite limited (Laws, 1976; Miller and Garrison, 1982).

Considerable evidence suggests that visible occupational sex segregation contributes to the formation of sex-typed occupational preferences in young people. First, knowledge of the sex-segregated nature of the workplace may lead young people, from an early age, to prepare themselves for careers in which they believe they would be welcome. Second, sex segregation may affect preemployment aspirations and skills by restricting the ability of parents and other adults to serve as models for nontraditional occupations. Limited empirical evidence (reviewed in Marini and Brinton, 1984) suggests that same-sex role models may influence college students' educational and career choices (Fox, 1974; Goldstein, 1979). For example, Douvan (1976) offers anecdotal evidence of the value to successful women of having a prominent same-sex role model, and Basow and Howe (1979) report that college seniors' career choices were affected to a significantly greater degree by same-sex than by opposite-sex role models. Third, growing up in a world in which educational materials and the mass media show men and women performing different roles may influence girls' and boys' expectations about the jobs they should fill. Television programs and commercials, projecting cultural ideals, depict women in fewer occupational roles than men (DeFleur, 1964; Women on Words and Images, 1975), and most of them are female occupations (Kaniuga et al., 1974; Tuchman et al., 1978; England and Gardner, 1983). The impact of television viewing on occupational aspirations has not been demonstrated, although elementary schoolchildren's identification with traditional sex roles is correlated with the amount of television they watch (Frueh and McGhee, 1975).

Both direct and indirect evidence points to the influence of young people's perceptions of occupational opportunities on their preemployment aspirations. Marini and Greenberger (1978) found that the sex composition of occupations influenced the degree to which white girls—but not boys—expected to realize their aspirations. Heilman (1979) found that high school students' occupational interests were a function of their perceptions of occupations as viable career choices, given their sex compositions. Research on the disparity between young people's aspirations and the occupations they expect to pursue is particularly instructive, because the latter are more likely to reflect the effect of constraints—including the sex labeling of the preferred occupations or market discrimination based on sex (Marini and Brinton, 1984). Girls, in particular, expect to be in more sex-typed occupations than the ones they prefer (Marini and Brinton, 1984). That young people's expectations are more sex-typed than their aspirations presumably reflects their perceptions of their actual options. Direct evidence for this presumption is provided by a study of the reasons for discrepancies between high school girls' expectations and aspirations. More than half of those whose expectations differed from their aspirations explained that the occupations to which they aspired were "inappropriate for females" (Burlin, 1976). In ad-

dition, almost one-third of the female high school students in a national sample (but only one-tenth of the males) thought that their gender would to some degree prevent them from getting the kind of work they would like (Bachman et al., 1980). Taken together these studies provide rather strong evidence that the existence of segregation contributes to the development of sex-typed occupational preferences.

Our second question is whether preemployment sex differences in aspirations, attitudes, and expectations lead to sex-typical occupational choices. Again we must distinguish values and traits from occupational preferences. Regarding the former, we quote from Marini and Brinton's (1984:208) review of sex typing in occupational socialization:

Although it is possible that sex differences, particularly in physical characteristics, may form the basis for some occupational sorting by sex, the relevance of most stereotypically ascribed sex differences in personality and ability, including physical differences, to occupational performance remains unknown. . . . It seems likely that the extent to which one sex is better suited to perform sex-typed jobs has been greatly exaggerated. Because sex differences in personality traits and abilities are both smaller than they are stereotypically ascribed to be and of questionable relevance to the performance of most jobs, their role in . . . [producing] sex segregation . . . is likely to be minimal.

Additional research is clearly necessary to determine to what extent links exist between sex-typed characteristics and values and sex-typical occupational outcomes. We also need to know more about the actual skill requirements of jobs and their effect on sex segregation, since differences in aspirations may lead to differences in the skills men and women acquire.

The evidence regarding the association between people's preemployment occupational aspirations and the occupations in which they end up is mixed. Marini and Brinton (1984) identify five studies, all done before 1971, that examined the congruence between high school aspirations and subsequent occupational attainment. The estimates ranged from 15 to 25 percent agreement for respondents reinterviewed 10 years after high school (Kohout and Rothney, 1964; Kuvlesky and Bealer, 1967) to between 50 and 80 percent among a group sampled six months after high school graduation (Porter, 1954; Schmidt and Rothney, 1955). Obviously these findings are sensitive to the number and fineness of the occupational categories the researchers used. We have uncovered no evidence linking the strength of children's sex-role socialization and the sex typicality of their occupational outcomes. One study (Spitze and Waite, 1980) found that although young women's career commitments were associated with the sex typicality of their first post-college jobs, their sex-role attitudes had no effect. Still, perhaps because of the general lack of longitudinal data, there is surprisingly little research on the connection between aspirations and outcomes. It is not impossible that appropriate studies would show a link between the sex-typing of one's aspirations and preferences (or traditional attitudes and values on sex-roles generally) and the sex-typing of one's occupational outcomes. It would be more to the point to discover whether having traditional attitudes or preferences tends to be correlated with being in female-dominated occupations in general, and not whether aspiring to a specific occupation leads to entering that specific occupation.

To conclude, the differential socialization of the sexes probably contributes to occupational segregation to some degree, both through the formation of sex-typed preferences in workers and the formation of preferences for workers of a particular gender among employers. Prospective studies of the same individuals over time are badly needed for a clearer understanding of the way in which socialization contributes to segregation through influencing preferences compared with its effect through influencing awareness of opportunities. At this time some

preliminary conclusions can be stated. We have learned that the effects of preemployment socialization are far from immutable. Socialization is a lifelong process that continues after one enters the labor force. Accounts of the experiences of women who entered heavily male occupations subsequent to their first work experience (Walshok, 1981a) reveal the women's resocialization. It is not clear, however, whether interventions in childhood socialization would alter perceptions or attitudes, but some studies suggest that they can. Experimental research indicates that children who were exposed to media presentations showing men and women performing nontraditional work tended to express views that were less sex-typed about adult occupations than children who saw neutral or traditional sex-role portrayals (Atkin, 1975; Flerx et al., 1976; Davidson et al., 1979). Children who for a semester watched a television series ("Freestyle") designed to show men and women performing nontraditional activities and occupations displayed less stereotyped beliefs and attitudes about adults' occupational and domestic roles nine months later. Evaluations of programs designed to increase college women's participation in science (discussed in the following chapter) indicate that attempts to resocialize women to different career interests can be successful. It is important to recognize that high school curricula—including vocational education—constitute interventions that usually encourage occupational preparation consistent with sex-typed cultural values. In the next section, we trace the implications of education and training for sex-segregated occupational choices.

Education

People's labor market outcomes are affected by the amount and kind of education they acquire as well as through more subtle processes within the educational system. On average, black women and men attain about the same amount of schooling, while Hispanic and white men have a slight edge over Hispanic and white women. However, men are overrepresented at the lower and higher levels of education. Level of education is linked to the kinds of jobs women and men obtain. For example, of women in the labor force in 1981, those who were high school dropouts were much more likely than graduates to work as operatives, laborers, private household workers, and other service workers. Of women in professional and technical occupations, 60 percent had completed four or more years of college (U.S. Department of Labor, Women's Bureau, 1983:116). Although historically men have been more likely to attend college and attain higher educational levels than women, recent data show that the enrollment rates of men and women have converged (Heyns and Bird, 1982).

Given the different historical experience of women and men with public education and the wide acceptance of beliefs about sex differences in both character traits and abilities, persistent sex differences in educational processes within the schools are not surprising. We discuss here two kinds of differences that are relevant for sex segregation: (1) sex-stereotyped educational materials and (2) teachers' and counselors' sex stereotypes and differential treatment of the sexes.

Sex bias in educational materials and those used for career counseling has been well documented. (See Marini and Brinton, 1984, for a detailed review.) As a rule, textbooks stereotype occupations as male or female (Vetter et al., cited in Evenson and O'Neill 1978). To illustrate, in 134 elementary school readers examined in one study, women were portrayed in only 26 occupations (all but one of which were stereotypically female), compared with almost 150 occupations for men (Women on Words and Images, 1975). Similar stereotyping has been found in foreign language and mathematics texts. The effects of sex-stereotyped educational materials on

children's occupational aspirations have not been determined, although Kimmel (1970) and Wirtenberg (cited in National Commission on Employment Policy, 1980) found at least short-run effects of children's books on stereotyped attitudes toward minorities. An intriguing study (reported in Bem and Bem, 1973) revealed that females showed no interest in jobs labeled "draftsman" but expressed interest in jobs labeled "draftswoman." Similarly, males were not attracted to telephone operator jobs when the accompanying text used the female pronoun but were interested when male pronouns were employed. Nilsen (1977) observed a direct correlation between children's exposure to a sex-stereotyped reading program and their propensity to classify activities as belonging to male and female domains. However, we still know very little about the effects of books and other teaching materials on children's occupational choices.

Differential treatment of girls and boys by teachers seems to reinforce sex stereotypical attitudes and behaviors (see Brenner, 1981). Many teachers are aware of concerns regarding sex stereotyping, but they also perceive boys and girls as radically different and believe that they want to be treated differently (Guttentag and Bray, cited in Evenson and O'Neill, 1978). According to Guttentag and Bray's findings, teachers see their role as meeting rather than shaping their students needs. Teachers' education texts themselves continue to present stereotyped portrayals of females (Sadker and Sadker, cited in Brenner, 1981).

Marini and Brinton's (1984) review of the literature confirms sex bias in high school career counseling that is consistent with sextypical occupational choices. High school counselors have tended to hold traditional attitudes about the appropriate occupations for female and male students, to discourage nontraditional aspirations, and to be ignorant of issues related to women's employment (Thomas and Stewart, 1971; Bingham and House, 1973; Medvene and Collins,

1976; Karpicke, 1980). In sum, the literature reveals considerable bias by counselors regarding the appropriateness of various occupational aspirations for women, and invariably recommends that school counselors be trained to provide women students with less biased counseling. Although the impact of counseling on students' aspirations has not been generally demonstrated (Marini and Brinton, 1984), a recent study by the American Institutes for Research (Harrison et al., 1979) revealed the effect of counselors on student curricular choices: 25 percent of the female students and 14 percent of the male students taking courses unusual for their sex had been advised against enrolling in them. Of those who entered traditional areas, 14 percent of the girls and 8 percent of the boys said that they had been dissuaded by counselors from enrolling in nontraditional areas. Others found that counselors were more likely to discourage than encourage women from enrolling in math and science courses (Levine, 1976; Casserly, 1979).

Because it is highly segregated by sex, the public school system offers students few role models for sex-atypical occupations. Elementary schoolchildren are three times more likely to be taught by women than by men (U.S. Department of Commerce, Bureau of the Census, 1983b), which may account in part for girls' preferences for teaching careers. In view of the lack of valid evidence regarding the stability of individuals' occupational preferences and the large numbers of factors that intervene between early school experiences and adult career choices, however, it is difficult to draw conclusions about any segregative effect. Secondary school teachers are somewhat more likely to be male, and men teach math, science, and social science courses disproportionately. They are even more likely to outnumber women in the various administrative roles visible to students—principal, assistant principal, and school superintendent (Howard, cited in Brenner, 1981). However, as is true for sex stereotyping in teaching ma-

terials and for teachers' and counselors' attitudes and behavior, the impact, if any, of same-sex role models has not been established.

The tracking of students into different curricula or specific subjects and away from others is common in many high schools, although it is often so subtle that students are unaware that it is occurring (Marini and Brinton, 1984). Teachers and counselors may recommend that female students avoid certain college preparatory courses, with the effect of restricting their subsequent occupational options (Marini and Brinton, 1984). This process has been documented most fully with respect to math and science. Girls have been underrepresented in mathematics and science classes in secondary school, although recently they have begun to enroll in these classes in greater proportions (National Commission for Employment Policy, 1980). Women undergraduate mathematics majors were more likely than men to report that their teachers had discouraged their pursuing math careers, although female mathematicians also often referred to a teacher's encouragement as important to their career decision (Luchins and Luchins, 1980). Researchers (Marini and Brinton, 1984; Fennema, 1983) have concluded that sex differences in mathematics and science training stem not from differences in ability or (for mathematics) in liking for the subject, but from the labeling of these subjects as male and perceptions of their utility (Wise et al., 1979; Armstrong, in National Commission for Employment Policy, 1980; for a contrasting view see Benbow and Stanley, 1983). For whatever reason, young women take fewer mathematics courses beyond algebra in high school and college. The implications for women's subsequent opportunities have been examined in several studies. In some schools math and science courses are prerequisites for some sex-atypical vocational courses (e.g., electronics— League of Women's Voters Education Fund, 1982). Moreover, students who fail to take high school mathematics tend to avoid remedial mathematics courses later (Brenner, 1981). Lack of high school preparation also seriously restricts the majors for which college students qualify (Sells, 1973). For example, of a random sample of freshmen at the University of California at Berkeley, almost 60 percent of the men but only 8 percent of the women had enough high school math to take the course that was required to major in every field except the humanities, social sciences, librarianship, social welfare, and education (Sells, 1973). Failing to take college mathematics ultimately affected women's employment options. Sells (1979) found that only 16 percent of companies planning to recruit employees at the University of Maryland in 1978 would consider job candidates without a calculus background.[14]

Sex differences in college majors also contribute to job segregation, inasmuch as some college education is directly occupationally relevant. Until recently women were heavily concentrated in education, the humanities, arts, and behavioral sciences; and men in business, engineering, physical and certain social sciences, and preprofessional training (Polachek, 1978; National Center for Education Statistics, 1981). But recent data show decreasing sex differentiation across college majors (Heyns and Bird, 1982; Beller, 1984). Between 1971 and 1979 the index of segregation computed for college majors for a national sample of college students declined from 46 to 36 (National Center for Education Statistics, 1981), paralleling declines in sex segregation in professional occupations among members of young cohorts of workers (Beller, 1984). During the

1970s the proportion of women baccalaureates who took their degrees in education decreased by half, while those in business and health professions increased substantially. Women's enrollments in law, medicine, business administration, and engineering all increased sharply over the past decade (U.S. Department of Education, 1981). As a result, the proportion of law degrees awarded to women between 1970 and 1980 increased from 8 to over 40 percent; the comparable gains for medical degrees and masters of business administration are from 10 to 33 percent and from 3 to 21 percent, respectively. In the last decade women earned an increasing share of degrees in such quantitatively based disciplines as biological, physical, and computer sciences, at every degree level (Berryman, 1983). In engineering, over 13 percent of bachelor's degrees awarded in 1983 were to women, compared with less than 1 percent a decade earlier (Vetter and Babco, 1984; U.S. Department of Education, 1981). These changes probably reflect efforts to improve sex equity in education as well as women's responsiveness to improved opportunities in these male-dominated professional occupations.

Vocational Education

Unlike most general education in the public schools, vocational education early received federal money and federal policy direction. Consequently it has been a particular target of change (see the following chapter for a full discussion of sex equity efforts). Vocational education programs have been sex-segregated since their inception in the late 1800s. In recent years, between 20 and 44 percent of high school senior women were enrolled in vocational courses (Grasso, 1980; Harnischfeger and Wiley, 1980; Hofferth, 1980b). Males and females have been differentially distributed across vocational courses, with females predominantly in health, home economics, and office and

---

[14] Math courses or a business major are not, however, always necessary to perform the jobs that require them. Some corporations have increased employment opportunities for women by eliminating educational requirements that did not prove to be necessary for job performance (Shaeffer and Lynton, 1979).

business programs, and males in technical preparation, the trades, and agriculture (Harnischfeger and Wiley, 1980). In fact, as recently as 1979, almost half the vocational programs in 10,584 public schools and colleges were still exclusively of one sex (Maeroff, 1982).[15]

Whether training should be available to women and what kinds have long been subject to debate (Kessler-Harris, 1982). Implicitly assuming that women's domestic role is paramount, advocates argued that training women would make them better homemakers. This rationale ultimately led to state laws requiring domestic science (home economics) courses for girls in publicly funded programs. The 1917 Smith-Hughes Act, which initiated federal funding for vocational education, made sex-segregated vocational education a matter of national policy by subsidizing training for female secondary students in domestic science but not in commercial office skills. World War I opened some publicly financed industrial training courses to female students, but by 1920 these had largely disappeared, and the sex-segregated nature of vocational education was firmly established (Kessler-Harris, 1982). Occupational training eventually became available to high school girls, but primarily for occupations already perceived as female. Hence, female students predominated in health and clerical programs, and males in the trades, agriculture, and technical programs (Harnischfeger and Wiley, 1980). Only

retail sales has attracted students of both sexes in any numbers.

It is not clear to what extent sex differences across vocational education courses reflect tracking by the schools, students' choices, and parent and peer influences (Brenner, 1981). Kane and Frazee (1978) found that mothers are particularly influential in the type of vocational program women take, and young women in traditional vocational education training were more likely than those in nontraditional programs to cite their mother as a very important influence in program choice. Senior high school personnel reportedly influenced women's decisions to select their training less than half as often as parents. Young women may be especially loath to deviate from sex-role norms during adolescence when most vocational education takes place, and the same peer pressures that deter them from taking math and science may dissuade them from enrolling in shop or technical courses (Gaskell, 1985). The attitudes of male classmates deterred some adolescent girls from taking classes judged to be inappropriate for them, according to a study by Entwisle and Greenberger (1972). In their study of adult women who entered postsecondary vocational training, Kane and Frazee (1979) found that women who had already been in the labor force were more likely to consider mixed and nontraditional occupations,[16] apparently in response to their firsthand knowledge of the disadvantages of predominantly female jobs. In contrast, women who had been out of the labor force and who were insecure about reentering sought training for sex-typical occupations.

For whatever reason, vocational education programs are substantially sex-segre-

---

[15] A substantial proportion of all vocational education enrollments in secondary schools is in nonoccupationally specific programs; that is, programs that do not attempt to prepare students for specific jobs (Golladay and Wulfsberg, 1981). Home economics is a prime example: in 1978 only 11 percent of the enrollments in home economics and homemaking classes were classified as employment-related, according to the U.S. Office of Education. Of all secondary vocational enrollments in 1978, 43 percent were in these courses (Brenner, 1981:Table 5).

---

[16] The researchers classified programs in which 0-25 percent of the national enrollments are women as "nontraditional," those with 25-75 percent women as "mixed," and those with more than 75 percent women as "traditional."

gated, and the evidence, although some-what weak, suggests that enrollment in such programs does affect one's subsequent employment.[17] Type of vocational curriculum is apparently linked to later occupation (Brenner, 1981; Golladay and Wulfsberg, 1981). A recent cross-sectional analysis of 1,539 workers ages 20-34 indicates that vocational courses are linked with being employed in related occupations (Mertens and Gardner, 1981). The evidence does not permit conclusions about causality, however. On one hand, students' occupational knowledge and preferences may dictate their choice of vocational courses; on the other hand, the vocational curricula open to them may in turn influence both their aspirations and their knowledge of available jobs (Mott and Moore, 1976; Kohen and Breinich, 1975), and hence affect the kinds of jobs they consider when they enter the labor market. Persons in postsecondary vocational training are considerably more likely than those in secondary school programs to enroll in employment-related programs (Brenner, 1981), so type of postsecondary vocational education is especially likely to be linked to subsequent occupation.

Assessment of the actual impact of vocational training on the sex typicality of students' subsequent jobs is hampered by data limitations. The federal Vocational Education Data System (VEDS), for example, includes job placement data only for students who either completed occupationally specific vocational programs and were available for placement or had terminated their training to take full-time jobs in the fields for which they were trained (Golladay and Wulfsberg, 1981). Thus, VEDS data exclude students who dropped out of the programs as well as those students enrolled in programs not considered vocationally specific, e.g., home economics and industrial arts.

The National Longitudinal Survey data are of higher quality but omit some variables necessary to assess the effects of vocational education on labor market outcomes (Brenner, 1981). These data show that young women who had enrolled in commercial programs were more likely than those in other vocational courses to hold sex-typical jobs four years later. In contrast, young women who had taken other than white-collar clerical vocational courses were less likely than female students in general, or those in college preparatory or other vocational courses, to hold sex-typed jobs (Grasso, 1980). Hofferth (1980b) observed the same pattern after 10 years.

Moreover, for both sexes, graduating from a trade or industrial program was associated with subsequent participation in and completion of an apprenticeship (Mertens and Gardner, 1981). Apprenticeship is the primary avenue into many skilled blue-collar occupations, and women have been almost totally excluded. In 1978 they constituted only 2.6 percent of the more than 250,000 registered apprentices and were thus underrepresented even relative to their presence (5.6 percent) in craft jobs (Ullman and Deaux, 1981). Several barriers contribute to women's underrepresentation in apprenticeship programs. They are less likely to learn about programs, to qualify, and to be selected (Waite and Hudis, 1981). An upper age limit of 24-27 years in many trades presents a significant obstacle to women who have children during their twenties. Moreover, many women who have spent several years in traditionally female jobs (Kane and Miller, 1981; Waite and Hudis, 1981;

---

[17] Three major longitudinal studies by Grasso and Shea (1979), Hofferth (1980b), and Harnischfeger and Wiley (1980) investigated whether vocational education improves the labor market outcomes of participants. These studies suggest that male participants fared no better than young men who had not been in vocational courses, net of other factors (see also Grasso, 1980). With respect to female students, Grasso and Shea found that those who were in vocational education courses were more likely to finish high school and earned higher wages than those in general education courses. The former were enrolled primarily in clerical programs that presumably led to clerical employment.

O'Farrell, 1982) do not consider skilled blue-collar work until divorce or other economic pressures prompt them to seek better-paying work. Large application and union induction fees may be beyond the budgets of the very women motivated by economic need to consider male occupations.

Conclusion

In sum, women's labor market opportunities are affected by the vocational education, general education, and other socialization and training influences to which they are exposed. The link to employment is most plausible for vocational education, which teaches job-specific skills needed in the labor market, but some connection is undoubtedly present for the other types of experiences reviewed above as well. While we have focused on the effect of socialization processes on aspirations and learned personality traits, the differential treatment and exposure of boys and girls in general education, and the sex segregation of occupationally specific programs in vocational education, a general outcome of the socialization and education process is to restrict information about job options that are most typical of the opposite sex. For example, Gann Watson testified before the Committee on Education and Labor of the House of Representatives (U.S. Congress, House, 1982:343-344) that

Most vocational students, particularly young women, opt for programs that are familiar to them. They do not know about . . . courses in areas consistent with their capabilities . . . which can lead to excellent employment opportunities. They choose to enroll in such courses as consumer and homemaking, industrial sewing and cosmetology because they conceive of them as women's programs and because they know what people in these jobs do. They do not know what machinists do, they do not know what industrial electricians do, so they go into cosmetology programs.

Interviews with female construction workers in a study of the industry sponsored by the Department of Labor illustrate this point. Before they had contact with a referral agency, the women were unaware of career opportunities in construction (U.S. Department of Labor, Employment Standards Administration, 1981).

It seems probable that occupational knowledge affects occupational outcomes. Parnes and Kohen (1975) have shown that this is the case for young black and white men, although knowledge of what workers in 10 occupations did was associated with only fairly small increases on the Duncan SEI score associated with their subsequent jobs. A similar study for young women (Mott and Moore, 1976) showed no effect of occupational knowledge on the prestige of their subsequent jobs. The 10 occupations on which the young women were questioned, however, were typically held by women, so we can draw no conclusions from this study about the effect of knowledge of a broad range of occupations on women's occupational choices or outcomes.

Providing students with information about sex-atypical occupations is probably not sufficient, however, to yield significant changes in their aspirations, in view of the importance of cultural norms and peer group and family pressures. For example, Verheyden-Hilliard (National Commission for Employment Policy, 1980) described a study in which a counselor provided a small group of girls with information regarding jobs not customarily held by women over an extended period. Although their awareness of the range of jobs open to women was enhanced, these subjects were not more likely to aspire to nontraditional occupations. Nevertheless, improved information is certainly a necessary, if not sufficient, step in ensuring equal opportunity in the labor market.

FAMILY RESPONSIBILITIES

We noted at the outset of this chapter that deep-seated cultural beliefs about appropriate activities for men and women undoubtedly have a strong influence on both workers themselves and employers in their attitudes about appropriate work for men and women. One of the most long-standing of these beliefs is that women belong at home raising children and caring for their families. And we noted that, in fact, women more than men undertake the duties associated with child, family, and home care—both because they do so within marriage and because, if single, they are much more likely than men to have children living with them. These family care activities are done by women whether or not they also work for wages. Despite the increasing participation of mothers of even very young children in the labor force in recent years, a substantial proportion of mothers do withdraw from the labor market to care for young children. It is not unreasonable to suppose that women's family responsibilities do affect their labor market behavior, and several theorists have argued that women choose to enter and work in occupations that accommodate their actual or anticipated family responsibilities and that such choices, in the aggregate, contribute to job segregation by sex.

There are other ways, too, that women may be influenced by their families in their work lives. Husbands, and possibly fathers, may have definite ideas about the appropriate type, hours, and location of work for the women in their families. For example, Weil (1961) reports that 69.3 percent of the husbands of women who work part time object to full-time employment for women. While the pervasiveness of this attitude has probably undergone some change since 1961, 29.2 percent of married women who were employed in 1983 worked part time (U.S. Department of Labor, Women's Bureau, 1983); and women who work part time are between 3.8 and 4.4 times less likely to be employed in male occupations (Beller, 1982b). Since there is a correlation between part-time work and the likelihood of being employed in a sex-segregated occupation, to the degree that part-time work is more ac-

ceptable to the husbands of married women in the labor force, this attitude may contribute to occupational sex segregation. Women may be constrained by their husbands' attitudes, not only about the number of hours they work but also about how much money it is appropriate for them to earn. Thirty percent of magazine readers surveyed in 1978 responded that they thought they would turn down a job that paid more than their husbands earned (Bird, 1979). Axelson (1970) found that 25.7 percent of white men and 38.8 percent of black men agree or strongly agree that a husband should feel inadequate if his wife earns more than he does, and 10.9 percent of white men and 24.2 percent of black men agree or strongly agree that a wife should refuse a salary larger than that of her husband.[18] These findings suggest that husbands' attitudes may constrain wives' labor market choices.

Women may be constrained by additional aspects of familial responsibility. Many careers require a willingness to relocate as new opportunities arise. Bird (1979) found that corporate officers find relocating difficult because of family responsibilities and that the husband's career may take precedence. In a study of the careers of academic men and women, Marwell et al. (1979) cite evidence that 49 percent of married women, compared with 4 percent of married men, viewed their spouses' jobs as a major deterrent to considering positions in other geographic areas. It is likely, then, that the requirement of mobility in certain careers restricts women more so than it does men and contributes to occupational segregation by sex. Ironically, husband's careers may not only con-

---

[18] These findings raise the intriguing question of whether low wages contribute to job segregation (rather than the other way around), if wives seek low-paying jobs because they fear their husbands' objections. Recent data reveal, however, that in 12 percent of all couples wives earn more than their husbands (U.S. Department of Commerce, Bureau of the Census, 1983c).

strain wives' choices but may also directly benefit from their wives' contributions. Benham (1975) concludes that a woman's college education does more to raise the income of her husband than it does to increase the income she can earn herself. And given the household division of labor, it is likely that jobs that seem to require spouses to serve in a support role, such as those in the upper ranks of corporate, political, or academic life, are more easily filled by men than women (Bird, 1979; Kanter, 1977). In a survey of married male college graduates (Mortimer, 1976) only 14 percent replied that their wives had no involvement in their careers, and 19 percent said their wives had participated directly in job tasks. Fully 91 percent of ministers' wives said they were involved in church-related work, but only 18 percent thought they would be equally involved if their husbands were not ministers (Taylor and Hartley, 1975).

The significance of all aspects of families—including pregnancy, childbirth, caring for children, housework, and husbands' attitudes—is undoubtedly large for many aspects of womens' work lives, but, as we have seen, the theory and the evidence concerning their implications for job segregation by sex is much more limited. We want to caution, too, against the common tendency in social science research to assume that family responsibilities are important only to women's work lives and not to those of men. As Feldberg and Glenn (1979) have pointed out, all too often women at work are studied as though family was all that mattered for their behavior (overlooking the influence of such factors as working conditions, wages, and promotion opportunities) and men at home or in their communities are studied as though work was all that mattered (while connections of family and community concerns to work-related issues are ignored). While the available research focuses on the effects of women's family responsibilities on their workplace behavior, we want to stress the

necessity for considering all the permutations of work-family interactions, for men as well as women.

Human Capital Theory

Mincer and Polachek (1974, 1978) and Polachek (1976, 1978, 1979, 1981a, 1981b) have argued that women's actual or expected family obligations dictate the choice of predominantly female occupations. This argument is derived from human capital theory and is based on the assumption that people make choices to invest in training or to pursue certain occupations with an eye toward maximizing their lifetime earnings. Women's expectations that they will interrupt their labor force participation to have children are thought to affect their decisions about education, training, and occupational choice in several ways. First, because women who do not plan continuous employment expect less return from any job-related investment in education or training, they might select female-dominated occupations, which are believed to require less investment in training. Second, women who anticipate a short period of employment might try to maximize their starting salaries by selecting female-dominated occupations, which hypothetically start at higher wage levels but yield lower long-run returns to experience than predominantly male occupations (which hypothetically pay less to start because they provide on-the-job training and advancement opportunity—Zellner, 1975). Third, women who anticipate intermittent employment might choose occupations requiring skills that do not depreciate rapidly with disuse or that do not penalize the depreciation.

Another possibility is that the household rather than the individual is the maximizing unit that allocates the time of its members according to their talents to realize the greatest economic benefit (Becker, 1974; Moore and Sawhill, 1976).[19] Regardless of their socialization, women's poorer earning prospects relative to their husbands—either because they plan discontinuous employment, have less education or experience, or because of sex discrimination in the labor market—would lead them to specialize in domestic work while their husbands specialize in market work. Wives would retain responsibility for child care and domestic work even when employed full time, because their primary orientation would be toward the family. They might then prefer jobs that do not require overtime, unanticipated work effort, travel, or geographic mobility or that permit flexibility and time off in domestic emergencies, all hypothetically characteristics of some predominantly female occupations.[20]

Unfortunately, we have few data either about women's preferences or the degree to which female-dominated occupations might accommodate them, but, before turning to the available empirical literature that attempts to test several variants of the human capital thesis, let us note several theoretical objections. First, even if women do seek jobs that require less training, there is no reason to expect them to cluster particularly in female-dominated jobs, since many male-dominated jobs also require little skill or training (Blau and Jusenius, 1976). Second, it is difficult to establish the direction of causation between labor force intermittency

and occupations with low wage growth (Welch, cited in Marini and Brinton, 1984)—have women in such occupations chosen them, or have they simply accepted what was offered? In general, is constraint a more accurate description of women's behavior than preference or choice? We now turn to the research results.

The human capital account of segregation has generated considerable research but conflicting findings. Mincer and Polachek (1974, 1978) attributed the observed relationship between women's work experience, home time, and wages to the depreciation of their skills while out of the labor force.[21] More recently, Polachek (1981b) cited the link between women's marital status and occupation as indirect evidence. He noted Andrea Beller's (1981) finding that being single increased women's probability of working in a male-dominated occupation and interpreted the different distributions of ever-married and never-married women in professional, technical, and administrative jobs in several industrialized nations in Roos's (1983) study as consistent with his thesis. Beller's own interpretation of these findings, however, is that single women had only a slightly greater probability (1 percent) of being employed in a nontraditional occupation (Beller, 1982b). Roos (1983) contends that the marital status differences are both

---

[19] The idea that the family is a utility maximizing unit has been criticized by feminist theorists (Folbre, 1982; McCrate, 1984). As Folbre points out, the potential for conflict of interest within the family is circumvented by the human capital approach. Much of feminist scholarship on the family has been devoted to reconceptualizing it from the separate vantage points of women and men rather than treating it as an undifferentiated unit (Hartmann, 1981; Rapp et al., 1979).

[20] The sexes do differ in the average distance they travel to work and their willingness to accept a job in another area (Niemi, 1974; Madden, 1978, 1981).

---

[21] The human capital approach has been criticized for failing to take into account the ways in which the attributes of jobs (rather than family responsibilities) affect women's behavior. Low wages (and discrimination) can affect the experience women (or men) choose to accumulate. And women, as well as men, may quit because of undesirable job features, such as lack of opportunities for promotion. On the effect of earnings on experience see Kahn (1980) and the exchange between Sandell and Shapiro (1978) and Mincer and Polachek (1978). For evidence of women's quitting, see Blau and Kahn (1981b) and Viscusi (1980); recent studies generally indicate that controlling for pay, occupation, industry, and personal productivity characteristics, men are as likely to quit as women.

minimal and inconsistent with the human capital explanation, and England (1982) found that single, childless white women were no more likely than other white women to be employed in sex-atypical occupations.

A more direct test examines the relationship between discontinuous participation and employment in a female-dominated occupation. Polachek (1981a) showed that years out of the labor force increased women's probability of working in female-dominated major occupational categories. In a simulation he also showed that if all women workers were employed continuously, their representation would increase in broad census categories for professional, managerial, and technical occupations and decrease in the operative and clerical categories. But Corcoran et al. (1984) pointed out that even under the assumption of continuous employment in Polachek's simulation, the index of segregation would decline by only two points.

Contrary to the human capital prediction, women's actual employment continuity does not appear to be related to holding a female-typed occupation. England's (1982) analysis of 3,754 mature women ages 30-44 in the National Longitudinal Survey found that the percentage of time they had been employed since completing school did not vary with the sex composition of their first or most recent occupation. Nor was the sex composition of their first occupation correlated with the proportion of (presurvey) years women eventually spent in the labor force (England, 1982). Moreover, the rates at which the earnings of women in predominantly female occupations appreciated with experience did not differ from those for women in less segregated occupations. England (1984) replicated these findings in a similar analysis of workers surveyed in the University of Michigan's Panel Study of Income Dynamics. If the human capital explanation is correct, the negative effect of time out of the labor force on earnings should have been greater in male-dominated oc-

cupations, but the sizes of the effect for more and less male occupations differed slightly or not at all. Polachek (1979) has demonstrated that time out of the labor force is positively correlated with wage loss, but not the crucial point that women's human capital depreciates less in predominantly female occupations. In sum, Polachek's thesis has little support. There is no clear evidence that female occupations penalize intermittence less than male occupations, nor is there much evidence that women who spend more time at home or expect to do so are apt to choose such occupations (England, 1984).

Mincer and Ofek (1982) have refined the human capital approach to women's labor market behavior to encompass the premise that workers recover skills that depreciated during a period out of the labor force more rapidly than they accumulate them from scratch. This implies that wage losses following a career interruption should be followed by a period of rapid wage growth. Corcoran et al. (1984) confirmed this for employed wives and female heads of households whose labor market behavior was observed over a 13-year period. These women displayed both the hypothesized wage loss after being out of the labor force and the hypothesized period of rapid recovery upon reentry, so that their net loss of wages was small. As Corcoran et al. point out, this rebound effect has important implications for the human capital explanation of segregation. If depreciation is quickly repaired, it is not economically rational for intermittent workers either to choose minimal investments or to postpone investing in job training until they have returned to the labor force on a permanent basis. And even if female-dominated occupations penalized women less than male-dominated occupations for dropping out, the long-run penalties are too small to support the inference that it is economically rational for women to choose such occupations, given their lower wages and lesser return to experience. In fact, England (1984) found that women in male-dominated occupations have higher lifetime earnings than women in female-dominated ones, suggesting that it is not economically rational to choose predominantly female occupations to maximize lifetime earnings.

The ability of the human capital approach to explain sex segregation ultimately depends on determining what women believe is true and how they make labor market decisions. Unfortunately, we know very little about the beliefs women hold with respect to their own investments in human capital or the extent to which their occupational choices conform to the model of economic rationality. In general, when behavior is subject to such strong structural and cultural constraints as women's work is, there is less reason to expect a theory that assumes economic optimization to hold. While further research on women's own views of the trade-offs between investments in training, wage gains, and time spent with children might illuminate some of the assumptions of this approach, the lack of empirical confirmation suggests that if women choose female-dominated occupations, they probably do not do so because they think such occupations will maximize their lifetime earnings. Though the empirical evidence is limited, women may choose to limit their work commitment because of familial arrangements. It is even more likely that such a choice is subject to considerable constraint, as we examine below with regard to child care.

Child Care and Occupational Segregation

The custom of assigning primary responsibility for child care to women has historically restricted their participation in the work force and in education and training programs. To a lesser degree it continues to do so. This can be seen in the differential labor force participation rates of women by the presence and age of their children. For example, in March 1982 half the women with children under age six were in the labor force compared with two-thirds of those with school-age children (U.S. Department of Labor, Women's Bureau, 1982b). The belief that young children whose mothers work suffer has contributed to the deterrent effect of having young children on women's employment, although the proportion of working mothers who believe that their employment will harm their children has declined markedly during the past decade (Bumpass, 1982). Recent reviews of research (Kamerman and Hayes, 1982; Hayes and Kamerman, 1983) indicate that the children of working mothers suffer no discernible ill effects from their mothers' employment (to the contrary, the added income demonstrably improves the lives of some children), that both wage-working and at-home mothers behave similarly toward their children (in such areas as school visits, for example), and that the children of both wage-working and at-home mothers also spend their time similarly (in play, homework, sports, television viewing, etc.).

Evidence also suggests, however, that the lack of adequate, affordable, and convenient child care prevents some women from participating in the labor force and limits others to jobs that they believe will accommodate their child care responsibilities. Estimates indicate that one in every five to six nonemployed women is not in the labor force because she cannot find satisfactory child care (Shortlidge, 1977; Presser and Baldwin, 1980). National Longitudinal Survey data from 1971 for mothers with children under age six suggest that these figures may be even higher for black women: 26 percent of black mothers surveyed reportedly were constrained from employment by the lack of adequate day care compared with only 5 percent of the white mothers, and 47 percent of the nonemployed black and 13 percent of white mothers said that they would look for jobs immediately if free day care were available (U.S. Department of Labor, Manpower Administration, 1975).

The absence of flexible child care alternatives may also restrict some women to jobs with certain hours, those that do not require overtime or weekend work, and those that permit time off for children's illnesses. The U.S. Commission on Civil Rights (1981b) reviews several studies indicating that the unavailability of adequate child care prevents women from increasing their hours of employment. The 1977 Current Population Survey on child care indicated that 16 percent of employed women would work more hours if they could locate suitable child care (Presser and Baldwin, 1980). Limiting their work hours can in turn reduce women's prospects for promotion, restrict them to jobs for which they are overqualified, or make it impossible for them to take courses that would improve their job options. Survey data confirm the problem child care presents for many employed women (Astin, 1969; National Commission on Working Women, 1979). One in 12 of the employed women surveyed in the 1977 special Current Population Survey on child care cared for their children while they were at work (U.S. Department of Commerce, Bureau of the Census, 1982:6). One in eight women in blue-collar and service occupations did so, many of whom managed by working in their own homes (U.S. Department of Commerce, Bureau of the Census, 1982:26). It seems likely that most of these women were restricted to low-paying, predominantly female occupations like direct mail or telephone sales.

The U.S. Commission on Civil Rights (1981b) details the ways in which the lack of child care restricts women's ability and, in the case of the Work Incentive Program (WIN), their legal right to take advantage of important federal job training programs. Although they discovered no estimates as to the number of women who are denied access to programs because they lack child care, the commission reports that since 1972 federal regulations have required that child care be available before a women is referred for employment or training and describes a 1977 study that identified the lack of adequate child care as one of two primary reasons why women WIN registrants were less likely than men to be assigned to either training or a job.

Employed women vary widely in the type of child care they both use (U.S. Department of Commerce, Bureau of the Census, 1982) and prefer (Presser and Baldwin, 1980). Many women prefer family-based care to group care (U.S. Department of Labor, Manpower Administration, 1975), although working women surveyed by Paskoff preferred day care at the workplace (cited in U.S. Department of Labor, Women's Bureau, 1982b). Moreover, as Presser and Baldwin (1980) have shown, it is often the most disadvantaged women—young, unmarried, minority, and low-income mothers—who are least likely to locate satisfactory arrangements that they can afford. Full-time blue-collar and service workers are less than half as likely as mothers in white-collar occupations to use group child care and more likely to depend on their children's fathers (U.S. Department of Commerce, Bureau of the Census, 1982), probably through arranging for parents to work different shifts (Presser, 1980). And finally, some parents do not find any arrangements. Sandra Hofferth (1979) estimated that 32,000 preschoolers were caring for themselves in 1975. The 1977 Current Population Survey (U.S. Department of Commerce, Bureau of the Census, 1982:42) revealed self-care for .3 percent of the children under five whose mothers worked full-time and .5 percent of the children of mothers employed part-time.

Unfortunately, none of the available studies tells us how many employed women might be able to work in less sex-typed occupations if they were not constrained by their need for child care, but the constraints on employment opportunities that inadequate child care presents for some women are indisputable. It is also important not to lose sight of the fact that some employers may make hiring decisions based on their beliefs about individual women's need for child care and the probable reliability of that care. Employers may sometimes be reluctant to hire or promote mothers, even those who have secured adequate child care, for certain jobs because they question whether their child care is adequate. We also noted above that male workers may attempt to reinforce women's sense of responsibility for housework and child care through their own behavior on the job and at home. Such behavior would also contribute to job segregation.

Conclusion

In sum, although the research evidence does not enable us to say that women's greater responsibility for child care, housework, and family care necessarily contributes to sex segregation in the workplace, it almost certainly plays an important role in limiting their employment opportunities in general. Some women (and men) may of course freely choose to place family responsibilities first in their lives and employment and work careers second or lower. Whenever women's choices and opportunities are constrained, however, as they most certainly are by familial responsibilities and the lack of alternative social arrangements for family care, we must be concerned. For some women, familial responsibilities are clearly not chosen but are a burden thrust on them. For others, especially those for whom economic need is greatest, family responsibilities contribute all the more to their need for equal opportunity and equitable pay in the workplace. Yet others may feel compelled to bear the greater share of home and family care because their own earning ability is limited compared with their husbands or other male providers. Finally, for most if not all women, the powerful cultural beliefs regarding women's "natural" responsibility for children, men, and homes enter the workplace unbidden, conditioning many aspects of their employment.

THE OPPORTUNITY STRUCTURE AND SEX SEGREGATION

We have reviewed evidence indicating that many factors on both the demand and the supply sides affect labor market outcomes for men and women. We have separately examined the influence of deeply ingrained cultural beliefs, of barriers to employment, of education and socialization, and of family responsibilities on the extent and persistence of the sex segregation of jobs. Such an approach runs the risk of losing sight of the interrelationship between opportunities and decisions that occurs within the labor market. Workers' occupational decisions are often influenced by what they find in the labor market. The labor market presents workers with an occupational opportunity structure that is affected not so much by the actions of any one employer but is rather the cumulated effect of the actions of many. Over time, of course, opportunity structures change, at least partly as employers respond to changes in workers' behavior. In this section we examine evidence regarding the role of the occupational opportunity structure in shaping workers' preferences, knowledge, and occupational outcomes, and thereby contributing to the perpetuation of sex segregation.

Lloyd Reynolds (1951), in a major contribution to the analysis of labor markets, noted that the vacancies to which people have access when they enter the labor market strongly affect the occupations in which they end up. Reynolds characterized the job mobility process as involving a job search (often based on tips from friends and relatives) that typically culminates in a worker taking the first acceptable job offered.[22] Because jobs are filled rapidly, workers are seldom in the position to choose among al-

---

[22] See Kahn (1978), Sandell (1980), and Gera and Hasan (1982) for further discussion of the job search process.

ternatives. Reynolds concluded that changes in demand induce the adaptation of the labor supply: opportunity must precede movement. Sociologists, too (White, 1970; Sorensen, 1975, 1977; Spilerman, 1977; Konda and Stewman, 1980), have stressed the importance of opportunities in determining workers' occupational outcomes. In this scheme, workers' personal characteristics are important primarily as a basis for rationing vacancies in better jobs among the supply of potential applicants, an idea further developed by Thurow (1975). When gender is used systematically by employers as the basis for selecting workers for certain occupations, sex segregation results.

This emphasis on opportunities is consistent with research on labor market behavior. Workers frequently do not make career plans until they have left school and entered the labor market. For example, more than half the workers that Lipset and his colleagues (Bendix et al., 1954) surveyed had no specific job plans while in school, and members of a national sample of college students who did have career plans changed them often (Davis, 1965). Once in the labor market, many young workers move from job to job seeking work that suits them through trial and error (Folk, 1968; Hall and Kasten, 1976; Sorensen, 1977; Rosenfeld, 1979), before settling into semipermanent positions.[23] Examining mobility data from the 1970 census, Rosenfeld and Sorensen (1979) found that young (ages 20-31) and, to a smaller degree, older (ages 32-41) workers of both sexes frequently changed occupations. During the previous five years, 35 percent of young men and 29 percent of young women moved from one to another of the 11 broad occupational categories, and 22 percent of older workers did so. More than one in nine people over age 18 who were employed in January 1977 worked in a different detailed occupational category a year later (Rosenfeld, 1979). Jacobs (1983) found that 55 percent of women ages 30-44 in 1967 worked in a different three-digit occupation 10 years later. Spilerman (1977) revealed similar results for male construction workers, truck drivers, and mail carriers: between 33 and 43 percent of workers in their twenties changed occupations during a five-year period, as did between 13 and 27 percent of those in their thirties. Such mobility suggests that career decisions made prior to entering the labor force are important for only a minority of workers. It is rather that their labor market careers are likely to be shaped by the opportunities they find.

Unfortunately, most systematic research on the effect of job openings on occupational attainment has been limited to men (Rosenfeld, 1982), so evidence of the effect of opportunities on women's labor market behavior is largely indirect. The evidence is of three types. The first shows women's responsiveness to labor market conditions and the actual availability of jobs—regardless of prior sex labeling. The second shows that the opportunity structure is highly differentiated by sex. The third demonstrates flexibility in workers' preferences and aspirations.

Substantial evidence suggests that women's response to labor market conditions and job availability is strong. Cain (1966), Mincer (1962a), and others have demonstrated that the unprecedented influx of women into the labor force since World War II was a response to increases in wage rates offered. Oppenheimer (1970) has argued that because many of the new jobs created since the mid-1940s were in occupations considered to be "women's work," the rise in female labor force participation can be understood as a response to job opportunities that had not previously existed for women. Moreover, once in the labor force, the decisions of women to move from one job to another are as strongly influenced as those of men by the wage rate in the current job

---

[23] Rosenfeld (1984) reviews these and other theories of labor market mobility for young male workers.

and by the long-run earning prospects offered by a job change (Blau and Kahn, 1981b).

Furthermore, women are responsive to particular occupational openings. When occupations have become open, women have responded by moving into them—regardless of their prior sex label. For example, within a 20-year period, the proportion of clerical workers who were women increased from less than 5 percent in 1880 to over 30 percent in 1900; 20 years later, women made up half of all clerical workers (Rotella, 1981). During World War II, when employers welcomed applications from women, their numbers in such jobs as welding that were formerly almost exclusively male increased tremendously.[24] Black women's rapid movement out of domestic service and into clerical occupations (Malveaux, 1982b) that opened to them during the 1960s and 1970s provides another example of women's responsiveness to the availability of occupations. During the 1970s, sharp increases occurred in the proportions of women obtaining professional degrees in fields such as law and medicine, which have been dominated by men. The rapid increase in the number of women mining coal (Hall, 1981; Clauss, 1982) indicates that nonprofessional and physically arduous occupations also attract women when they believe they have a chance at jobs. In 1972, no women applied for mining jobs at Peabody Coal Company in Kentucky, the nation's largest coal producer; by 1978, after it had become known that women were being hired, 1,131 women applied for mining jobs

(Working Women, 1981). A similar growth occurred in applications by women for jobs in shipbuilding yards, when the Maritime Administration began requiring the shipbuilding contractors to establish goals and timetables for the increased employment of women. The shipbuilding contractors found that as more women were hired, more women applied. Unquestionably, the key reason for the increase of women in this case was goals and timetables (*Federal Register* 42, No. 158:41379-80), but while equal employment opportunity policies played a role in many of these examples, their effect is hard to document. A more systematic effort is left for the next chapter.[25]

This is not to say that large pools of women are available for all male-dominated occupations. Employers sometimes claim that they cannot comply with federally mandated affirmative action requirements because the pool of eligible women is too small (U.S. Department of Labor, Employment Standards Administration, 1981). But shortages are probably most common in occupations that require preemployment training. Of course, women may lack enthusiasm for occupations in which they believe they will encounter hostility or other difficulties or those in which their femininity might be questioned (Strober, 1984). As Wolf (1981)

---

[24] Milkman (1980:103) quotes a 1943 billboard:

"What Job is mine on the Victory Line?"
If you've sewed on buttons, or made buttonholes, on a machine,
    you can learn to do spot welding on airplane parts.
If you've used an electric mixer in your kitchen,
    you can learn to run a drill press.
If you've followed recipes exactly in making cakes,
    you can learn to load shell.

[25] Several researchers have attempted to assess the impact of equal employment opportunity laws on the labor market outcomes of minorities or women (Ashenfelter and Heckman, 1976; Goldstein and Smith, 1976; Heckman and Wolpin, 1976; Beller, 1978, 1979, 1980, 1982a, 1982b; Flanagan, 1976; Butler and Heckman, 1977; Brown, 1982; Osterman, 1982; Leonard, 1984a,b,c). We discuss their conclusions in the next chapter. Here it is sufficient to mention the difficulty involved in demonstrating the impact of the passage of equal employment laws and regulations on the actual availability of opportunities. The dramatic effect of the passage and enforcement of the 1965 Voting Rights Act on voting by blacks (U.S. Commission on Civil Rights, 1981a) provides some evidence of the impact on people's behavior of legal changes that open up opportunities.

notes, young women, for whom norms about appropriate female behavior are salient, may be especially reluctant to take jobs labeled male. After their middle twenties, however, women are less likely to be deterred by the possibility that they may appear unfeminine and more likely to be influenced by the fact that predominantly male jobs are better paid.

That women have generally responded to opportunities as they became available does not mean that they are not also constrained in their behavior and does not belie the basic sex-differentiated structure of opportunities. For example, as noted above, family obligations may constrain women's responses to particular types of openings. Moreover, despite the opening of new occupations to women, some areas are still explicitly closed to women and many others are implicitly so, as the evidence of barriers in the workplace reviewed above demonstrates. In particular, opportunities at the establishment level are apparently extremely sex-segregated. As Bielby and Baron (1984) found for a sample of California firms, nearly 60 percent were totally segregated, i.e., were either all male or all female or had a job structure in which each job category was occupied by a single sex. Within establishments, particularly large establishments, rules govern workers' opportunities. Rules governing seniority, job bidding rights, transfer, leaves, and so on have often contributed to restricting women's career advancement and concentrating them in female-dominated jobs. Throughout the economy, the index of segregation remains over 60—women often work with women and men with men, and women's occupations are lower paid. An individual could not fail to notice the sex-typing of jobs and the differential opportunities apparently available to women and men. And he or she might conclude, rightly or wrongly, that their choices are severely constrained.

Finally, flexibility in workers' preferences and behavior (and in the labor market as well) is demonstrated by both a fair amount of mobility by men and women between sex-typical and sex-atypical occupations, as measured at the level of detailed census occupations, and the continuing influence of structural factors on their preferences and aspirations. In one recent study of women ages 30-44 in the National Longitudinal Survey who changed jobs between 1967 and 1977, Jacobs (1983) found the sex type of their jobs at these two points uncorrelated (sex type was trichotomized into less than 30 percent female, 30-69.9 percent female, and over 70 percent female). When he replicated his analysis with 1980 and 1981 Current Population Survey data for job changers of both sexes and across the full range of adult ages, Jacobs observed only small correlations between the sex type of jobs at the two points ($r = .10$ for the women, $.15$ for the men). Rosenfeld's (1984) analyses of a sample of workers who changed jobs during 1972 revealed that about 15 percent of women who worked in jobs that were over half female moved to jobs that were dominated by men, and about 40 percent of women in jobs in which men were the majority moved to similar jobs, with the remaining 40 percent moving to jobs that were at least 50 percent female. It is important to note, however, that the sex type of these job shifts is generally measured for the occupational aggregates in which the jobs fall. For example, a shift from food server in a cafeteria to crossing guard might be measured as a shift from female-typed work to sex-neutral work, because food servers are in an occupational category that is predominantly female while crossing guards are in an integrated occupational category (made up of female crossing guards and male traffic enforcement officers). Nevertheless the actual move is from one female-typed job to another. Because sex segregation is pervasive at the level of jobs within firms, many of the moves noted in these studies may be more sex-typical than is apparent. Despite these data problems, however, these recent studies, confirmed by other researchers (e.g., Corcoran et al., 1984), suggest that a moderate amount of mobility occurs across sex-typed occupations.

Evidence also shows that structural factors continue to influence workers' behavior and attitudes after they enter the labor market. Theorists of labor market segmentation argue that workers' motivation and behavior are governed both by their position in labor market segments and, within organizations, on job ladders (Stevenson, 1978; Harrison and Sum, 1979). For example, the turnover rates of both sexes are affected by the type of job they hold, so controlling for the latter accounts almost completely for sex differences in turnover (U.S. Department of Labor, Women's Bureau, 1975; Lloyd and Niemi, 1979; Haber et al., 1983). Recent evidence indicates similar effects of job characteristics on the psychological functioning of both women and men (Miller et al., 1979; Krause et al., 1982; Kohn et al., 1983). People's jobs socialize them to certain attitudes toward work. It follows that exposure to various work opportunities and experiences affects workers' occupational preferences. For example, longitudinal analysis of mature employed women revealed that their attitudes toward work became more favorable in response to their employment experiences (Ferree, 1980). The opportunity structure can also be expected to have an effect on workers' occupational aspirations. To illustrate, about half the women in traditionally male skilled craft jobs whom Walshok (1981a) studied had some childhood access to nontraditional work skills, but, according to Walshok, because they also realized that these fields offered no opportunities for women, they did not seek craft jobs until opportunities opened up. For example, a plumber described her experience: "I've always liked tools . . . (but) it never occurred to me that I would ever be a plumber until somebody handed me a wrench and said 'Hop to it.' I just happened to run into that particular opportunity . . ." (p. 169). It seems likely, then, that women's aspirations and

preferences change as their perception of opportunities changes and that the occupational opportunity structure is an important determinant of their preferences.

These findings suggest a fluidity in the labor market, in workers, and in their occupational preferences. Apparently, workers can and do circulate in and out of sex-atypical occupations. Our discussion of informal barriers above suggested some reasons why workers might leave sex-atypical occupations, but further systematic longitudinal research is clearly needed to understand the circulation of workers across sex-typed occupations. These frequent job changes belie the claim that segregation reflects the relatively stable choices of women and men stemming from their childhood sex-role socialization but support the thesis that workers' job outcomes reflect the available opportunities. The amount of movement between sex-typical and sex-atypical occupations and the responsiveness of women workers to new opportunities makes the continued high degree of sex segregation in the economy even more remarkable. Clearly, theories of occupational sex segregation and of discrimination will have to take into account the movement of workers of both sexes in and out of sex-atypical occupations. Further research will be needed to ascertain to what extent these occupational changes actually involve movement across sex-typed jobs. In any case, however, the mobility is a significant aspect of the labor market for women and men.

Two additional aspects of the occupational opportunity structure merit discussion. First, the occupational opportunity structure affects workers' decisions by affecting their knowledge of job opportunities as well as their preferences. As we noted above in discussing institutionalized barriers in the workplace, many employers use referrals from other workers as an important recruitment technique. Thus potential applicants hear about available jobs from friends and other informal networks that tend to be sex-segregated. Women are more likely to hear about available jobs from other women, and, because of the sex-segregated occupational structure, these women are likely to be in women's jobs. Second, it is important to remember that while the occupational opportunity structure results in part from employers' actions, taken together, workers also participate in its development. Employers determine whom to hire and in what position, but workers sometimes play an active role, for example when whites or men object to minorities or women (Bergmann and Darrity, 1981), or when applicants accept or refuse jobs that are offered. As Strober (1984) notes, if white men refuse a job at the wage offered, employers may try to hire women or minority men. If some women or minority men accept it, their acceptance will signal to yet others that this job is now available to them.

CONCLUSION

From our examination of the evidence for several alternative and interrelated explanations of sex segregation, our primary conclusion is that women's occupational choices and preferences play a limited role in explaining occupational segregation by sex.

Both explanations for occupational segregation that focus on women's own choices—sex-role socialization and human capital theory—recognize that cultural values about men and women condition their socialization and their subsequent educational choices. Sex-role socialization is thought to contribute to labor market segregation by encouraging girls to be primarily responsible for domestic work and boys for breadwinning and by identifying sex-appropriate occupations. Each gender is not only socialized to perform sex-specific primary adult roles, but each is also taught the skills, values, and occupational aspirations compatible with them. The socialization process also encourages the development of different sex-linked personality traits that may ultimately affect the occupations to which women and men feel suited. The occupational aspirations of boys and girls continue to differ as do some occupationally related skills and values, although these differences have declined in the recent past. These differences are consistent with what we know of the content of sex-role socialization: parents, teachers, and counselors treat girls and boys differently and hold different goals for them. Tracking still occurs within the public school system, as does sex stereotyping in children's books, including textbooks, and the mass media. Although the link is not established unequivocally, it seems likely that socialization contributes to sex differences in aspirations, preferences, skills, and values and therefore probably contributes to occupational segregation, but we are unsure about the size of any contribution and the value of focusing on sex-role socialization as a locus of change. Our literature review suggests that the impact of preemployment sex differences in abilities and values on occupational outcomes is probably small, except in those occupations that require skills that are usually acquired prior to employment. Further research to clarify the role of occupational aspirations in producing sex-typed occupational outcomes is clearly indicated.

The sizable amount of mobility that occurs across occupations, and more specifically across sex-typical and sex-atypical occupations, is inconsistent with the view that outcomes reflect fixed occupational preferences. Rather we have seen that preferences are likely to change over a lifetime, particularly in response to new opportunities. The shifts that have been observed in women's occupational aspirations in recent years are consistent with expanding job opportunities for women in a broader range of occupations. That young women often expect to pursue more traditional occupations than those to which they aspire reinforces our argument that the perceived opportunity structure is of central importance in determining both preferences and outcomes. The educational system also contributes to segregation by tracking students in sex-typical vocational courses. The failure of schools to present a wide range of occupational possibilities to students regardless of their sex necessarily narrows the job possibilities that they are likely to pursue later.

Advocates of the human capital theory of sex segregation, a second major explanation that attributes sex segregation to women's choices, have constructed an internally plausible account of how segregation could result from the economically rational decisions by women who plan to raise families to limit their investments in training and pursue certain occupations. Women do fail to acquire the training necessary for many jobs, but it is not clear how much this reflects their own choices, lack of encouragement, or the existence of obstacles to their doing so. Attempts to assess the theory by examining patterns of sex segregation by marital status have yielded conflicting results. The results of studies based on panel data that provide the most direct tests have been inconsistent with the theory's predictions. Women who spend more time out of the labor force are no more apt to choose female-dominated occupations than those who plan continuous employment, and female occupations do not penalize intermittent labor force participation less than male-dominated ones. Furthermore, any depreciation in women's occupational skills that does occur when they leave the labor force seems to be quickly repaired, so that long-run income losses are too small to motivate women to postpone investing in training or to select low-paying occupations that require little training. The connections between familial responsibilities and work deserve additional research attention, however, because it seems likely that family care obligations do influence people's labor market behavior.

The limited effect of socialization and related factors that can be demonstrated directs our attention to the role of forces within the labor market that limit the set of occupations from which women workers can choose. This approach recognizes the active role employers play in the labor market as well as the existence of other barriers that reduce women's options. A variety of barriers prevent women from exercising free occupational choice. Some barriers were codified into laws, and others were permitted by the courts. Most such laws are now invalid, but their legacy lingers in both employment practices and the current segregated occupational structure. It is important to recall that cultural beliefs about women's proper roles influence decisions by employers and male coworkers. Their behavior as well as institutionalized personnel practices also create barriers in the labor market. On these grounds we conclude that sex segregation cannot be ascribed primarily to women's choice of female-dominated occupations.

As we have shown, women's exclusion from many occupations has unquestionably contributed to segregation. An examination of the operation of labor markets and of the importance of the occupational structure reviewed indicates that the labor market outcomes of both men and women commonly depend on the opportunities that are known and open to them. These opportunities have been largely determined by employers and other decision makers in influential positions. Employers have in many instances structured their workplace and personnel policies in ways that have established and reinforced job segregation, but employers also respond to changes in women's and men's attitudes as well as to government initiatives. Consequently the opportunities available to women expand at the same time that public and private awareness of changing attitudes grows. As opportunities have expanded in the past, women have rapidly responded. This seems to be the best explanation for some rather dramatic changes over the past decade in women's representation in a variety of occupations, which we examined in Chapter 2.

These conclusions have implications for different types of intervention. If it were possible and desirable to do so, reducing sex differences in personal traits produced by socialization without changing the labor market would probably reduce segregation only slightly. Moreover, early sex-role socialization is probably less amenable to policy intervention than are some factors that come into play later, such as tracking in schools and barriers women encounter in the labor market. Eliminating the latter factors should contribute to changes in women's occupational aspirations, as well as an increase in their opportunities, and thus both directly and indirectly modify women's distribution across occupations. In the next chapter our examination of the effectiveness of a variety of interventions further demonstrates the close relationship between opportunities and workers' behavior and illustrates important sources of further change.

4 Reducing Sex Segregation in the Workplace

Interventions which reduce Sexual Segregation

In Chapter 2 we noted that over the past decade women have increased their representation in some occupations and industries that historically had been predominantly or exclusively male. This chapter presents evidence that at least a portion of this increase resulted from direct interventions in training and labor market processes, in the form of either prohibitions against sex discrimination or programs designed to enhance women's occupational opportunities. The best examples of the former are Title VII of the 1964 Civil Rights Act, which prohibits sex discrimination in several conditions of employment, and Executive Order 11246 (11375), which requires nondiscrimination and positive action by federal contractors. Positive actions include the affirmative action programs instituted by some professional schools and special programs for women by some private employers.

Although the threat of enforcement action by government agencies can be a powerful incentive for employers to change their practices, incentives need not come from government or the courts. They may also emanate from female employees, women's organizations, or changing public opinion about permissible behavior. The evidence we review in this chapter suggests that laws and regulations, legal action, and private programs have facilitated women's progress in several fields. Of course, not all deliberate efforts to reduce sex segregation have produced measurable effects. Interventions by government may be ineffective if they are misdirected or when enforcement is weak and evasion easy. By examining the effectiveness of various programs whose goals included promoting sex equity, we identify strategies that are likely to be effective in the future as well as barriers to the effectiveness of some existing programs.

Most of the interventions to reduce sex segregation have been directed at the workplace and applied specifically to hiring practices, on-the-job training, and promotion opportunities. Others, such as the 1976 Vocational Education Amendments and the 1978 reauthorization of the Comprehensive Employment and Training Act (CETA), mandated sex equity in job training. Laws or programs established to eliminate sex inequity in education, such as Title IX of the 1972 Educational Amendments, may also have implications for sex segregation in the workplace.

Drawing conclusions about the effective-

83

ness of any particular intervention is difficult. Even sophisticated research methods cannot isolate the extent to which changes in women's occupational status can be attributed to a particular intervention as opposed to other changes that occurred during the period in which the intervention was instituted. Of course, the lack of an improvement in women's occupational status does not necessarily mean that an intervention was ineffective. The implementation might have prevented a decline that otherwise would have occurred. Assessing the effectiveness of a law presents an additional difficulty. Under one theory of law enforcement, a law propels "voluntary" actions that would not occur in its absence: enforcing a law in one instance deters others from violating it. As a result, the indirect result of a single law enforcement action on other employers cannot be adequately isolated from other effects. Standard social science methods such as cross-sectional and time-series regression analyses of aggregate-level data are considered inadequate to discover the impact of changes in law enforcement practice on compliance behavior.

We emphasize particularly the difficulty of attributing any difference in a group's employment status to enforcement rather than other forces operating during the same period. The civil rights and women's liberation movements of the 1960s and 1970s highlighted job discrimination and reshaped social values about how minorities and women should be treated. The women's movement influenced attitudes about the kinds of occupations women should be able to pursue. Women in customarily male occupations were featured in news stories, advertisements, and to some extent in popular television programs. The aspirations of individual women expanded. The women's movement unquestionably contributed also to the passage of laws and regulations, the issuance of guidelines with respect to sex, and the carrying out of enforcement activities. During the same period, sex discrimination in employment became both morally suspect and

illegal, and employers, unions, and educators were also subject to direct pressure from women's groups to provide equal opportunities and compensatory training. Both the women's movement and the threat of federal sanctions encouraged women to press employers for better jobs and made the increasing numbers of women interested in "male" jobs visible to employers whose normal hiring practices may have missed them.

The difficulty of isolating the effects of alternative explanations for change limits the conclusions we can draw about enforcement effects. Our review of the evidence, however, has convinced us that enforcement of existing antidiscrimination laws has contributed to reducing sex segregation. To support conclusions about the impact of interventions, we draw on a variety of evidence, including time series data; statistical studies; case studies of specific establishments, occupations, and training or educational programs in which litigation occurred or policy changed; and surveys. Where we can, we also review what is known of the enforcement practices for laws and regulations. We begin by considering intervention within the workplace—federal laws and regulations aimed at eliminating sex discrimination and efforts by employers to promote sex equity. Next, we examine remedies involving job training and vocational and general education. Finally, we consider interventions that enhance access to jobs for people with family responsibilities—child care and work scheduling. Throughout this chapter we emphasize federal laws and federal programs; our resources did not permit the examination of numerous state and local initiatives.

INTERVENTIONS DIRECTED AT THE WORKPLACE

Laws, Regulations, and Enforcement Efforts

During the 1960s and early 1970s, several federal laws and regulations were enacted prohibiting sex discrimination in employment. Most important in setting out the principle of equal employment opportunity is Title VII of the 1964 Civil Rights Act. The act forbids employers from discriminating in several conditions of employment on the basis of race, color, sex, national origin, or religion. The second important instrument for reducing employment discrimination based on gender is Executive Order 11246 (1965; amended by Executive Order 11375 in 1967). As amended, Executive Order 11246 prohibits federal contractors from employment discrimination on account of race, color, religion, sex, or national origin (certain contractors are, however, exempted). Under subsequent regulatory revisions, contractors must also pledge to take affirmative action to ensure nondiscriminatory treatment of minorities and women, including recruitment and training, employment, and upgrading. In view of the large number of workers employed by covered contractors—31 million (Women Employed, 1982)—the order's potential impact is great. In the next sections we describe these laws and regulations in more detail, assess their implementation, and review evidence regarding their effectiveness in expanding women's job opportunities.

Title VII and the Equal Employment Opportunity Commission

According to Title VII of the 1964 Civil Rights Act, employers can neither refuse to hire nor discharge any person on the basis of color, race, sex, national origin, or religion. Neither may they discriminate on these bases with respect to compensation, terms, conditions, or privileges of employment, nor limit, segregate, or classify employees or applicants in any way that deprives them of employment opportunities or otherwise adversely affects their employment status. The law applies also to labor organizations and forbids discrimination by employers, labor organizations, and joint labor-management committees that control apprenticeship and

other training programs. As amended in 1972, it covers the federal government, state and local governments, and most firms with at least 15 employees; in October 1981 the Pregnancy Discrimination Act included within the scope of Title VII discrimination based on pregnancy. The Civil Rights Act also created the Equal Employment Opportunity Commission (EEOC) to administer the employment provisions of the law. In 1969 the EEOC issued guidelines on sex discrimination that barred, among other discriminatory acts, hiring based on stereotyped characterization of the sexes, classifying jobs as "men's" and "women's," and advertising under male and female headings (U.S. Department of Labor, Women's Bureau, 1978).

The EEOC monitors employers through annual reports required of those with at least 100 workers. Although the reports do not provide detailed occupational breakdowns, substantial race and gender disparities in the large categories reported have been used by the EEOC to target employers for investigation of systemic discrimination (U.S. Department of Labor, Women's Bureau, 1982a). Initially, the EEOC had limited enforcement powers: its functions were to investigate charges of discrimination and to attempt to resolve them through conciliation, but the EEOC could not bring suit if conciliation failed until 1972, when the Civil Rights Act was amended by the Equal Employment Opportunity Act.

Some observers have questioned whether the agency carried out its functions of investigation and conciliation effectively in the early years (U.S. Commission on Civil Rights, 1975; U.S. Comptroller General, 1976). Two General Accounting Office studies (U.S. Comptroller General, 1976) indicate little follow-up after conciliation agreements and suggest that agreements did not always improve women's employment status.

In gaining the right to sue for complainants in court in 1972, the agency obtained enforcement power. Most charges are, of course, settled without going to court through the agency's administrative processes. By the early 1970s almost 50,000 new charges of discrimination were being filed annually, on average, and a large backlog had accumulated. By 1977, 130,000 charges were awaiting action by the EEOC. Between 1965 and 1975 the courts were not very likely to grant class relief and did so half as often in sex cases as in race cases (Dunlap, cited in Greenberger, 1978). When the EEOC went to court, however, settlements outnumbered cases dismissed without appeal by a three to one ratio (U.S. Comptroller General, 1976). It is important to note that litigation in Title VII class action cases is very complicated and often takes several years.

A variety of performance measures have been used to assess the effectiveness of the EEOC: predeliberation settlement rate, conciliation success rate, case resolution rate, processing time, etc., but few time-series data are available to assess activity levels or effectiveness over time. Some evidence suggests improved performance after the EEOC was reorganized in 1977 with new case processing procedures and increased budget and authorized staff (more than 3,500 positions at the peak between 1979 and 1981; Burbridge, 1984). Approximately 70,000 charges were being filed each year. The agency implemented a procedure to expedite new charges and to reduce the backlog ("rapid charge processing"), first in model offices in three cities and then, after determining its effectiveness, nationwide. Rapid charge processing enabled the agency to emphasize cases of systemic discrimination. Expedited procedures for rapid settlement also led to more settlements and fewer complaints dismissed for no cause (Women Employed, 1980). By July 1981 the backlog had fallen to about 15 percent of its size in 1977. After 1981, however, the budget fell in real terms, authorized positions decreased somewhat, and more important, the settlement rate fell from 43 percent in 1980 to 28 percent in

1983, and the no-cause rate increased from 29 percent in 1980 to 41 percent in 1983. During the same period, however, the number of cases closed annually increased about 25 percent and the remaining small backlog shrank further (Burbridge, 1984). In fiscal 1981 the EEOC filed 368 lawsuits (which included charges of discrimination based on race, religion, or national origin as well as sex). Between 1981 and 1983, the number of cases filed in court fell dramatically. Only 110 cases were filed in 1982 and 136 in 1983. The number of systemic cases filed also fell, from 25 in 1981 to 10 in 1983; in 1982 none was filed (Burbridge, 1984).

Conclusions about the agency's effectiveness must be drawn cautiously. When the EEOC pursued systemic cases involving large employers, the visibility of such cases presumably had a deterrent effect, and, in fact, a survey of major employers revealed that managerial awareness of enforcement efforts at other companies was positively related to having effective programs to enhance women employees' opportunities at their own companies (Shaeffer and Lynton, 1979; Wallace, 1979).

The major contributions of the EEOC in advancing women's occupational opportunities may have been in establishing such principles as disparate impact, pregnancy discrimination, and a narrow definition of bona fide occupational qualification in the courts and in shaping the remedies and personnel changes to be undertaken by discriminating firms (O'Farrell and Harlan, 1984). Consent decrees tended to take a comprehensive approach to developing intervention strategies that included improving women's access to sex-atypical jobs, job upgrading, allocating resources to train women for male-dominated jobs, and developing monitoring procedures (O'Farrell and Harlan, 1984). Case studies (described below) illustrate the implementation of these strategies. Most extensively studied are the events at American Telephone and Telegraph, Inc. Other important cases litigated by the EEOC under Title VII led the courts to overrule state protective laws specific to women (usually maximum hours or weight laws) and company policies against hiring women with preschool children. In a challenge to Pan American Airlines' refusal to hire male flight attendants, the court ruled that customer preferences are irrelevant unless a business's essential purpose is to satisfy them.

Successful individual and class action suits brought under Title VII also led organizations to make their operating procedures more equitable. Between 1964 and 1981 federal district courts decided more than 5,000 cases, of which about one-third were class actions (Leonard, 1984a). Certainly many times this number were settled through conciliation or in the state courts. Thus, conciliation and litigation under Title VII have led to changes in the practices of individual employers as well as to an increasingly broad interpretation of the statute that restricted employers' rights to consider sex in employment decisions.

Whether the EEOC's impact will continue over the next few years is an open question. In a recent Urban Institute report, Burbridge (1984) concludes, from changes in the types of cases filed and other information, that the EEOC has shifted its enforcement effort toward the investigation and settlement of individual charges and away from systemic or class action cases that affect larger numbers of workers at lower cost with larger deterrent effects. Early in 1985, the EEOC announced at a press conference that it was shifting its enforcement policy from systemic to individual cases (Evans and Fields, 1985). The EEOC also seems to be moving away from earlier policies that established a broad interpretation of Title VII. It has declined to pursue a broad policy on comparable worth, for example (U.S. Congress, House, 1984; Williams, 1985c), has reduced the number of filings of amicus briefs, and has cut back the number of attorneys in appellate litigation by 20 percent

when budget cuts sustained were 5.5 percent (Burbridge, 1984). In one instance, the EEOC withdrew, at the request of the U.S. Department of Justice, an amicus brief it had filed in support of a New Orleans Police Department quota-based consent decree providing a remedy for past discrimination when it was challenged in federal court. In spring 1985 the Department of Justice filed suit against the District of Columbia Fire Department challenging its affirmative action plan because it uses sex and race quotas (Saperstein, 1985). Other Justice Department suits against state and local governments have followed.

These policy shifts point toward an emphasis on getting redress for "identifiable victims" of discrimination, deemphasizing class actions and quotas. These shifts are consistent with statements of senior officials of the Justice Department and reflect the recent broad and significant change in civil rights policy (Peterson, 1985a; Williams, 1985b; Knight-Ridder, 1985).

Executive Order 11246 and the Office of Federal Contract Compliance Programs

Executive Order 11246 (11375) extended the prohibition of discrimination based on sex, race, color, national origin, or religion to federal contractors. The executive order differs from Title VII in three important ways. First, noncomplying contractors can have their federal contracts terminated, and violators can be debarred from future contracts. Second, contractors are required to take affirmative actions to ensure nondiscriminatory treatment in recruitment, training, and upgrading of minorities (under Order Number 4, 1970) and women (under Revised Order Number 4, 1971). Third, individuals do not have the right to initiate private legal actions in court.

Originally 13 federal contracting agencies were responsible for ensuring that their contractors did not discriminate before contracts were signed, for monitoring compliance, and for investigating discrimination complaints. The Office of Federal Contract Compliance in the U.S. Department of Labor coordinated their activities, but a mechanism to implement these regulations did not exist until December 1971, when Revised Order Number 4 extended the affirmative action requirement to women (Wallace, 1979). In 1978 all federal contract compliance activities were consolidated within the Office of Federal Contract Compliance Programs (OFCCP) in the Department of Labor. In the same year special OFCCP regulations directed at sex discrimination by construction contractors became effective. In June 1970 the OFCCP issued guidelines that forbade advertising under sex-labeled classifications, using sex-based seniority lists, denying jobs to qualified applicants because of state protective laws, distinguishing marital status among one sex but not the other, setting different retirement ages for the sexes, and penalizing women with children (U.S. Department of Labor, Women's Bureau, 1978).

In the first few years after the executive order was amended to include sex discrimination, this provision was essentially ignored. Sex was not included in the first rules issued to implement the order, and guidelines regarding sex discrimination were not available until Revised Order Number 4 was issued (Simmons et al., 1975). Federal contracting agencies appear to have been reluctant to invoke available sanctions for either sex-based or race-based discrimination. Until 1971 no federal contractor in violation of the order was debarred from future contracts, and only about two contractors were debarred per year over the next seven years (Brown, 1982). Only 27 contractors have ever been debarred, and over half of these were in the last three years of the Carter administration. At least through 1978 no federal contracts were terminated or contractors debarred because of discrimination by sex (Greenberger, 1978). However, as a result of a nationwide effort by the Women's Eq-

uity Action League, which brought a large number of complaints in 1970-1971, by July 1972 the U.S Department of Health, Education, and Welfare had temporarily withheld funds from 11 universities that failed to comply with the order (Simmons et al., 1975). The U.S. Department of Justice has authority to bring suit directly against Executive Order 11246 violators, bypassing OFCCP enforcement procedures, but has seldom used it.

The primary tools to enforce the executive order have been compliance reviews and voluntary conciliation, but for many years compliance reviews were infrequent. Between 1970 and 1972 fewer than one contractor in five were reviewed (Goldstein and Smith, 1976).[1] In addition, some compliance agencies approved affirmative action plans that did not meet the guidelines (Ahart, 1976). In each of fiscal years 1981 and 1982 the consolidated OFCCP in the Department of Labor completed over 3,000 reviews and investigated over 2,000 complaints, but over 2,000 complaints remained backlogged at the end of fiscal 1982 (OFCCP, *Quarterly Review and Analysis Reports* for 1981, 1982). A standard of six reviews per month encouraged compliance officers to focus on small contractors (Ahart, 1976). Some analysts have surmised that the effects of the executive order may have declined as contractors learned how to show good-faith efforts without significantly changing their personnel policies (Brown, 1982). However, a 1976 Bureau of National Affairs survey indicates that the overwhelming majority of firms subject to OFCC regulations had af-

---

[1] Different federal contracting agencies varied in their propensity to review contractors. The National Aeronautics and Space Administration, the Environmental Protection Agency, and the U.S. Department of Commerce reviewed at least half, whereas the U.S. Department of Agriculture and the U.S. Department of the Treasury reviewed about 2 percent of their contractors (U.S. Commission on Civil Rights, in Brown, 1982, note 10).

firmative action plans and one-third of them evaluated managers in terms of EEO performance (Freeman, 1981). While we cannot conclude from these data that the establishments were making effective efforts to improve job options for women and minorities, they show that employers were aware of their responsibilities and were taking at least the minimal steps required.

The system in which individual federal contracting agencies were responsible for enforcement contributed to the initial low use of sanctions (Ahart, 1976). When the compliance program was consolidated into a single office in 1978, it targeted banking, insurance, and mining for special attention. Subsequent gains in women's representation in largely male occupations in these industries demonstrate the agency's potential. To illustrate, the proportion of female underground miners increased from 1 in 10,000 in 1978 to 1 in 12 in 1980 (Betty Jean Hall, Director, Coal Employment Project, Sept. 4, 1981; Byrne, 1983). Data for the banking industry indicate that the small gains women had been making among financial managers rose sharply after the special enforcement effort, almost doubling from 17.4 percent in 1970 to 33.6 percent by 1980. This increase, however, may partially reflect job title inflation as well as the rapid expansion in small bank branches, which helped to create lower-level managerial positions for women.[2] In insurance, women's representation increased the most among adjusters, an occupation that was 9 percent female in 1961

and 58 percent female 20 years later (Working Women, 1981).

Budget and authorized positions for the OFCCP increased markedly during the two years following the 1978 consolidation. In real terms the budget fell after 1981, as did positions; both have since remained relatively stable. The estimated 1985 budget is approximately $50 million, with 1,000 authorized positions (compared to $160 million and 3,100 positions for the EEOC). Since 1980, the number of complaint investigations and compliance reviews completed annually has increased steadily, but the number of administrative complaints filed and debarments has fallen. No debarments occurred in 1982 or 1983, compared with five in 1980. Back pay awards have also decreased dramatically, from $9,300,000 in 1980 to $600,000 in 1983. The U.S. Commission on Civil Rights reported that the proportion of investigations and reviews that resulted in findings of discrimination or conciliation when fault was found had fallen, and the proportion of cases closed without a full investigation had risen. As Burbridge (1984) points out, the pattern is similar to that of the EEOC. Less thorough attention is given to an increased number of cases. The agency has decreased its use of its more stringent enforcement tools.

Policy shifts are also illustrated by a series of proposed changes in regulations that would reduce federal contractors' affirmative action obligations and exempt certain previously covered contractors from the regulations. A set of changes proposed in 1983 would limit back pay awards to identifiable victims of discrimination and limit the retroactivity of the awards to two years. The OFCCP did not consult with the EEOC as required by law until substantial time had elapsed, and, although it has not yet posted the final rules, the OFCCP may already be implementing these changes (Burbridge, 1984). These policy shifts at OFCCP, like those at the EEOC, are consistent with stated objectives of the current administration

---

[2] Beller (1984) considers whether the increase during the 1970s in the number of women in managerial occupations represents the upgrading of job titles. She cites Current Population Survey data that show almost no improvements in the ratios of female to male median weekly earnings for full-time wage and salaried workers in managerial occupations between 1973 and 1978 (.582 and .586, respectively), an indicator that is consistent with—although it does not demonstrate—job title inflation.

(Knight-Ridder, 1985; Saperstein, 1985; Williams, 1985a). More recently, in the fall of 1985, a fundamental change in the executive order was proposed by the Justice Department; it would virtually eliminate the use of goals and timetables.

Construction Contractors

The OFCCP monitors construction contractors in a separate program. In 1978 the OFCCP published regulations requiring construction contractors to carry out equal employment and affirmative action programs for women and minorities. Contractors were required to ensure that work sites were free of harassment, assign at least two women to each project, notify recruitment sources for women in writing of job opportunities, notify the OFCCP if the union referral process impedes affirmative action efforts, and actively recruit women for apprenticeship and other training. As a result of a lawsuit by women's groups, *Advocates for Women* v. *Marshall*, the OFCCP initially set employment goals for construction contractors of 3.1 percent women for the first year, 5 percent for the second year, and 6.9 percent for the third year. The 6.9 percent goal still stands.

Between 1978 and 1980 the proportion of women construction workers increased from 1.5 to 2 percent. In 1980 women construction workers were twice as likely to be laborers as craftworkers—2.6 and 1.3 percent, respectively (U.S. Department of Labor, Bureau of Labor Statistics, 1981c:Table 27). But it may be too soon to expect much progress in construction, particularly in view of the lengthy apprenticeship programs through which workers often obtain craft jobs.

Two recent studies of OFCCP efforts to increase women's participation in the construction trades, one by an investigator at a training organization for women (Westley, 1982) and one done in-house (U.S. Department of Labor, Employment Standards Administration, 1981), concluded that goals and timetables have created a small increased demand for women construction workers and are essential to achieving equal access for women in the construction industry. Each examined OFCCP compliance review files and interviewed OFCCP and Bureau of Apprenticeship and Training officials, women construction workers and applicants, women's training program providers, contractors, union business agents, and joint apprenticeship and training council coordinators. According to both studies, most of the contractors and unions favored eliminating the goals and timetables, yet they admitted that without them women would not be hired.

Observers agree that conscientious enforcement provided construction jobs for women but that enforcement was not uniform and that staff lacked procedures for uncovering discrimination. The OFCCP inhouse study cited its lack of an enforcement strategy and haphazard compliance activities as tending to dissipate its efforts (U.S. Department of Labor, Employment Standards Administration, 1981). None of the agency staff whom Westley (1982) interviewed had ever found a company not in compliance, and the majority of contractors interviewed reportedly felt no pressure from OFCCP to adhere to the contract compliance provisions in their federal contracts. Of 2,994 reports on file at the OFCCP for October 1980, only one-fifth even indicated the number of hours female construction workers were employed, and of these only 5 percent met the 6.9 percent goal (U.S. Department of Labor, Employment Standards Administration, 1981). According to the OFCCP's own study, compliance reviews resulted in increased employment of women, but the gains were sometimes short-lived. In view of the generally weak enforcement efforts it is not surprising that few contractors achieved the 6.9 percent goal (*Federal Register*, 1981:46[134]).

Federal Employees

Executive orders also prohibit discrimination against federal employees, and in 1972 the Equal Employment Opportunity Act brought federal employees under the protection of Title VII. Although it is not possible to determine whether these regulations directly affected women's opportunities, women have increased their representation in higher-level federal government jobs during the period in which the directives have been in force. In 1974 women were only 18.9 percent of the full-time work force in grades GS 9-12 and 14.8 percent in grades 13-15; in 1980 women constituted 26.9 percent and 8.2 percent, respectively; by 1983 women constituted 30.4 percent and 10.3 percent, respectively (U.S. Comptroller General, 1984:33). A detailed investigation of women attorneys (Epstein, 1981) found that their recent advancement into government law positions resulted from concerted efforts by government agencies to recruit minorities and women. Epstein reported that the percentage of women lawyers in the Office of the U.S. Attorney General went from 3.7 in 1970 to 17.3 in 1979. By 1980, 31.5 percent of the newly hired lawyers in the Justice Department were women. It seems probable that affirmative action requirements were a factor, both through influencing agency behavior and, by publicizing new opportunities or creating the impression that jobs existed, through encouraging women to train and apply for such jobs.

Conclusion

From the outset, enforcement of both Title VII and Executive Order 11246 was uneven and often inadequate. For several years enforcement agencies lacked real enforcement powers. They were also hampered by insufficient budgets, lack of personnel, and administrative difficulties (Greenberger, 1978; Brown, 1982). In addition, some have argued that the enforcement agencies did not take the prohibition against sex discrimination seriously in the early years (Greenberger, 1978). For example, in early published guidelines the EEOC explicitly permitted sex-labeled classified advertisement columns (Eastwood, 1978). Finally, detecting violators may be difficult under the best conditions. Nevertheless, these accounts of EEOC and OFCCP enforcement practices suggest that when Title VII and Executive Order 11246 (11375) were enforced, significant numbers of jobs were opened to women.

We turn next to an examination of evidence from case studies of enforcement actions directed toward particular establishments and findings from statistical studies that have attempted to examine the more general impact of the laws and regulations.

The Effectiveness of Enforcement

Evidence From Case Studies

The consequences of the EEOC intervention at American Telephone and Telegraph (AT&T), the country's largest company in 1970, provide compelling evidence for the effectiveness of a single enforcement action on women's job opportunities. In 1970, in 92.4 percent of all jobs at AT&T at least 90 percent of all workers were of one sex. The following year the EEOC petitioned the Federal Communications Commission to deny AT&T a rate increase. Ultimately AT&T agreed to provide salary adjustments and back pay to employees who had been injured by discriminatory employment practices. They also agreed to modify hiring, promotion, and training policies and to develop an affirmative action plan with targeted goals for women and minorities for jobs from which they had been excluded. As a result, female employment in several male-dominated occupations increased markedly between 1973

TABLE 4-1 Changing Women's Employment in AT&T Operating Companies, December 31, 1972, and September 30, 1978

Job Class	Description	Total Workers			Women			Black Women		
		1972	1978	% Change	1972	1978	% Change	1972	1978	% Change
1	Middle management and above	15,780	17,711	12.2	338	1,374	306.5	5	81	1,520.0
2	Second-level management	43,138	52,415	21.5	4,830	11,078	129.4	183	1,151	529.0
3	Entry-level management	95,949	116,458	21.4	29,543	40,976	38.7	2,285	6,338	177.4
4	Administrative	32,716	32,468	-0.7	27,380	24,774	-9.5	2,737	4,600	68.1
5	Salesworkers, nonmanagement	5,813	8,455	45.5	1,539	3,720	141.7	156	801	413.5
6	Skilled craft (outside)	65,107	70,884	8.9	38	1,928	4,973.7	1	319	31,800.0
7	Skilled craft (inside)	76,542	74,584	-2.6	2,619	8,830	237.2	238	1,459	513.0
8	General service (skilled)[a]	11,347	703	-93.8	540	176	-67.4	114	51	-55.3
9	Semiskilled craft (outside)	66,104	63,767	-3.6	206	3,386	1,543.7	24	642	2,575.0
10	Semiskilled craft (inside)	18,011	21,907	21.6	3,554	7,779	118.9	496	1,815	265.9
11	Clerical, skilled	82,392	104,065	26.3	77,633	91,206	17.5	11,005	19,916	81.0
12	Clerical, semiskilled	74,689	87,030	16.5	73,409	79,453	8.2	13,988	22,976	64.3
13	Clerical, entry level	45,140	34,890	-22.8	42,929	30,400	-29.2	11,100	8,963	-19.3
14	Telephone operators	148,622	104,134	-29.9	146,562	96,348	-34.3	34,770	24,347	-30.0
15	Service workers, entry level	12,365	10,296	-16.7	4,641	4,254	-8.3	1,549	1,429	-7.7
	Total	793,715	799,785	0.8	415,761	405,682	-2.4	78,651	94,888	20.6
	Percentage of total				52.4	50.7		9.9	11.9	

[a]Later dropped from the classification.
SOURCE: Wallace (1982:19).

and 1979. The proportions of women who were officials and managers or worked in sales, crafts, and service all increased by at least 5 percentage points; while men's representation in predominantly female administrative, clerical, and operator jobs increased from 3 to 6 percentage points (Northrup and Larson, 1979). Women's increased representation across a finer breakdown of occupations is shown in Table 4-1.

A 1974 consent decree signed by nine major steel companies[3] and the United Steelworkers of America illustrates changes in employment practices that facilitate women's integration into traditionally male production and maintenance jobs. In order to meet the hiring goals for minorities and women in craft jobs that the agreement called for, one firm began a preapprenticeship training school for certain craft apprenticeships that was open both to current female and minority employees and to CETA participants (Ullman and Deaux, 1981). One plant also arranged for a nonprofit agency experienced in recruiting and training minorities for construction apprenticeships to recruit and screen prospects for craft apprenticeships. Consistent with findings for other crafts and industries (Briggs, 1981; Kane and Miller, 1981), these special outreach and pretraining programs were highly effective in attracting women to craft jobs. The consent decree also required firms to restructure their seniority systems from departmentwide to plantwide systems so that women in typically female jobs would be competitive bidders for male-dominated jobs in other departments (and could make such moves without losing seniority; Ullman and Deaux, 1981). The need for this kind of modification is demonstrated by women's lack of

progress in one plant in which seniority changes were delayed because of collective bargaining agreements. In that plant most of the women whose bids for craft jobs were unsuccessful lost because they lacked sufficient seniority. The effects of the consent decree can be seen clearly in women's increased representation in certain jobs. In the less than four years between 1976 and the end of 1979, the numbers of women in production and maintenance positions in two steel mills increased almost threefold from 763 to 1,938, while their number in craft jobs increased from 27 (0.4 percent of all craft workers) to 197 (2.2 percent; 4.7 percent in the plant whose program had been in existence longer). One company hired more than 1,500 women for production jobs between 1977 and 1979, and in the other women were 32 percent of the new hires in 1979. Moreover, the aluminum industry voluntarily accepted the steel industry's consent decree virtually verbatim in their own collective bargaining agreement (Brown, 1982).

Other large firms that have entered into consent decrees with the EEOC include United Airlines (1976), Merrill Lynch (1976), General Electric (1978), and General Motors (1983). These are the largest firms in their industries, and smaller firms may follow the industry leader in their labor practices (Wallace, 1979).

A review of case studies of firms subject to litigation and consent decrees that the committee commissioned (O'Farrell and Harlan, 1984) concluded that the federal presence significantly motivates companies to facilitate women's movement into nontraditional jobs. In general an increase in the numbers of women in traditionally male jobs corresponded to pressure by federal agencies, either through direct actions against large companies or through the indirect effect of companies complying rather than risking federal action (as occurred in the aluminum industry). Many companies reported that federal enforcement activities

---

[3] One company withdrew from the consent decree negotiations, claiming that it had not discriminated in hiring and placement, but it subsequently signed two conciliation agreements with the EEOC after four years of negotiation (Ullman and Deaux, 1981).

had a major effect on their organizations' employment practices. Awareness of federal laws and the financial costs of violating them were cited repeatedly as primary factors in stimulating change.

A Conference Board survey of about 250 large corporations (Shaeffer and Lynton, 1979) confirmed the importance of management commitment for increasing women's employment opportunities. Top management awareness of federal laws and regulations related to equal employment policy was perceived as an important determinant of the success of the company's efforts. Few of the firms said that an actual complaint, investigation, or lawsuit had spurred their efforts, but they often mentioned awareness of large back-pay awards in class-action suits against other employers, and they deemed the risk of a Title VII class action suit a very real one.

Evidence From Statistical Studies

Several researchers have attempted to assess statistically the effectiveness of antidiscrimination regulations. Researchers seeking to probe the impact of the EEOC's enforcement of Title VII typically use time series data to compare the relative employment status of women and/or minorities before and after Title VII was implemented. Using this method, Freeman (1973, 1977) found that the earnings of blacks relative to those of same-sex whites increased more rapidly after 1964, when Title VII was passed. Later work (Vroman, 1975; Ginsburg and Vroman, 1976) partially replicates Freeman's findings, but critics (Butler and Heckman, 1977) point out that Freeman's conclusions could be the result of selection bias; the lowest-paid blacks may have dropped out of the labor force in increasing proportions during these years.

Beller (1979, 1980, 1982a, 1982b) has estimated the impacts of Title VII on sex and race differences in employment outcomes using cross-sectional as well as longitudinal designs. Several studies examine the male-

female earnings differential and the probability of being employed in a male-dominated occupation before and after EEO laws were implemented. These studies reveal that enforcement of Title VII (as indicated by number of investigations and ratio of charges to settlements) increased female earnings slightly between 1967 and 1974 and narrowed the sex differential in the probability of working in a predominantly male occupation. While subject to some procedural criticisms (see, for example, Brown, 1982), Beller's results hold across various measurement techniques.

Recently Leonard (1984a) attempted to determine whether Title VII litigation affected the employment status of blacks within manufacturing industries. Using 1966 and 1978 EEOC data, he found a significant improvement in the representation of black males and an even stronger effect for black females, both of which could be attributed to litigation.

Individually these statistical studies of the effectiveness of Title VII for minorities and women have various limitations, but on balance they suggest more rapid improvement in employment status for blacks and sometimes women than would have occurred in the absence of enforcement.

Most studies of the impact of Executive Order 11246 (11375) and its enforcement by the OFCC compare the proportions of minorities or women or both employed by federal contractors and noncontractors at a single point in time, or rates of change in these proportions between federal contractors and noncontractors. Differences may be attributed to the executive order, if other relevant variables (size of firm, type of industry, region, condition of the local labor market, and so on) are controlled statistically. Unfortunately, it is not always possible to control for all relevant variables, and even if it were, interpretation of cross-sectional comparisons can be difficult. For example, if enforcing antidiscrimination orders leads contractors to hire protected workers from noncontractors, the cross-sectional comparison will overestimate any effect that exists or show a positive effect even if there is no net gain in employment status of the relevant groups. (This would also occur if enforcement sorts firms into contractor and noncontractor groups according to their desire to discriminate.) Some biases will work in the other direction. If enforcement of the executive order leads noncontractors to refrain from discriminating, then cross-sectional comparisons will indicate little or no effect when the opposite is actually true.

Three studies analyzing data for the late 1960s and early 1970s and focusing primarily on racial discrimination (Ashenfelter and Heckman, 1976; Goldstein and Smith, 1976; Heckman and Wolpin, 1976) illustrate the basic approach.[4] Using EEOC data for race and sex distributions across nine broad occupational categories,[5] they found modest effects of OFCC activities on total black male employment, very small effects on black female employment, and no effects on the proportion of blacks in skilled occupations.

On one hand, because these data do not tap changes within the broad occupational categories, they probably understate the impact of the executive order. On the other hand, if women and minorities whom contractors employ are concentrated in the least-skilled, most poorly paid jobs within occupational categories, which is probably the case, effects would be overstated. In reviewing these studies, Brown (1982) notes that problems with the data and with the use of noncontractors as the control group can give rise to potential biases in both directions, but that none of the studies seems uniquely persuasive. He concludes that they

point to a positive "but hardly revolutionary effect (probably no more than 10 percent in the 'long run') of OFCC activities" on relative employment of black men in contractor firms and very little effect for black women. The small effects found in these early years are understandable because effective implementation (including the development of concepts such as the available labor pool and a system of accountability within the OFCC) began about 1971. Later studies tend to show larger effects.

Beller (1982b) estimated that between 1967 and 1971 affirmative action required by the OFCC reduced barriers to white women's entry into male-dominated occupations. By 1974 black women began to gain relative to black men, but by then almost half of white women's gains had eroded. Beller suggested that poor economic conditions caused newly hired white women to be laid off, although it is not clear why black women were not similarly affected. Elsewhere Beller (1980) showed that increases in the unemployment rate in the early 1970s substantially hampered the effectiveness of Title VII with respect to equalizing the earnings of men and women.

A study based on more recent data provides evidence that the federal contract compliance program is generally effective in improving employment opportunities for minorities and women. When he examined almost 70,000 establishments in 1974 and 1980, Leonard (1984b) found that the employment shares of women and minorities grew more rapidly among contractors than noncontractors. The effect was largest for black men and smallest for white women. He also found that compliance reviews contributed significantly to black and other minority representation in the sampled establishments, above and beyond contractor status alone, but their effect for white women was negative. As Leonard notes, the entrance into the labor force during this period of massive numbers of white women who took jobs with both contractors and noncontractors could have obscured any effect the

---

[4] During most of this period, compliance efforts were directed primarily at racial discrimination, and the evaluation studies accordingly focus on changes in black-white differences.

[5] EEO-1 data are drawn from the reports that all federal contractors and certain other employers must submit annually to the EEOC. They provide occupational distributions across nine broad occupational groupings by race and sex.

contract compliance regulations had. Without evidence supporting this interpretation, however, the available data suggest that the contract compliance program has been most effective for blacks of both sexes and least effective for white women. Contrary to the findings of earlier studies, Leonard, in another study using the same data (1984c), found that minority men made particular gains in skilled white-collar occupations.

One other cross-sectional study (Osterman, 1982) deserves mention both because it measures OFCCP effect in a slightly different way and because it focuses on women. Osterman assumes that quit rates measure job contentment and thus might contain information about the effectiveness of affirmative action. Using 1978-1979 data from the Panel Study of Income Dynamics, he found that several indicators of OFCCP activity statistically reduced women's (but not men's) propensity to quit, when personal and job characteristics were controlled. He concluded that affirmative action enforcement makes women more willing to stay with their jobs, perhaps through higher wages or improved aspects of the job. If OFCCP activity were simply correlated with something attractive about an industry, then men's quit rates should also have responded to OFCCP activity. That they did not reduces the likelihood that the effect for women is spurious.

Finally, using a sociologically realistic model that took into account changes in popular attitudes toward blacks' and women's rights to work, unemployment rates, and aggregate educational levels, Burstein (1983) found that total federal enforcement expenditures and the percentage of final appellate court decisions favoring women and minorities were associated with strong gains in the incomes of black women relative to white men and slightly smaller gains for black men and white women.

Conclusion

The statistical studies of the effects of Title VII and the federal antidiscrimination reg-

ulations, coupled with the case studies, suggest that they have made a difference. The effects that can be demonstrated statistically in the early years are not large; this is not surprising because it took some time for implementation to become effective. Studies based on data since the early 1970s show stronger effects, a finding in accord with strengthened regulations and their more effective implementation in the 1970s. In general, however, positive effects occurred most often for black men, somewhat less so for black women, and were least evident for white women.

But some studies did show positive enforcement effects for women, and the case studies demonstrate that women's entry into new occupations that were targeted for enforcement effort was significant. As Beller and Han (1984) have shown, occupational sex segregation declined during the 1970s. The existence and enforcement of antidiscrimination regulations almost certainly contributed to this decline, both directly and by fostering attitude changes among both employers and workers about what kinds of work should be available to women. Evidence that enforcement works demonstrates that behavior and beliefs are not immutable. Since 1981, however, enforcement efforts have declined. The effects of this reduced level of effort on future employment opportunities of women and minorities remain to be seen. The committee is concerned that the reduced effort will make further positive change less likely. The reduced effort, or even the perception of it, could affect the behavior of employers and others in many ways, ranging from subtle to overt changes in policy and practice.

Efforts by Employers to Reduce Sex Segregation

During the 1970s many companies set out to increase female employees' job opportunities, and toward the end of the decade social scientists investigated the impact of some of these efforts. These studies provide information about the effectiveness of a variety of mechanisms for enhancing women's employment opportunities. Ullman and Deaux (1981) investigated the aftermath of a 1974 steel industry consent decree, and O'Farrell and Harlan (1982) studied the experience of blue-collar women in a large electrical products firm. To increase women's job options, some companies used general EEO strategies; others implemented specific mechanisms that emphasized recruiting and preparing women for sex-atypical jobs. We discuss these two types of strategies below.

The efforts of some companies stemmed directly from consent decrees or other actions that followed from efforts by federal enforcement agencies and private parties. Others established EEO programs voluntarily. Women's job options did not improve "naturally." Committed top managers had to pursue this goal just as they would any other organizational goal—by analyzing the problem, devising strategies, and taking concrete steps to ensure their implementation. According to a Conference Board survey of 265 large corporations, the most important factors for increasing women's opportunities were top-level commitment to equal opportunity, implementation and dissemination of an equal employment policy that included goals and timetables, analysis of how the company used women and the modification of personnel practices as necessary, the monitoring of organizational performance, and the identification of and response to particular problems (Shaeffer and Lynton, 1979). Other studies confirm these results. On the basis of their study of 10 public utilities, Meyer and Lee (U.S. Department of Labor, Employment and Training Administration, 1978) noted the importance of both high-level commitment to EEO—which apparently was fostered by awareness of the legal consequences of noncompliance—and publicizing the company's EEO efforts.

On the basis of their review of several case studies, O'Farrell and Harlan (1984) out-

lined the operation of an effective internal administrative structure for setting and implementing EEO policy. It must include centralized accounting and control but also provide for line responsibility. Because line managers must implement policy that they may personally oppose, their involvement is critical (U.S. Department of Labor, Employment and Training Administration, 1978). It has been suggested that their resistance can be minimized by recognizing and compensating line managers for their extra efforts (McLane, 1980). Involving line managers in setting standards and screening also reduces the risk that they will feel that unqualified women are being foisted on them (Schaeffer and Lynton, 1979). Obviously, adequate resources are essential. O'Farrell and Harlan (1984) and O'Farrell (1981) also stress the need to involve unions, claiming that consent agreements that do not involve unions have sometimes impeded women's progress. The steel industry agreement was one of the few major consent agreements in the 1970s to which the union was a party. Corporations that responded to the Conference Board survey reported more disappointing attempts to integrate women into blue- than white-collar jobs, and a much higher proportion of the "failures" involved unionized employees. Although by no means conclusive, this result suggests that union cooperation can facilitate integrating women into blue-collar, formerly all-male jobs.

Specific mechanisms that have been used successfully to attract and qualify women for jobs that had been predominantly or totally male include using outside agencies as well as modifying internal personnel practices. To inform women of opportunities, employers must use aggressive recruitment tactics such as job fairs (O'Farrell and Harlan, 1984), advertise jobs broadly, and post them throughout the plant. Job posting has been required in some consent decrees; posting sex-atypical jobs in areas where women work may convince them that these jobs are open to them (Shaeffer and Lynton, 1979). Posting is not effective, however, when seniority governs job allocation and women's seniority is not transferable to another department. In fact, some companies reported that bad feelings were generated when notices provided inadequate information, jobs were already filled by the time interested female employees responded, or unsuccessful candidates were not told why they were passed over (Shaeffer and Lynton, 1979).

When the pool of interested female employees proved inadequate, some companies recruited women through skilled trades training programs (Kane and Miller, 1981; Ullman and Deaux, 1981). Another effective strategy was to list employees who might be candidates for sex-atypical jobs. Others encouraged supervisors to identify women interested in shifting to a predominantly male job (Shaeffer and Lynton, 1979). Some companies included women who had not expressed any interest in male-dominated jobs, in recognition that women's perceptions about appropriate work roles were changing. Some firms assisted female employees with career planning, described opportunities in nontraditional blue- or white-collar jobs, or gave women a chance to observe women already employed in predominantly male occupations. Many companies broadened the pool of female candidates by eliminating unnecessary job requirements. Using female recruiters and innovative recruitment practices was also effective (Shaeffer and Lynton, 1979).

Several firms found recruiting women to blue-collar jobs a greater challenge than recruiting them to nontraditional white-collar jobs. Some reportedly found it very difficult to recruit women for totally unskilled heavy physical labor jobs, even when these were entry-level jobs leading to better positions, because many women believed that they were likely to have that job permanently (a perception that is often realistic for typically female occupations). Companies were more successful in moving women directly into semiskilled jobs that led to highly skilled jobs or into training programs for skilled craft

jobs. Some firms devised their own programs to train women who were already employed in typically female jobs for new work. The presence of a few women in skilled jobs showed others that it was worth the initially unpleasant work (Shaeffer and Lynton, 1979). Employers also found that women were more willing to transfer to an atypical job if they had the right to return to their former job (O'Farrell and Harlan, 1984).

Because conventional seniority and job-bidding systems often prevent women from bidding for jobs that have been dominated by men (Roos and Reskin, 1984), modifications have been necessary to bring about change in many instances, such as the steel industry consent decree described above. The AT&T-EEOC consent decree included a seniority override that allowed women and minorities to pass more senior white men. Used over 35,000 times at the nonmanagerial level during the six years of the consent decree (O'Farrell and Harlan, 1982), the override provision contributed to AT&T's reaching at least 90 percent of its hiring targets after the first year.

Devising mechanisms to enhance women's chances for success on blue-collar jobs in which they are pioneers is particularly difficult (U.S. Department of Labor, Employment and Training Administration, 1978). Women who moved into blue-collar heavily male jobs typically encountered more opposition from both coworkers and supervisors than women who moved into managerial jobs. Prior training with the tools, skills, and vocabulary necessary to do the job raised their level of competence when they began the work and reassured male coworkers. This is particularly important because some male employees who initially supported hiring women changed their minds when some of the first women did not measure up. Since only one or two women often enter a male work group, each woman's performance is taken as typical of what all women are likely to do. Equally important was careful screening. Part of the differential success rates for moving women into white- and blue-collar jobs was linked to the more careful screening for the former. The more thorough the screening, the more likely women were to succeed (U.S. Department of Labor, Employment and Training Administration, 1978; Shaeffer and Lynton, 1979).

Management has successfully intervened in response to coworker opposition or harassment. Some companies sensitized shop stewards and supervisors and trained them in dealing with these problems. Extending probationary periods was effective in some blue-collar jobs. Women who moved into managerial jobs were less likely to experience harassment, but they still encountered resistance to their acceptance (Harlan and Weiss, 1981). One study found that women managers encountered sex bias regardless of their numbers (Harlan and Weiss, 1981). Thus, increasing the number of women in nontraditional roles may provide support and minimize isolation but may not necessarily reduce the risk of sex bias. Although some stress the importance of mentors, company-assigned mentors were not effective in one study (U.S. Department of Labor, Employment and Training Administration, 1978; McLane, 1980). Communications from top management to the coworkers of new women managers that clarified their status as equals rather than as upgraded secretaries sometimes helped (Shaeffer and Lynton, 1979). Management intervention or group discussions to identify problems and arrive at solutions salvaged some initial failures.

In sum, companies that increased women's representation in jobs previously held predominantly by men used a wide range of mechanisms that were outside their normal personnel procedures. Nearly all progress in hard-to-fill blue-collar jobs resulted from nontraditional recruitment and training programs, often with the assistance of private agencies. Both job analysis and new recruiting techniques increased the pool of applicants. Often aspects of internal labor

markets—especially seniority systems and job requirements—had to be modified. Simply placing women in atypical blue-collar jobs was not enough: careful screening of pioneers was clearly critical, and pretraining often made the difference between co-worker acceptance or rejection and ultimately success or failure. Management minimized or remedied on-the-job problems such as coworker hostility when they monitored men's reactions to integration by women. Generally companies were much more successful at increasing women's representation in predominantly male white-collar jobs than in blue-collar jobs. Women did not invariably need special training, but companies that ensured that women obtained the same training and support that men did showed the most success. Most important for overall success was commitment to equal employment opportunities for women, manifested in specific policies, goals, and timetables and coupled with a monitoring system and sufficient resources. Since managerial commitment is linked to awareness of federal regulations and of federal enforcement efforts, these findings provide additional grounds for the importance of maintaining federal EEO programs.

INTERVENTIONS DIRECTED AT JOB TRAINING AND VOCATIONAL AND GENERAL EDUCATION

Changing the behavior and practices of employers as described above leads primarily to changes in the demand side of the labor market. In effect, employers increase their demand for previously excluded or restricted groups by removing barriers to their hiring and advancement. Such changes also induce supply-side changes, since workers will respond to available opportunities. But change can also be initiated on the supply side. If, for example, women train to be computer programmers and there is a critical need for computer programmers, employers will probably hire them even if they

would prefer men. Moreover, the availability of women with the appropriate skills
for a predominantly male job suggests that
the job is perhaps not so intrinsically male
after all. Because many of the better-paid
traditionally male-dominated jobs require
considerable acquisition of skills, many organizations have emphasized improving
training and education opportunities for
women and girls. Here we review the results
of some of these efforts, particularly those
that are related to federal laws and regulations.

Apprenticeship Programs

Apprenticeship programs—a primary
route of entry into skilled trades—have always been extremely segregated, with a small
number of women concentrated in a few of
the several hundred apprenticeship programs registered with the U.S. Department
of Labor. As early as 1964 sex discrimination
in apprenticeship was outlawed, and Executive Order 11246, as amended, prohibits
discrimination in programs supported by
federal contractors. Prohibiting discrimination has not been very effective in bringing women into apprenticeship programs,
however, because of many remaining formal
and informal barriers to their participation,
such as upper age limits and lack of familiarity with the programs (Kane et al., 1977).[6]

Scattered early efforts were made to increase women's participation in some all-
male programs. For example, between 1970
and 1973 the State of Wisconsin conducted
a women-in-apprenticeship project. At the
beginning of that period most female apprentices were in cosmetology; only 13
women were apprenticed in fields that were
not traditionally female. By the end, 67

women had begun apprenticeships in other
fields, and women were apprenticed in 30
occupations in which they had not been represented in 1970 (U.S. Department of Labor, Women's Bureau, 1975; Briggs, 1981).
At the national level, in 1974 the Manpower
Administration with the assistance of the
Women's Bureau in the Department of Labor initiated a pilot outreach project with
three contractors to apprentice women in
nontraditional occupations. At the same time
the language was changed in all other outreach contracts to include women as well as
minorities and to require efforts to place
them in apprenticeable nontraditional occupations (U.S. Department of Labor,
Women's Bureau, 1975). Given the small
scale of these early efforts, it is not surprising
that the increase in the representation of
women was small through 1978 (see Table
4-2).

In 1978 two federal agencies issued rul-
ings mandating efforts to increase women's
representation. The first, the OFCCP's
Equal Employment Opportunity in Construction regulations (discussed above), required most federal contractors to provide

TABLE 4-2 Female Apprentices, 1973-
1984

Year	Apprentices		Percentage Female
	Total	Women	
1973	283,774	1,986	.7
1974	291,049	2,619	.9
1975	266,477	3,198	1.2
1976	254,968	4,334	1.7
1977	262,586	5,777	2.2
1978	290,224	8,997	3.1
1979	323,866	13,343	4.1
1980	320,073	15,363	4.8
1981	315,887	18,006	5.7
1982	286,698	17,202	6.0
1983	253,187	16,710	6.6
1984	232,583	15,583	6.7

SOURCES: For 1973-1978: U.S. Department of Labor, Employment and Training Administration (1979a).
For 1979-1984: unpublished data from the Bureau of
Apprenticeship and Training, U.S. Department of Labor.

---

[6] Wolf (1981) and Roos and Reskin (1984) discuss how
the organization and selection standards in apprenticeship programs have the effect of reducing women's
participation in apprenticeship.

on-the-job training opportunities for women or to participate in area training programs that included women and minorities. Federal contractors also had to publicize apprenticeship openings to women and minority group members. One month later the Department of Labor issued regulations requiring apprenticeship programs registered with the Department of Labor's Bureau of Apprenticeship and Training (BAT) to take affirmative action to recruit women. For nonconstruction apprenticeships, the ruling set a goal of 50 percent of the proportion of women in local labor markets, which was about a 20 percent goal for most parts of the country (U.S. Department of Labor, Women's Bureau, 1980a). The immediate goals, however, required 11.5 percent of apprentices to be female by April 1979 and 12.5 percent a year later (Kane and Miller, 1981).

The sharp rise in the number of women in registered apprenticeship programs between 1978 and 1979 shown in Table 4-2 suggests that the goal had some effect. Although women's share of apprenticeships increased only from 3.1 to 4.1 percent, 4,346 more women were apprentices in June 1979 than at the start of the year, a 48 percent increase.

Proportionally, women's representation increased most in the graphic arts trades, and slightly smaller increases occurred in personal service trades and construction trades (U.S. Department of Labor, Employment and Training Administration, 1982). The change in construction is especially noteworthy because it presumably stems primarily from the OFCCP regulations. Table 4-3 shows consistent gains in the percentage female in 12 building trade programs between 1975 and 1979. In 1975 in all but one of the building trades, fewer than 1 percent of the apprentices were women. Four years later, the total number of women had increased tenfold, and in two trades—painters and operating engineers—women approached 10 percent of the num-

ber of apprentices. These figures mask wide variation across states (Kane and Miller, 1981), which is not surprising since most monitoring occurs at the state level. Apprenticeship remained virtually closed to women in some northeastern cities as recently as 1981 (U.S. Department of Labor, Employment and Training Administration, 1982). Even during the recent recession, the share of apprenticeships held by women continued to increase; from its 4.1 percent level in 1979 it reached 6 percent in 1982 and 6.7 percent at the close of fiscal 1984 (unpublished data from the Bureau of Apprenticeship and Training, U.S. Department of Labor).

The available data suggest that goals and timetables have produced remarkable results when they were fully implemented (Kane and Miller, 1981). In the year after the new regulations were issued, every state but one showed an increase in the number of women apprentices. A detailed study in Wisconsin (Briggs, 1981) further demonstrates the importance of the Department of Labor goal. Excluding barbers (which had become predominantly female in Wisconsin over the decade), women's representation among new apprentices in traditionally male fields varied between 0.7 and 2.1 percent between 1970 and 1977. In 1978, the year the regulations became effective, women were 2.6 percent of the new starts; the following year they were 3.1 percent (Briggs, 1981).

Little evaluation of enforcement of the apprenticeship goals has been carried out. As noted above, one study of construction industry programs (Westley, 1982) suggested that noncompliance was the norm. Of the two regulatory agencies, the Bureau of Apprenticeship and Training (BAT) has no sanctioning power except deregistration, which it rarely exercises, and the OFCCP has no oversight responsibility for unions, so unions have little incentive to actively recruit women for their apprenticeship programs. A stipulation that limits the regula-

TABLE 4-3   Female Apprentices in Registered Building Trades Programs, 1975-1979

Trade	1975			1979		
	Total Apprentices	Female Apprentices	Percentage Female	Total Apprentices	Female Apprentices	Percentage Female
Boilermakers	2,660	10	.4	4,083	82	2.0
Bricklayers	7,832	5	.1	8,462	188	2.2
Carpenters	36,594	159	.4	43,832	1,973	4.5
Cement masons	3,034	10	.3	3,118	212	6.8
Electricians	32,640	129	.4	34,584	1,257	3.6
Glaziers	1,390	2	.1	1,160	13	1.1
Lathers	1,268	1	.1	1,483	18	1.2
Operating engineers	6,187	20	.3	6,051	553	9.1
Painters	6,650	87	1.3	6,760	604	8.9
Plumbers	18,405	23	.1	17,554	299	1.7
Roofers	4,070	4	.1	5,745	91	1.6
Sheet metal workers	11,647	48	.4	11,154	293	2.6

SOURCE: U.S. Department of Labor, Employment and Training Administration (1975, 1979b).

tions to programs with at least five apprentices has permitted programs to evade the ruling by training only four apprentices at a time or calling their apprentices "helpers." Locally administered plans in some cities may be a more effective mechanism for women because they often screen and orient women whom they recommend for apprenticeships (U.S. Deparment of Labor, Employment Standards Administration, 1981). The Division of Program Analysis of the OFCCP concluded from an extensive evaluation of women in construction that the relative success of these "hometown" plans demonstrates the necessity of some authority to encourage cooperation among all the institutions involved in apprenticeship training.

Two studies of women in apprenticeship programs provide some guidelines regarding what kinds of mechanisms increase women's participation and success in apprenticeship programs. Kane et al. (1977) pointed out that while plant postings have not succeeded in attracting women, company efforts to contact and recruit female production workers were more successful. They also stressed that age limits, although ruled

by the courts to be illegal under Title VII,[7] continue to keep women out of apprenticeship programs. Women's lack of mechanical skills and vocational training in secondary school also hampered them, according to Kane and her colleagues.

Female apprentices in traditionally male programs reported serious difficulties in getting trained by journeymen (Kane et al., 1977; Walshok, 1981b). A study at General Motors (Walshok, 1981b) showed that journeymen's impressions of female apprentices affected their willingness to help the women improve their performance. As a result, GM established a successful pilot program in which supervisors and journeymen identi-

---

[7] See Kane et al. (1977) for a full discussion of this issue. Among the relevant cases are: *Pettway* v. *American Cast Iron Pipe Co.*, CA5 (1974) 7 FEP Cases 1115; *Stevenson* v. *International Paper Co.*, Mobile, Alabama, CA5 (1975) 10 FEP Cases 1386; *U.S.* v. *Steamfitters Local 638*, DC NY (1973) 6 FEP Cases 319; *Judson and Judson's* v. *Apprenticeship and Training Council of the State of Oregon*, Ore Ct App (1972) 4 FEP Cases 747; EEOC No. 71-1418 (March 17, 1971) 3 FEP Cases 580; EEOC No. 72-0265 (August 6, 1971) 4 FEP Cases 68.

fied skills and concepts that apprentices had to master, then provided testing and feedback on their acquisition. Crucially important was the involvement of plant management and journeymen in the program's design. Preliminary evaluation indicated that the performance of apprentices improved and journeymen were reassured that incompetent apprentices were not moving through the program.

In sum, Department of Labor regulations requiring equal employment opportunity in apprenticeship seem to have contributed to women's small gains in customarily male apprenticeship programs. Most observers contend that more active enforcement by BAT and greater involvement by the OFCCP would yield additional progress. It seems clear that genuine affirmative efforts required by the regulations are necessary to attract enough women to apprenticeships in what are currently among the most sex-segregated of occupations.

Federal Job Training Programs

Two federal job training programs had the potential to prepare women and men for sex-atypical occupations. The first, the Work Incentive Program (WIN), which was established by Title II of the 1967 Social Security Amendments, was designed to provide job opportunities and training for persons receiving Aid to Families With Dependent Children (AFDC). All adult AFDC recipients under age 65 are required to register for WIN except those with children under six and women whose husbands have registered. A larger program was the 1973 Comprehensive Employment Training Act (CETA), amended in 1978, which was established to improve the employment options of economically disadvantaged Americans through job training and public service employment. Regulations issued in 1979 required all programs to help eliminate sex stereotyping in training and employ-

ment (Berryman and Chow, 1981). May 1980 regulations stipulated that prime sponsors[8] should take affirmative steps to recruit and train women for occupations with skill shortages that were at least 75 percent male and men for traditionally female occupations (*Federal Register* 1979:44[65]:20026-27). To achieve these ends, CETA regulations permitted various support services (health care, child care, and transportation) that would facilitate women's participation (U.S. Department of Labor, Women's Bureau, 1980c). Given its size, CETA had considerable potential to train workers for sex-atypical jobs.[9] But both WIN and CETA contained provisions that reduced the likelihood that they would prepare many women for customarily male occupations. WIN's explicit priority for male family heads resulted in women's substantial underrepresentation both in the program and among those who eventually found jobs (U.S. Department of Labor, Women's Bureau, 1975; Barrett, 1979). Eligibility standards and preferences for household heads and veterans in CETA programs implicitly favored men (Barrett, 1979; Jacobus, 1980). As a result, during the 1970s veterans comprised 7 percent of the unemployed, but between one-third and one-half of CETA public service employment participants (Harlan, 1980). For these reasons and others, women were underrepresented in CETA programs relative to their eligibility (Harlan, 1980; Wolf, 1981; Waite

---

[8] A prime sponsor was the unit of government that was the recipient of the federal CETA grant to provide comprehensive employment and training services. Basic programming responsibility lay with prime sponsors (U.S. Department of Labor, Women's Bureau, 1980c; Guttman, 1983).

[9] In 1978 CETA served over 3 million people with a $10 billion budget (U.S. Department of Labor, Employment and Training Administration, unpublished data, 1979, cited in Harlan, 1980). In fiscal 1979 CETA spent $9.4 billion training over 4 million people (Zornitsky and McNally, 1980).

and Berryman, 1984). The Job Corps program within CETA initially included no provisions for women, and even after provisions were made, women were underrepresented relative to their proportion among unemployed youth (Barrett, 1979).

CETA expired in 1981 and was replaced by the Job Training Partnership Act, effective in 1983, which included no public service employment and emphasized private sector leadership. Little evaluation of programs sponsored under this act is yet available.

The Work Incentive Program

According to an Urban Institute study (Underwood, 1979), the WIN program required 1.5 million people to enter the labor force but could provide services for only one-fifth of them, jobs for less than one-tenth, and training or public service employment for only 7 percent. Statistical analyses show no evidence that WIN has contributed to reducing sex segregation among participants. In fiscal 1980, 75 percent of WIN registrants and 69 percent of those who found jobs through WIN were women. The job assignments of WIN participants mirrored the sex composition of the labor force. Fewer than 7 percent of the women who participated were assigned to jobs in the machine trades, construction, and transportation, compared with 40 percent of men. In contrast, two-thirds of the women were placed in clerical, sales, and service occupations, compared with one-fifth of the male participants (Underwood, 1980). As recently as 1980, over 68 percent of female participants were concentrated in these three occupational categories, and there is no evidence of declining occupational segregation in WIN (Underwood, 1980).

The Comprehensive Employment and Training Act

Evaluations of CETA's impact on women's job options suggest that prime sponsors seldom administered CETA in a way that fulfilled its mandate to train workers for nontraditional jobs. Analyses of the Continuous Longitudinal Manpower Survey data on CETA participants over a three-year period show sex differences in program assignments, with women concentrated in the shorter-duration, lower-paying, and often part-time "adult work experience" assignments and in classroom training rather than public service employment and on-the-job training (Wolf, 1981). These differences are relevant because most classroom training was for typically female jobs (Waite and Berryman, 1984), although the majority of women in on-the-job training were also in predominantly female occupations (Berryman et al., 1981). CETA's emphasis on quick placement precluded training women for predominantly male blue-collar trades. In addition, the emphasis on training as many people as possible discouraged sponsors from using funds for the support services that the legislation permitted (Wolf, 1981; U.S. Commission on Civil Rights, 1981b).

An evaluation of six Massachusetts CETA programs (Zornitsky and McNally, 1980) illustrates how CETA outcomes differ for the sexes. Upon leaving the programs, 60 percent of the women obtained work in clerical and service jobs, compared with 22 percent of the men. In contrast, 61 percent of the men and 21 percent of the women found positions as craftsmen, operators, or laborers. Presumably as a result, the women earned 88 percent of what the men did.

The level of sex segregation within CETA declined slightly between 1976 and 1978 (Wolf, 1981). Increasing proportions of adult women were employed in traditionally male CETA jobs, and decreasing proportions held traditionally female jobs. This pattern was slightly stronger for young women, though young men showed very little change. It is not clear whether these changes reflected CETA sponsors' efforts to eliminate sex stereotyping or changes in participants' preferences (Berryman and Chow, 1981). The percentage of women desiring mixed or customarily male occupations increased over this period, and CETA programs only partly succeeded in meeting these preferences. Depending on the year, between 33 and 60 percent of the women who requested placement in mixed or male-dominated occupations were not assigned to them, and only 40-56 percent of the men who requested traditionally female jobs were assigned to a predominantly female occupation. For both sexes, the probability of receiving a requested nontraditional job declined between 1976 and 1978 (Berryman et al., 1981). Moreover, more than half the women surveyed in the Continuous Longitudinal Manpower Survey who had previously worked in a job that was not traditionally held by women were placed in a typically female job in CETA. Only one-quarter of the women whose prior jobs were female-typed were assigned to a mixed or male occupation (Waite and Berryman, 1984). Unfortunately, no programwide evaluations are available of the effects of regulations to implement the 1978 amendment that required programs to try to eliminate sex stereotyping. Nor do we know much about whether nontraditional training within CETA was associated with sex-atypical employment in post-CETA jobs.

The across-the-board evaluations of CETA obscure the success of many small programs that CETA funds helped to support (Shuchat with Guinier and Douglas, 1981). Some examples are a Denver program that placed almost 900 women in 70 different trade occupations over a nine-year period (Carruthers, 1980) and a Washington, D.C., program that trained and placed about 400 women in technical jobs in electrical, mechanical, and automotive trades between 1977 and 1980 (Gilbert, 1980). In both programs retention rates ranged from 70 to 80 percent. The Women's Technical Institute (WTI) of Boston has informed and counseled approximately 10,000 women about nontraditional technical jobs and trained almost 500 for

technical jobs since 1976. Working closely with Boston-area technical employers, WTI placed over 90 percent of the graduates of its six-month electronics course and two-thirds of all its graduates. Providing placement services in nontraditional training programs is of paramount importance. Navari's survey (cited in Walshok, 1981a:280-281) of over 100 women workers indicated that programs such as CETA and WIN were less successful than they could have been in part because they did not provide access to permanent jobs.

Shuchat's (1981) survey of 166 community colleges and private organizations revealed that mechanisms to identify job openings were associated with successful programs to prepare women for nontraditional blue-collar and technical occupations. These often emerged from developing and maintaining ties with local employers.

Many of the programs that provided training for women for jobs that were usually predominantly male were model programs supported by federal funds that are no longer available. The success of some of them suggests that job training programs for adult women, when they provide for placement, can open male-dominated occupations to women. Large-scale federal programs appear to have been less successful at achieving this outcome. It is important to consider why most training programs were quite segregated, despite the regulations. Most were administered by the same organizations that had carried out earlier federal training policies (e.g., the U.S. Employment Service, vocational schools, previous Manpower Administration programs—Harlan, 1979), which had neither the experience nor the community support to create programs that would recruit workers for or place them in sex-atypical jobs. Within the local communities in which CETA was administered, the same social forces and cultural beliefs existed that have impeded occupational desegregation in educational institutions and the labor market.

The evaluations we have reviewed support two conclusions regarding the effectiveness of federally funded training programs. First, regulations requiring nondiscrimination and affirmative action are not likely to be sufficient to achieve desegregation within job training programs without both federal assistance in developing operating mechanisms and strong enforcement to ensure their implementation. Second, small programs specifically geared toward training women for jobs that men have dominated have been effective; their superior effectiveness in realizing the federal goals of reducing occupational sex stereotyping suggests that in the short-run most progress in training women for sex-atypical occupations may have to come from specially structured innovative programs.

A recent evaluation of implementation by the states of the Job Training Partnership Act suggests that enforcement of equal employment opportunity principles may be ineffective. Eighty percent of the states lack any regulations concerning equal opportunity for their programs, and the Department of Labor has also not issued regulations, nor has it taken any action against the states. The Labor Department's EEO enforcement staff has been reduced by more than two-thirds. Consequently, machinery for the prevention of sex (and other) discrimination is lacking in the largest federally funded job training program (Illinois Unemployment and Job Training Research Project, 1985).

Vocational Education

The only education curriculum to receive federal funds, vocational education draws almost half of all federal money allocated to secondary education (Brenner, 1981). Since the 1970s, vocational education has been included in prohibitions against sex discrimination, most specifically in the 1976 amendments to the Vocational Education Act, which mandate sex equity. It has been estimated that vocational education directly or indirectly prepares up to 62 percent of the labor force for entry-level jobs and up to 75 percent of women for the jobs they presently hold (Kane and Frazee, 1978). Thus, vocational education has substantial potential to perpetuate or to reduce sex segregation in the labor force.

In Chapter 3 we showed that throughout this century vocational education has been strongly segregated by sex. Moreover, the data, although they have certain weaknesses, suggest that vocational curricula are linked to people's subsequent jobs. It is likely that if more women were trained for occupations that men currently dominate, their representation in such occupations would increase. In this section we examine the impact of laws passed in the 1960s and 1970s that prohibit sex discrimination and mandate sex equity in public vocational education.

Laws, Regulations, and Enforcement Efforts

The first law that addressed discrimination in vocational education, Title VI of the 1964 Civil Rights Act, prohibited discrimination based on race, color, or national origin. In 1972, Title IX of the Education Amendments extended the prohibition to include sex discrimination. However, the authorized enforcement agency, then the Office of Education in the Department of Health, Education, and Welfare (HEW) failed to enforce either law until ordered by the court to do so following a 1973 suit (*Adams* v. *Califano*). Among other things, HEW was directed to carry out compliance reviews of state vocational education programs and issue guidelines indicating how the two laws applied to vocational education (Brenner, 1981). Three years later Congress amended the Vocational Education Act (Public Law 94-482) explicitly to promote sex equity. The 1976 amendments required states to develop and implement policies and procedures to eliminate sex discrimination and stereotyping in federally funded vocational education programs and provided federal funds to promote equal access of the sexes to vocational education.[10] In recognition of the fact that high school girls were often subtly discouraged or even overtly excluded from taking shop and technical courses, the amendments also called for the states to promote equal access of the sexes to all vocational education programs. Each state was required to employ a full-time sex equity coordinator, to allocate at least $50,000 for that position, and to assess and meet the needs of special groups such as displaced homemakers, single heads of households, and people moving into nontraditional jobs.

Regulations for implementing the amendments were not issued until October 1977, and not until 1979 did the Office for Civil Rights of the Department of Education (newly separated from the old HEW) issue guidelines that outlined state responsibilities for monitoring local programs and provide them with technical assistance to implement the law. Thus, it may be rather soon to expect substantial progress. Moreover, the historically highly segregated nature of vocational education, as well as the fact that when most vocational educators and administrators established their careers sex segregation in vocational education was seen as natural and desirable, would retard the speed with which changes would occur.

The states have varied widely in their progress in implementing the regulations. On the basis of interviews with vocational education personnel in 49 states and the District of Columbia, Harrison (1980) characterized state responses as largely "passive." Only one-third of the states reported that they were attempting to correct problems

they discovered in the required compliance reviews, and some had not used all the federal funds that were allocated because they required state matching funds (National Commission for Employment Policy, 1980; Brenner, 1981). Brenner cites the example of Ohio, which spent only $2,000 of the $42,000 allocated for model projects in 1978. A study of 15 states revealed that only infrequently did the states' 1980 annual plans required by the vocational education amendments contain specific methods for carrying out stated intentions to promote sex equity (National Advisory Council on Vocational Education and the National Advisory Council on Women's Educational Programs, 1980). For example, only four states required local agencies to recruit women and men for sex-atypical programs in order to receive federal vocational education funds (Brenner, 1981). A case study of the successful New York State program, in contrast, indicated that the office was established as soon as the amendments were passed, it was adequately staffed and funded, and the director reported directly to the State Director of Vocational Education (National Commission for Employment Policy, 1980).

An in-depth evaluation of the extent to which state and local school districts in five states (Idaho, Iowa, Massachusetts, Pennsylvania, and Wisconsin) have implemented the sex equity provisions of the Vocational Education Act (VEA) (League of Women Voters Education Fund, 1982) revealed that compliance at the local level was passive at best. The districts they examined had done little to recruit students to or to ensure their retention in programs atypical to their sex or to aid them in finding jobs. They found slow but growing support for sex equity in vocational education, largely at the state level through the efforts of the sex equity coordinators. Prior to the VEA, these states had made few if any efforts toward sex equity in public vocational education, whereas within a few years after regulations and guidelines were issued, all had taken con-

---

[10] Steiger et al. (1979) provide a comprehensive review of the legislative history and goals of the 1976 Education Amendments (Public Law 94-482) of which Title II contained the provisions for sex equity in vocational education.

crete steps and some had allotted over $150,000 toward sex equity. The report points out that recent federal and state budget cuts retard or eliminate the changes in some states, however.

The permissive rather than mandatory form of some of the guidelines and the lenient federal compliance procedures and inadequate enforcement mechanisms, which have had little if any impact at the local level, all make it unlikely that change will occur more rapidly or more uniformly. Ultimately, of course, change must occur within local schools. At the local level, between 20 and 38 percent of the educational agencies in one study took positive steps, including: sponsoring relevant research; educating students, employers, and community organizations about inequities; encouraging student participation in sex-atypical programs; providing guidance, counseling, or job placement services for students in nontraditional programs; and offering day care for the children of vocational students (Harrison, 1980). As one teacher observed, "There needs to be a conscious decision and commitment to the ideas of sex equity from the superintendent of the school district on down." Yet most of the local administrators who were interviewed thought that the regulations were unnecessary, and some also said that they would not do anything to promote sex equity unless required to by federal or state laws.

School districts have had more time to implement the Title IX requirements for sex equity in vocational education. Of 100 local educational agencies surveyed by the American Institutes for Research (Harrison, 1980), 81 percent reportedly had conducted or planned to conduct the self-evaluations regarding vocational education required by Title IX. Slightly over 70 percent had reviewed recruitment materials, 63 percent had examined admissions practices, and half had reviewed curriculum materials. Thus, the districts were more likely to have carried out reviews required by Title IX than those required by the Vocational Education Act.

In sum, state and local efforts to implement the provisions of the 1976 amendments as well as the provisions regarding vocational education in Title IX have been uneven. Within states that took the regulations seriously, however, changes have occurred.

Changes in the Sex-Typing of Vocational Education

It appears—although causal links have not been established—that when schools encouraged students to take sex-atypical courses, more students did so. Indeed, significant although modest changes have occurred during the 1970s in female students' distribution across vocational programs. Two national studies (Steiger et al., 1979; National Advisory Council on Vocational Education and the National Advisory Council on Women's Educational Programs, 1980) and the five-state study cited above (League of Women Voters Education Fund, 1982) have been carried out to assess changes in women's distribution across vocational programs since the implementation of the 1976 amendments.

Four points must be borne in mind in examining their results. First, the quality of some of the data, particularly those from the federal Vocational Education Data System (VEDS), is questionable (Brenner, 1981). For example, the VEDS data do not provide unduplicated tabulations of student enrollments, nor do they distinguish students who took a few vocational courses from those who pursued a vocational program. Second, in both the national and the state data, gains in some states and localities are offset by the absence of change in others. Third, as we noted earlier, the regulations implementing the laws are quite recent, so it may be too soon to observe much change. Fourth, we cannot expect to see immediate consequences of changes in vocational education in the labor market. The proportions of women enrolled in nontraditional vocational education programs are expected to increase faster than women's representation in related occupations because of the time required to complete training and find jobs (National Commission for Employment Policy, 1980), and barriers in the workplace may prevent some women from pursuing nontraditional occupations for which they trained. With these qualifications in mind, we turn to the data.

In general, women continue to dominate the programs that have been overwhelmingly female since their inception and men those that were originally reserved for men. Although women's concentration in business and office, occupational home economics, and health programs declined between 1972 and 1976, the percentages leveled off over the next two years. Table 4-4 shows trends across comparable data sets for 1972, 1976, and 1978. Of the traditionally male fields, women increased their representa-

tion in technical fields and agriculture between 1976 and 1978, but entered trade and industrial fields in only small numbers. Much less marked has been men's movement into occupationally linked home economics programs.

Federally collected data show that a higher proportion of women are enrolling in courses geared to paid employment. Between 1972 and 1978 the proportion of all female vocational students enrolled in non-employment-related home economics programs dropped by 12 percent (U.S. Congress, House, 1982). Enrollment data from 15 states that account for 55 percent of the national enrollment in high school and adult vocational education programs showed an overall rise in vocational education enrollments of 4.4 percent between 1972 and 1978, but a 60 percent increase in the number of women enrolled (National Advisory Council on Women's Educational Programs, 1982). Nationally, between 1972 and 1978 the percentage of women students in traditionally female courses fell from 90.4 to 83.4, while

TABLE 4-4   Percentage Female Enrollment in Vocational Education Programs by Program Area, 1972-1980

Program	1972	1976	1978	1980[a]
Employment-related	41.1	36.6	45.7	
Agriculture	5.3	11.3	17.3	17
Distribution	45.2	40.8	51.5	52
Health	84.6	78.7	78.0	75
Occupational home economics	86.0	84.7	82.4	76
Office	76.3	75.1	75.6	72
Technical	9.7	11.3	17.6	20
Trades and industry	11.6	12.7	15.4	18
Consumer and homemaking	92.1	83.2	80.2	71
Special programs	44.7	33.8	32.5	
Guidance	[b]	48.8	46.5	
Remedial	42.3	44.1	45.0	
Industrial arts	[b]	11.4	17.2	
Others not elsewhere classified	[b]	21.2	33.3	
Total	55.3	51.2	50.4	

[a]As of January 1985, 1978 was the latest year for which national summary data for vocational education were available in detail.

[b]Not provided in summary data for these categories in 1972.

SOURCE: National Commission for Employment Policy (1981:66).

the percentage in mixed and nontraditional classes increased from 52.8 to 56.8 percent and from 5.4 to 11.1 percent, respectively (National Advisory Council on Vocational Education and National Advisory Council on Women's Educational Programs, 1980). The ratio of female to male enrollment in agriculture increased by almost 14 percent between 1972 and 1979 and that for technical programs grew by 7.8 percent, while the proportion of young men in home economics rose by 13 percent. Women's enrollment in nontraditional programs increased significantly faster at the postsecondary and adult education levels than in high schools.

The data from 15 states point to some determinants of these changes. Women's enrollment in nontraditional programs grew fastest in states in which detailed plans involving specific goals and timetables were formulated. The closer the states scrutinized schools, the more action they took to achieve sex equity (National Advisory Council on Vocational Education and National Advisory Council on Women's Educational Programs, 1980). Also, female role models in courses with a male or a "mixed" image and male role models in courses with a female image may encourage both sexes to consider broader career options (Rieder, 1977). One effective project in North Carolina (A. Smith, 1976) trained teachers in summer institutes and made consultants available who helped teachers implement innovative plans. The results were dramatic: 1,000 women enrolled in agricultural courses in the state and 700 in trade and industrial courses, and 1,300 men enrolled in home economics courses.

The Vocational Education Equity Study (described in National Advisory Council on Vocational Education and the National Advisory Council on Women's Educational Programs, 1980) used case studies to identify promising approaches for achieving sex equity in vocational education. Effective strategies include establishing liaisons with employers; thoroughly orienting participants as to what to expect in the program

and the job market; obtaining full support from the host organization, especially in community college settings, to maximize the program's visibility and legitimacy; providing support services to participants, especially women who have children, using existing services when possible; carefully planning and evaluating; and recruiting a competent staff who are dedicated to sex equity, know the local labor market, and can serve as role models for participants.

Students in Sex-Atypical Programs

The experience of students in sex-atypical programs is not always without difficulties and the outcomes of participating in such programs are somewhat unclear. We know more about the experiences and outcomes of women in traditionally male programs than we do about those of men in traditionally female programs.

Women in both secondary and postsecondary sex-atypical programs felt that male students had trouble adjusting to female classmates, and believed that their teachers expected more of them than of male students (Kane et al., 1976; Kane and Frazee, 1978). They also felt that males were better prepared, having had more technical subjects in high school. More than half the women in sex-atypical postsecondary programs felt that their own high school education had not prepared them for such training, although those who had taken several math and science courses felt better prepared. (In contrast, only 25 percent of women in sex-typical programs felt unprepared; Kane et al., 1976.) The proportion of women who expressed problems depended on the number of women in a class. In classes with six or more women, 56 percent experienced problems, compared with 78 percent of women in classes with fewer than four women. It appears that the experiences of women being trained in predominantly male areas are similar to those of women who take jobs in which they are in the minority.

Unfortunately, we do not know very much about the labor market outcomes of women who enrolled in customarily male vocational courses. Two early studies (Wilms, 1974; Lewis and Kaltreider, 1976) reported that only one-fifth to one-third of the women enrolled in nontraditional courses found jobs closely related to their training. However, these ratios are still higher than the probabilities of working in male-dominated occupations among the general population of working women. Data for 1972 through 1976 show that both female and male students in sex-typical vocational curricula were more likely to plan to enter the occupation for which they were training or to seek more vocational training than were students in sex-atypical programs (Harrison et al., 1979). Women enrolled in traditionally male programs were less likely than men to select a traditionally male occupation as their first choice (from a list of occupations provided them). With respect to wages, Grasso and Shea (1979) found that women in sex-typical jobs, particularly those in clerical programs, outearned those in sex-atypical jobs at the point when earnings were measured. Enrollment in a vocational track that prepared students for typically male blue-collar jobs did not yield higher wages for the women studied, who were in a high school in the late 1960s. The negative wage effect of sex-atypical vocational education could mean these women faced more slowly accelerating (but ultimately steeper) wage curves. Alternatively, they might have experienced wage discrimination in heavily male occupations. We do not know whether the wage effect of taking male-oriented courses improved for female high school graduates in the 1970s, when more women were doing so.

Despite these mixed findings, there are good reasons to expect that sex-atypical programs do benefit women and contribute to reducing sex segregation in the workplace. We know that over a lifetime, male-dominated occupations pay better than female ones, and consequently women who enter male-dominated occupations stand to gain relative to those who do not. Although the immediate employment impact of vocational education may be small as measured to date, there are other important reasons to reduce sex segregation in vocational education. First, sex-segregated public school curricula—particularly courses designed to prepare students for employment—reinforce cultural assumptions of the propriety of women and men doing different work. Sex-integrated classes implicitly challenge these assumptions and thus prepare young men and women for working side by side on the same jobs. Second, integrating vocational courses can raise the awareness of sex stereotyping of school counselors, vocational educators, parents, and employers and provide a model for sex equity. Third, sex-atypical vocational education may enhance women's access to male-dominated jobs by teaching them necessary mechanical skills and exposing them to occupations of which they are often unaware, as well as by putting them into pools from which employers often recruit for blue-collar jobs (Roos and Reskin, 1984). Most important, for access to highly paid skilled craft jobs, taking vocational education courses contributes to the successful completion of apprenticeships (Mertens and Gardner, 1981). We expect that the importance, particularly for women, of participating in sex-atypical education will become increasingly clear as programs improve and sufficient numbers of women have participated to demonstrate measurable effects.

Conclusion

Sex segregation across the major vocational program areas has declined significantly, almost certainly at least partly as a result of the implementation of the Vocational Education Act and Title IX of the 1972 Education Amendments. We can draw several conclusions about the effectiveness of federal legislation in providing a more sex-equitable environment in the schools. First, the differential success of various states in implementing the 1976 Vocational Education Amendments suggests that a legislative mandate coupled with federal money is not enough. Active monitoring of schools, particularly the administration of pre- and in-service courses for teachers and counselors, seems to be important. The data support the conclusion reached in the study mandated by the 1976 Vocational Education Act and executed by the American Institutes for Research (Steiger et al., 1979): vocational educators cannot assume that opening traditionally male programs to female students will neutralize family and peer group pressures; rather, affirmative programs will be necessary to attract women to these programs. Second, for training to be effective, programs must also have placement provisions. Third, state programs that were most successful in attracting females to less traditional specialties established a broad base of support for them by setting up orientation programs and providing connections with potential employers (Evenson and O'Neill, 1978).

General Education

In Chapter 3 we concluded that sex stereotyping in teaching materials, the behavior of teachers and counselors, and tracking lead to sex differences in education and training, which in turn tend to perpetuate sex segregation by limiting women's knowledge of, interest in, and preparation for occupations that have been labeled male. In addition, sex differences in high school mathematics training, type of vocational training, college major, professional training, and postgraduate study all have implications for students' subsequent occupational opportunities.

Laws, Regulations, and Enforcement Efforts

During the 1970s, Congress passed several laws designed to reduce sex stereotyping and sex discrimination in federally supported education. These laws may contribute to reducing sex segregation in employment by modifying women's occupational socialization and by specifically preparing them for jobs typically held by males. Most important of these laws is Title IX of the 1972 Educational Amendments. Title IX was the first law specifically designed to protect students from sex discrimination. It covers admissions, financial aid, and access to and treatment in curricular and extracurricular programs sponsored by educational institutions and agencies. Thus, courses of study, counseling, and extracurricular activities are all included. It also prohibits discrimination in the treatment of workers in educational programs that receive federal funds.

Federal agencies that provide financial assistance to educational institutions are responsible for enforcing Title IX and may terminate funding if the recipients fail to comply. Originally HEW had primary enforcement responsibility. In 1977 the Office for Civil Rights (OCR), first in HEW and after 1980 in the Department of Education, assumed that responsibility. OCR investigates complaints and carries out compliance reviews. When violations are detected, the agency seeks voluntary compliance. If negotiations are unsuccessful, OCR may initiate proceedings to terminate financial assistance or refer the case to the Department of Justice for prosecution. In *Grove City College* v. *Bell* (104 S. Ct. 1211 [1984]), the Supreme Court narrowed the scope of Title IX to only those specific programs that received federal funds whereas OCR had been applying an institutionwide definition of the impact of federal funding. The Justice Department's position in the Grove City case provides another illustration of the significant shift in civil rights policies between the current and previous administrations (Peterson, 1985a). Whereas previously the OCR had applied Title IX broadly, the Justice Department in 1983 entered the Grove City case on the side of limiting the applicability of Title IX, changing the government's position by submitting a second brief. The Department of Education immediately announced plans to drop many pending cases against colleges and universities. Since the Grove City decision, a congressional resolution supporting the broader interpretation has been passed and legislation to mandate a broader interpretation, called the Civil Rights Restoration Act of 1985, is pending. The administration opposes the proposed legislation; debate has been intense, and how the issue will be resolved is not clear.

In the Women's Educational Equity Act (WEA) of 1974 and 1978, and in subsequent reauthorizations in 1981 and 1984, Congress authorized funding for model programs to eliminate sex stereotyping and promote educational equity for women and girls. The WEA provides grants, contracts, and technical assistance for developing materials and model programs to achieve educational equity for girls and women. It also provides grants to help school districts and other institutions meet the requirements of Title IX (U.S. Department of Labor, Women's Bureau, 1982a). Thus, Title IX prohibits discrimination and the Women's Educational Equity Act is geared toward encouraging intervention strategies to promote sex equity.

Implementation of the sex equity and antidiscrimination laws directed at educational institutions was slow. Although Congress approved Title IX in 1972, final regulations implementing it were not issued by HEW until 1976. The Project on Equal Education Rights (1978) of the National Organization for Women's Legal Defense and Education Fund outlined other reasons why Title IX had little effect during its first four years. A large backlog of complaints had accumulated by 1976. Students change schools frequently, so complainants could not be located and complaints were often moot by the time HEW responded. Investigations were allegedly often perfunctory, and 22 percent of the cases filed during the period were closed without an investigation. When HEW did obtain commitments from school officials to eliminate illegal practices, OCR did not monitor whether they actually did so. The large number of school districts against which no complaints had been filed were not adequately monitored. It is difficult to determine how much enforcement has improved subsequently, but the OCR director commented that HEW's enforcement efforts had been neither widespread nor energetic (U.S. Commission on Civil Rights, 1980).

In December 1977 in *Adams* v. *Califano*, the Court directed HEW and the Department of Labor to institute enforcement proceedings. Approximately 20,000 school districts and institutions of higher education receive federal assistance, but the OCR completed only 5 compliance reviews in 1978 and 24 in 1979 (U.S. Commission on Civil Rights, 1980). Between 1972 (when Title IX was enacted) and 1980, OCR issued 33 notices of intent to initiate administrative proceedings to terminate funds and actually proceeded to hearings in only a few cases (U.S. Commission on Civil Rights, 1980). Five cases that involved employment discrimination were referred to the Department of Justice for prosecution through 1980, but the department declined to act on any of them (U.S. Commission on Civil Rights, 1980). As of 1980, no school had ever lost federal funds for noncompliance (Project on the Status and Education of Women, 1981). In 1981 the U.S. Commission on Civil Rights reported that, although the Office for Civil Rights, then the authorized enforcement agency, had made improvements, enforcement of Title IX was still unduly slow and at times inadequate (Project on the Status and Education of Women, 1981). In the same year, an evaluation by the National Advisory Council on Women's Educational Programs (1981) concluded that progress had occurred, but offered only anecdotal evidence documenting this conclusion.

Studies of particular enforcement regions

trace the consequences of enforcement in-activity (Miller and Associates; Michigan Department of Education; both cited in U.S. Commission on Civil Rights, 1980). A study of one region found few of the schools in full compliance and many exerting only minimal efforts to comply. This poor record resulted partly because they had not received adequate information regarding their obligations or the guidelines for implementing the requirements, but also partly because they did not take the threat of sanctions seriously. The U.S. Commission on Civil Rights (1980) found that when both OCR staff and recipient institutions knew that sanctions would not be imposed, the former pressed in negotiations for compromise rather than full compliance. According to the Commission on Civil Rights, several studies have shown that adequate technical assistance, particularly in self-evaluation, promotes voluntary compliance, but that this assistance has not often been offered by OCR staff.

In sum, the OCR has been criticized as being slow to issue guidelines and process complaints and for showing little commitment to discovering violations or helping institutions prevent them (U.S. Commission on Civil Rights, 1980).[11] No research exists

that has statistically estimated the impact of Title IX on sex equity in higher education. The law was passed when strong political pressure pushed for sex equity in education, and its passage may have fueled that movement. Women's participation in professional and postgraduate education has increased, and sex segregation across college majors has declined (see Chapter 3). Research has not established, however, the extent to which Title IX has contributed to these changes.

Exemplary Programs

We located little research assessing specific programs to combat occupational sex-role stereotyping in secondary schools. According to a review by Evenson and O'Neill (1978), the following factors contribute to the effectiveness of such programs: in-service training for school staff, basing course content on students' actual experiences, early intervention, providing follow-up support, and involving parents in support networks. For example, Project Eve in the Houston school system, which provided information, counseling, and encouragement to high school girls, resulted in increased female enrollments in every vocational course, and dramatic increases in auto mechanics, metals, radio and television, plumbing, and air conditioning courses (Evenson and O'Neill, 1978). The importance of institutional involvement is suggested by the fact that one review (Beach, 1977) could locate no instance in which individual teachers or counselors initiated change on their own.

Evaluations of programs to increase girls' enrollment in mathematics courses and to encourage women's participation in science and engineering suggest that some have been quite effective. For example, in an experiment in which fourth through sixth graders were asked to figure out how science toys worked (described in Rossi, 1965), some girls were reluctant to take part, explaining that girls were not supposed to know about such

---

[11] In view of the minimal enforcement efforts, it is perhaps not surprising that changes regarding employment in educational institutions covered by Title IX have not been dramatic. In 1974 women were 13 percent of elementary and secondary school principals; four years later their share of these jobs had increased by 1 percentage point (National Advisory Council on Women's Educational Programs, 1981). Between 1972-1973 and 1980-1981, the number of female school superintendents increased from 65 in 13,000 (Brenner, 1981) to 154 in 16,000 (National Advisory Council on Women's Educational Programs, 1981). Women college faculty, usually covered by Title IX as well as the amended Executive Order 11246 and Title VII of the 1964 Civil Rights Act, showed progress on some dimensions, such as salary, but the sex disparity in the percentage who were tenured widened (Astin and Snyder, 1982).

things. The children's teachers and parents were informed of this result and its implications for the girls' understanding of science. When the experiment was repeated the following year, girls did the task willingly and with apparent enjoyment, and the sexes performed almost identically. Some remedial programs serve adult women who are either returning to school or in the labor force; others at the secondary level attempt to change the learning environment or attitudes of girls, their teachers, or parents. A model remedial program demonstrably increased women's career aspirations (Ernest, 1976; MacDonald, 1980).

Effective programs use various techniques, including female instructors who serve as role models or mentors and preinstruction counseling to reduce any anxiety toward mathematics. Casserly (1982) surveyed several high school programs to determine what factors were most effective in encouraging girls' study of mathematics. More important than parents or peers were teachers, especially those with a mathematics or science background (rather than a background in mathematics education), with advanced degrees, and with prior professional employment that used their math skills. Adult role models also apparently illustrate the value of mathematics. Fennema (1983) found that young women avoided mathematics courses because they were less likely than men to believe that math is useful, and that a brief intervention changed that belief. The evidence that all-female classes are more effective is rather strong (Fox, 1981; Casserly, 1982). At the aggregate level, several data sets show a narrowing of the sex differential in mathematics background: 1960 Project Talent data revealed that 9 percent of the girls and 33 percent of the boys took four years of high school mathematics; the 1977-1978 National Assessment of Educational Progress data for 1,776 high school seniors showed considerable convergence: 31 percent of the boys and 27 percent

of the girls had four years of math (Brenner, 1981). It seems unlikely that these changes are due primarily to special programs, but many such programs have been demonstrably successful (Fox, 1981).

Since 1974 the National Science Foundation (NSF) has supported experimental programs to encourage women to pursue careers in science, mathematics, and engineering. In 1976 Congress authorized NSF to develop methods to increase the flow of women into scientific careers. Over the next four years, NSF funded programs at 99 colleges and universities as well as a Visiting Woman Scientist Program for high school students. Evaluation indicated that high schools welcomed the women scientists' visits, which encouraged girls to seek information about scientific careers (Lantz et al., 1980). NSF also supported programs to prepare women with bachelor's or master's degrees in the sciences to enter and find employment in fields in which women were markedly underrepresented. Extensive evaluation indicates that these programs also were very successful. Lantz's conclusions regarding successful programs to encourage women to pursue scientific careers probably hold also for nonscience programs: they should identify and eliminate barriers in the workplace, alter management's perceptions of women's potential contributions, increase women's understanding of what employers want, and create support systems for women.

In 1981 the National Science Foundation Authorization and Science and Technology Equal Opportunities Act was passed to further encourage full participation by women and minorities in scientific, engineering, and technical fields. Preliminary evaluations of some of the programs NSF has supported under this and the 1976 act suggest that model projects designed to increase women's participation in engineering have been more effective than those oriented toward science (Lantz et al., 1982). Several explanations for this difference are possible. Not only did the engineering schools as a group cooperate, but a bachelor's degree in engineering is often a terminal degree that qualifies the holder for a job, and job opportunities recently have been excellent.

Conclusion

The impact of federal laws prohibiting discrimination in federally supported public education on reduced sex segregation in the workplace is difficult to measure, but it is probably not large. Implementation of Title IX has been slow, and few school districts or universities have been reviewed for compliance with the law. The decline in sex differences in various educational achievements during the 1970s cannot be directly attributed to the existence or enforcement of antidiscrimination laws, although some state and regional studies show a link between amount of enforcement of Title IX and changes in certain indicators. In general, little scientific research has been carried out to evaluate the effectiveness of various programs to combat occupational sex stereotyping in the schools. Sundry evidence suggests that when decision makers are committed to sex equity, staff are more cooperative and change more likely. Evaluation of programs designed to encourage girls and women to study mathematics and science have shown them to be effective. Generally, the evidence suggests that small programs funded under sex equity laws have been more likely to succeed than large-scale interventions, probably because of the difficulties in ensuring the implementation of the latter at the local level.

INTERVENTIONS TO ACCOMMODATE FAMILY RESPONSIBILITIES

We noted in the previous chapter that, despite mixed empirical evidence linking women's work in family care to specific labor market outcomes such as job segregation and lower wages, it seems likely that the tradi-

tionally greater responsibility of women for family and child care and housework affects their labor market participation in a variety of ways. Interventions by the federal government aimed at changing the traditional division of labor between the sexes have been virtually nonexistent, but in recent years some effort has been directed toward attempting to accommodate women's responsibilities, particularly for children, to their wage-work lives. For the most part, these accommodations have also been available to men.

Before turning to them, however, we point out that several long-established areas of federal policy actually reinforce the traditional division of labor between women and men. The federal income tax system (and many state systems as well) treat the family as the tax-paying unit and use a progressive rate structure. As Gordon (1979a) and others have pointed out, these two practices tend to discourage the labor market participation of secondary family earners, usually women. Because wives generally earn less than their husbands, their earnings are viewed as the additional or marginal earnings, which are taxed at higher rates because of the progressivity of the tax structure. Although the joint taxation of the husband and wife and the income-splitting provisions of the federal tax code benefit families with a non-wage-earning wife, they actually provide a disincentive to the married working couple who pay higher taxes together than if they were not married. This marriage penalty is generally greatest when husbands and wives earn similar incomes in the middle and upper income ranges. It has come under increasing scrutiny in recent years, as increasing numbers of women work for wages. Despite the recent addition of a tax credit for working spouses, however, the penalty has not been entirely eliminated. The social security system also rewards the traditional family at the expense of the working couple (Gordon, 1979b). Again because women's earnings tend to be lower than those of their husbands, women often receive higher retirement benefits by claiming the benefits they are entitled to as spouses rather than those based on their own earnings. In essence this means that the return a wife gets on her payments as a worker over her lifetime are nil. In general, working couples get a lower return to their social security payments than do single-earner couples. Such policies, while they may not contribute directly to job segregation by sex, provide negative incentives to women's paid employment in general and accordingly probably affect women's careers at work as well.

Child Care

Except during periods of war and depression, the role of the federal government in providing organized child care has been small (U.S. Department of Labor, Manpower Administration, 1975). Over the past 20 years, however, the federal government and some private employers have tried to reduce the constraint that the lack of child care represents for many women. The federal efforts have included both direct subsidies to child care centers as well as tax credits to parents and tax incentives to employers. Federal legislation that provides funds for child care services sought to reduce poverty by enabling low-income mothers to participate in job training programs or enter the labor force. These programs included Head Start, Aid to Families With Dependent Children, WIN, and CETA (U.S. Department of Labor, Manpower Administration, 1975; U.S. Department of Labor, Women's Bureau, 1982b).[12] But these programs have been helpful to varied and often limited degrees (U.S. Commission on Civil Rights, 1981b). For example, CETA programs were locally

administered, and under block grants most local programs preferred to use their resources in other ways that provided more visible payoffs. No national data exist on the number of women who received child care under CETA since it was grouped with other social services supported with CETA funds. Because these programs have been geared toward low-income women, eligibility requirements involve maximum income levels that may actually restrict women's opportunities. The U.S. Commission on Civil Rights report on child care and equal opportunity for women (1981b) noted instances of women forced to turn down better-paying and less sex-stereotyped jobs to avoid exceeding the allowable income and thus losing eligibility for child care assistance.

Recently the federal government's policy toward child care has shifted from providing direct support or subsidies to child care centers to offering tax credits to individuals and providing incentives to employers. Depending on their income, employed parents can deduct between 20 and 30 percent of child care expenses from the taxes they owe, thereby reducing the financial burden child care represents. Not everyone can afford the remaining costs or obtain acceptable care, however. The 1971 Revised Order 4 that the Office of Federal Contract Compliance issued as a guideline for Executive Order 11246 recognized that federal contractors can provide child care to employees as a form of affirmative action. It does not require them to do so, however, and it seems unlikely that many have implemented the suggestion. Branches of the military, in contrast with other federal employers, have often provided extensive child care facilities (U.S. Department of Labor, Women's Bureau, 1982b). Other public and private employers also address employees' child care needs through direct subsidies, on-site facilities, sick-child programs, and participation with other employers in child care consortia. In 1981 the Economic Recovery Tax Act revised the Internal Revenue Service code to

---

[12] Other federal programs are discussed in greater detail in reports on day care by the U.S. Commission on Civil Rights (1981b) and the Women's Bureau (U.S. Department of Labor, Women's Bureau, 1982b).

allow employers to provide child care services as a tax-free benefit to employees (Kamerman and Kingston, 1982). Both employees and employers report benefits from workplace child care facilities (U.S. Department of Labor, Women's Bureau, 1982b), including a decline in turnover and absenteeism, improved employee morale and productivity, and public relations and recruiting benefits to the company.

Flexible Work Scheduling

Employers can also mitigate the constraints that women's child care responsibilities place on their access to certain jobs by permitting workers of both sexes flexibility in scheduling their working hours. The potential benefit to working parents of "flexitime" or related alternatives such as job sharing and voluntary compressed workweeks is obvious. A wide range of public and private employers have experimented with permitting employees more flexibility in scheduling their working hours (Barrett, 1979). Many federal agencies have instituted various forms of flexitime and recent civil service legislation requires that a certain proportion of federal jobs be available on a part-time basis, with all of the protections and benefits accorded full-time workers. While we discovered no assessment of the impact of flexible work scheduling on women's access to traditionally male jobs, workers as well as supervisors overwhelmingly judge experimental programs as successful (Krucoff, 1981). One project that sought to encourage employers to permit flexible work scheduling for welfare mothers participating in WIN garnered considerable cooperation (U.S. Department of Labor, Employment and Training Administration, 1977). Part-time work is more frequently available in traditionally female jobs than others and is often penalized by the lack of fringe benefits and advancement opportunities. Barrett (1979) points out the importance of improving the working conditions of part-time

workers, not only because many women depend on these jobs for income, but also because the availability of well-paying, career-enhancing part-time work would contribute to a general reassessment of the allocation of paid employment and family work between husbands and wives. Of course, flexitime and job sharing cannot foster women's integration into predominantly male jobs or men's greater participation in family work if they are available primarily in the traditionally female sectors.

CONCLUSION

During the 1960s and 1970s numerous federal laws and regulations were enacted and promulgated prohibiting certain forms of discrimination in employment, training, and education. Assessing their effect is not easy. Enforcement agencies have had inadequate resources and enforcement has been uneven. Evaluation has not had a high priority for agencies, and statistical attempts are weakened by the difficulty of ruling out alternative explanations. In particular, the prominence of the women's movement during these same years, and its contributions not only to the passage of the laws but also to changes in attitudes and behavior, complicates the study of cause and effect. Nevertheless, a variety of evidence suggests that these remedies have contributed to observed decreases in occupational segregation.

Several types of evidence, both direct and indirect, demonstrate the impact of antidiscrimination laws and regulations in the employment area. First, information about particular establishments against which enforcement agencies brought action or about industries that were targeted for special enforcement efforts provide the most direct evidence. Although compliance agreements have often not been adequately monitored, evidence for some cases (e.g., AT&T, the steel industry) shows clear increases in women's representation in jobs that had been held almost exclusively by men. Considerable change has also occurred in women's participation in formerly predominantly male jobs in the three industries that the Office for Contract Compliance Programs targeted for special enforcement efforts: banking, insurance, and mining. Second, in-depth studies of federal contractors in construction revealed a broad consensus that the goals required by contract compliance regulations accounted for women's small gains in construction jobs. Third, increases—sometimes dramatic—in women's representation in several male-dominated professions (for example, accounting, engineering, law) have been credited by many either directly or indirectly to affirmative action. Fourth, after the Equal Employment Opportunity Act (1972) extended the protection of Title VII to federal employees, the representation of women in higher grades increased. Fifth, surveys of large establishments indicated that awareness of federal enforcement by top management is common and is associated with successful programs to integrate male-dominated jobs. Finally, statistical studies of the effect of Title VII or the executive order barring discrimination by federal contractors show positive enforcement effects. Although some of these studies can be individually criticized, taken together they suggest that antidiscrimination laws have modest effects in the intended direction.

With respect to employer initiatives, companies have used a wide variety of mechanisms that were outside their normal personnel practices to place women in jobs seldom held by them. Sometimes internal labor markets—including job requirements, seniority systems, and job ladders—had to be restructured. In blue-collar jobs, success required innovative recruitment programs, in some cases involving outside agencies that specialized in preparing women for such positions. Pretraining and on-the-job training proved to be very important, as did support systems and involving immediate supervi-

sors in developing tactics. Increasing women's representation in managerial jobs demanded fewer special practices. In organizations that were most successful in broadening the occupational outcomes of women, top-level management was typically committed to equal employment opportunity. Successful organizations set goals and timetables, established monitoring systems, and allocated sufficient resources.

Studies of women in apprenticeship programs indicate that genuine affirmative efforts, required by guidelines issued by the Department of Labor in 1978, are effective in attracting women to male-dominated programs, but that typical features of apprenticeship programs, such as age limits, discourage women from participating in them. Pretraining appears to enhance women's chances to qualify for programs and to succeed within them. Available evidence suggests that the regulations requiring equal employment opportunity for women in federally registered apprenticeship programs have contributed to women's small gains in customarily male programs. Although enforcement has reportedly been minimal, where good faith efforts have been made, women's representation has increased. In a few instances in which strong efforts were documented (e.g., the maritime industry, the construction industry in Seattle), women's gains have been more impressive. The least progress has occurred in construction-related programs, in which informal barriers and employer resistance are reportedly high. Since many of these programs fall under the executive order for federal contractors, established goals and enforcement tools exist; their implementation has apparently been problematic.

Federally funded employment training programs, evidence indicates, have done little to reduce segregation. Although a 1978 amendment to the 1973 Comprehensive Employment and Training Act (CETA) stipulated that all programs contribute to eliminating sex stereotyping, most CETA programs were segregated by sex. Nevertheless, CETA supported some very effective small programs specifically geared toward training women for sex-atypical occupations. Federally sponsored training programs have demonstrably fostered women's integration into certain occupations when they were administered with this goal. The new programs under the Job Training Partnership Act (effective in 1983) do not generally have effective EEO enforcement mechanisms.

Vocational education in the public schools, which prepares many students for jobs, has been highly sex-segregated since its inception. Although the effects of vocational education on students' subsequent employment outcomes are not well documented or understood, it seems likely that vocational education has helped to prepetuate sex segregation in the workplace. The 1976 Vocational Education Amendments addressed this by requiring federally funded vocational programs to eliminate sex stereotyping and sex discrimination and specifying mechanisms for the individual states to achieve these goals. The states have varied considerably in their responses. In those that implemented the regulations fully, female enrollment in sex-atypical courses increased. States with detailed plans including goals and timetables have shown the greatest decline in segregation. The varying degrees of progress across the states indicate that federal funds for desegregating along with a legislative mandate is not enough. Active monitoring of schools is essential.

Overall, segregation across major vocational program areas has declined. Women continue to be concentrated in stereotypically female programs, however, and most integration has occurred in programs without a strong masculine image, such as drafting and graphic arts. The most successful state programs have established a broad base of support for women in mixed and nontraditional courses. Effective local programs have used affirmative action to attract students and have developed procedures, such

as female role models and counseling, to neutralize peer group pressures. They have also developed ties with the community, fostered contacts with prospective employers, and provided special training and support services for vocational instructors.

Title IX of the 1972 Educational Amendments was designed to protect students from sex segregation in educational programs at all levels, but its implementation was slow and few school districts or universities have been reviewed for compliance with the law. Sex differences in various educational outcomes (years of mathematics, college major, graduate and professional study) did decline during the 1970s, however. Although these declines cannot be directly attributed to the existence or enforcement of antidiscrimination laws, some state and regional studies observed a link between enforcement of Title IX and women's gains on certain indicators. Generally, however, little scientific research has been carried out to evaluate the effectiveness of programs geared toward increasing sex equity in the schools. A few evaluations do suggest the importance of commitment by decision makers for genuine efforts by staff and for real progress. In contrast to the limited assessments of the impact of Title IX, evaluations of programs designed to increase girls' and women's participation in scientific and mathematics education—in particular, programs funded by NSF—show them to have effectively trained women in these fields. We know less about their indirect impact on women's subsequent entry into these fields, but in view of the strong link between training and professional employment in science, it seems likely that they have helped to reduce sex segregation in scientific and technical occupations. The results for programs aimed at reducing sex stereotyping and promoting sex equity in education are consistent with those we have seen for job training programs: small but adequately funded programs are more likely to show measurable success than large-scale interventions, probably because of the difficulties in ensuring the implementation of the latter at the local level. We must point out, however, that despite the success of several exemplary programs, there is no evidence that the effects on sex segregation in the workplace of federal laws prohibiting discrimination in federally funded education are large.

Improving women's employment opportunities by seeking to better accommodate women's family responsibilities to the demands of the work world has not been a common domain of federal interventions. Indeed, many federal policies, particularly in income taxation and social security benefits, tend to reinforce a division of labor within the family in which one adult takes primary responsibility for wage earning and one takes primary responsibility for family care. These policies are increasingly problematic in an era when the majority of women work for wages throughout much of their lives. In several surveys, women state that lack of adequate child care limits their participation in the labor market. While it is not clear to what extent inadequate child care contributes directly to sex segregation, improved availability of child care would no doubt improve women's employment opportunities generally. We note that the improved availability of child care is important for fathers and children as well as mothers.

Finally, we report and comment on recent changes in civil rights policy and enforcement. Several measures indicate that the federal enforcement effort has decreased since 1980. According to the Office of Management and Budget, total government outlays for civil rights enforcement have declined in real terms by 15 percent between 1980 and 1983. Moreover, since 1980, as reported by Burbridge (1984), the number of employment discrimination cases filed in the courts has grown by more than 50 percent, but cases filed by the U.S. government have declined by more than 25 percent. Burbridge also reports that, in the OFCCP, although the number of complaint investi-

gations and compliance reviews completed annually has increased steadily, the number of administrative complaints filed and debarments has fallen, and the proportion of cases closed without investigation has risen. Similarly in the EEOC, the agency's budget and number of authorized positions were significantly reduced, the settlement rate fell nearly 20 percent, and the no-cause rate increased about 10 percent.

The evidence reviewed above suggests that, in the employment area, quotas, goals, and timetables have been important in increasing opportunities for women and minorities. At the same time, public opinion is divided with respect to their efficacy and fairness. With recent changes in the philosophy and practice of federal civil rights enforcement, the current administration is moving away from these remedies. Since 1981, for example, the Department of Justice has joined several cases to argue against the use of quotas in hiring, promotion, and layoffs. It has interpreted the Supreme Court's decision in *Firefighters* v. *Stotts* (104 S.Ct. 2576 [1984]) broadly, arguing that it suggests that all court-ordered quotas are illegal. Many civil rights lawyers believe the decision applies only to court orders that go beyond original consent decrees and that the major impact of the decision will be on seniority and layoffs. To date the Justice Department view has been rejected by the federal district and appellate courts.[13] The

_____

[13] See *EEOC* v. *Local 638 . . . Local 28 of Sheet Metal Workers' International Association*, 759 F.2d 1172, 1185-86 (2d Cir. 1985); *Turner* v. *Orr*, 759 F.2d 817 (11th Cir. 1985); *Vanguards of Cleveland* v. *City of Cleveland*, 753 F.2d 479 (6th Cir. 1985); *Diaz* v. *AT&T*, 752 F.2d 1356, 1360 & n. 5 (9th Cir. 1985); *Janowiak* v. *Corporate City of South Bend*, 750 F.2d 557 (7th Cir. 1984); *Van Aken* v. *Young*, 750 F.2d 43 (6th Cir. 1984); *Johnson* v. *Transportation Agency*, 748 F.2d 1308, 1314 (9th Cir. 1984); *Wygant* v. *Jackson Board of Education*, 746 F.2d 1152 (6th Cir. 1984), cert. granted 104 S. Ct.___(1985); *Kromnick* v. *School District of Philadelphia*, 739 F.2d 894 (3rd Cir. 1984),

Department of Justice also changed its position on the Grove City College case, arguing, in its second brief, for a narrow interpretation of Title IX.

The evidence also shows that leadership and commitment to equal opportunity and affirmative action are important to their effective implementation. The recent changes in the direction of federal civil rights policy clearly signal a shift in the philosophy of appropriate enforcement and remedies. Although this shift is viewed by its proponents as more effective in advancing their concept of equal opportunity, some observers have interpreted these changes as reduced commitment to equal opportunity (Peterson 1985a, 1985b; Williams, 1985b). Obviously, evidence about the effectiveness of the new policy directions in terms of employment opportunities for women and minorities is not yet available. However, the evidence discussed above suggests that policies introduced during the preceding two decades have been effective in improving employment opportunities for women and minorities when adequately enforced.

---

cert. denied, 104 S. Ct.___(1985); *Grann* v. *City of Madison*, 738 F.2d 786 (7th Cir. 1984).

5 Findings and Recommendations

We began our examination of sex segregation in the workplace by describing why it is costly for both individuals and society. Sex segregation affects the lives of many Americans. Women of all racial and ethnic backgrounds are increasingly likely to be in the labor force and to work for more of their adult lives; more than half of all women are now in the labor force in any year. The vast majority of these women work in predominantly female occupations. The most serious consequence of this segregation is the persistent wage gap between the sexes.

In 1981 white women who were employed full-time year-round earned less than 60 percent of what white males earned; black women earned 76 percent of what black men earned; and Hispanic women earned 73 percent of what Hispanic men earned. In addition, black women earned 54 percent and Hispanic women earned 52 percent of what white men earned. Approximately 35-40 percent of this wage gap can be attributed to occupational segregation, and sex segregation *within* occupations apparently accounts for much of the remaining disparity. Hence, in the absence of occupational-level segregation, women would earn about 75 cents for every dollar a man earns rather

than the well known 59 cents, and in the absence of job-level segregation the gap would be still smaller.[1]

These economic consequences must be considered in light of the fact that the majority of employed women either support themselves and their dependents or contribute their earnings to the income of families in which husbands have below-average earnings. This is especially true for minority women. Working in a predominantly female occupation lowers the wages of both female and male workers, but women in such occupations, on average, earn even less than their male counterparts. The consequences of women's income loss due to job segregation extend beyond their years in the labor force. Because segregation depresses their wages, upon retirement women receive lower social security and pension benefits.

Nonwage consequences of sex segregation have been less fully documented, but evidence clearly shows that female-dominated occupations provide less on-the-job training

---

[1] This computation is based on data in "20 Facts on Women Workers" (U.S. Department of Labor, Women's Bureau, 1982).

and fewer opportunities for advancement. Some people have also argued that women's resulting lower income and occupational status reduce their bargaining power in the household and contribute to the unequal division of domestic work. In addition to these adverse consequences for individuals and their families, human resources are wasted when workers are allocated to jobs on the basis of gender (and often race or ethnicity) rather than ability.

Whenever sex segregation reflects barriers and constraints rather than choice, it is at odds with American values regarding equality of opportunity. We do not believe that full equality of opportunity necessarily requires the policy goal of eliminating all segregation in employment, so that all jobs would have equal proportions of women and men. How much job segregation would exist in the absence of artificial barriers of various kinds is unknowable, but it is our judgment that job segregation by sex would be substantially reduced if barriers were removed.

In this chapter we summarize our findings, which appear in somewhat greater detail at the end of each of the preceding chapters, and make recommendations for reducing sex segregation. We also identify issues that require further research.

SUMMARY OF FINDINGS

Measuring Sex Segregation

During the past decade women's occupational options have unquestionably expanded. Their participation has increased sharply in several occupations previously predominantly male by tradition or policy: for example, lawyers, bank managers, insurance adjusters, postal clerks, bus drivers, and janitors, among others. In other occupations, women's representation is small but increasing rapidly, for example: coal miners, police officers, and engineers. The overall index of occupational sex segregation de-

clined by nearly 10 percent between 1972 and 1981, more than it had during any previous decade in this century. Much of this decline was due to women's increased participation in many occupations that were 20-60 percent female in 1970 as well as to the decline in the size of some female-dominated occupations, rather than to the entry of women (or men) into the most atypical jobs for their sex.

Nevertheless, sex segregation continues to characterize the American workplace, despite the changes that have occurred in some occupations. Millions of women continue to work in a small number of almost totally female clerical and service occupations, and men continue to make up the majority of workers in the majority of occupations. The segregation index computed across several hundred detailed census occupational categories stood at 62 in 1981, indicating that 62 percent of all female or male workers would have to shift to an occupation currently dominated by members of the other sex in order for the distributions of female and male workers across occupations to be identical and for occupational sex segregation to be totally eliminated. This measure of segregation understates the amount of sex segregation in jobs, since it does not capture the considerable amount of segregation within many occupations and across establishments.

As successive generations of young black women have found jobs in clerical and professional occupations, rather than in the low-paid service occupations to which their mothers and grandmothers were largely restricted, the occupational distribution of black women increasingly resembles that of white women. Racial segregation in the workplace among both sexes has declined sharply over the past 40 years. Younger cohorts of all races experience somewhat less sex segregation in the workplace than the general population. Moreover, over the past 10 years the sexes have increasingly selected similar college majors, and the proportions of students in professional schools who are female have increased dramatically. It is too soon to know how these young women entering new occupations will fare, but women's very presence in these formerly male occupations signals an important social change that should make the path for their successors easier.

At the same time, over the remainder of this decade the overall level of segregation is projected to decline only very slightly—between 1 and 5 points, to somewhat less than 60 in 1990—primarily because most of the occupations in which the greatest absolute growth in jobs is expected are still predominantly of one sex. Although the projections of employment growth may be incorrect and some sex-neutral occupations may grow especially rapidly, only under the most optimistic assumptions is the index expected to continue to decline at the same rate as it did in the 1970s. The overall persistence in the aggregate level of segregation, contrasted with changes that have occurred in some occupations, suggests the metaphor of the half-empty/half-full glass: focusing on the increases in women's occupational opportunities suggests important social changes in women's aspirations and expectations and employers' receptiveness to them; focusing on the continued high levels of sex segregation points to the need for greater change in workplaces and other institutions and in the attitudes of employers and coworkers to eliminate the barriers and restrictions that we believe cause much of the sex segregation observed.

Explaining Sex Segregation

Several explanations have been proposed to account for the persistence of sex segregation in the workplace; they emphasize different factors and differ strongly in the interventions they imply. Not surprisingly, the evidence neither provides full confirmation nor warrants full rejection of any single explanation. The scientific evidence we reviewed, however, fails to support the argument that women's occupational outcomes result primarily from free choices that they make in an open market. It suggests rather that women face discrimination and institutional barriers in their education, training, and employment. Often the opportunities that women encounter in the labor market and in premarket training and education constrain their choices to a narrow set of alternatives.

In reviewing explanations for sex segregation, we considered the role of cultural beliefs; barriers to employment, including discrimination; socialization, education, and training; family responsibilities; and the opportunity structure.

Cultural Beliefs

Beliefs about differences between the sexes that are grounded in Western cultural values contribute to the persistence of sex segregation. These beliefs take as axiomatic that women's primary sphere is the home—and that of men is the workplace—and assume innate sex differences in personality and physical characteristics that are supposed to suit women and men to different kinds of work and militate against their working together except under certain conditions. As a result, employers and job seekers share attitudes about what kinds of work are appropriate for each sex, and many occupations have come to be labeled male or female. Although the sex labels of particular occupations have changed in the past, the rationalizations for these shifts seldom challenge the underlying assumptions that have resulted in the classification of most occupations as either women's or men's work.

Yet attitudes about women's roles, their right to do wage work, and appropriate relations between the sexes have changed substantially over the past 40 years, hand in hand with increased public awareness of changes in women's actual labor market behavior. The growing participation of women in the labor market, particularly large increases among women with young children, and the entry of women into highly segregated occupations, even in small numbers, challenge implicit assumptions about women's work lives and about appropriate jobs for women and men. Even small changes signal to future workers that society now permits them to pursue occupations customarily held by the other sex in the past. Although definitive demonstration is not possible, theories of social change suggest that the increasing recognition by lawmakers and the courts of women's right to equal opportunity in the workplace reinforce attitudinal changes. As a result, as integration takes hold, occupational sex stereotyping declines, and policies that facilitate the movement of persons of either sex into sex-atypical occupations should foster further declines in segregation.

Barriers

Despite recent changes in attitudes and new challenges to old beliefs, we found that a variety of barriers—legal, institutional, and informal—still limit women's access to occupations in which men have customarily predominated. These include recruiting systems that either depend on worker referrals or hire from male-dominated preemployment settings (e.g., vocational education classes, the military); requirements for non-essential training or credentials that women often lack; veterans' preference policies; promotion and transfer rules, such as department- rather than plantwide seniority systems, that hamper women's movement between jobs and departments; preemployment barriers to relevant job training, such as age restrictions for apprenticeship; and factors such as work climate, harassment, and sponsorship. Employers' acceptance of cultural stereotypes about the appropriate gender for certain jobs or their beliefs about women's and men's characteristics lead some to discriminate—to consider gender in hiring workers and assigning them to jobs. Sta-

tistical discrimination—the practice by which employers judge the costs of potential employees based on beliefs about the groups to which they belong—may also play an important role in narrowing women's occupational opportunities, although its effect has not been quantified.

The weight of scientific evidence indicates that discrimination has played a significant role in maintaining a sex-segregated work force. That women believe they face discrimination is evidenced by the tens of thousands of sex discrimination complaints filed under Title VII of the 1964 Civil Rights Act (which prohibits sex discrimination in many employment practices). A number of statistical studies of large employers show that equally qualified men and women are often assigned different jobs, with long-term effects on their subsequent careers. Case studies of some employers against which complaints have been filed and of certain industries provide corroborative evidence of the occurrence of sex discrimination in employment practices.

Socialization, Education, and Training

On the supply side, socialization, education, and training are important because they affect the attributes and qualities that people bring to the labor market. Early socialization is thought to contribute to sex segregation at work because it appears to lead to the development of sex differences in personality traits and skills that may be relevant for certain occupations; to sex differences in values, aspirations, and preferences; and to differences between the sexes in knowledge about occupations. But the link between socialization and occupational outcomes and the direction of causation are not well established. For example, considerable evidence suggests that perceptions of occupational opportunities influence expressed preferences. We have also seen that sex-typed aspirations and preferences change. Among adults, people pursue sex-atypical occupations when new opportunities appear. Socialization is a lifelong process, and adult vocational education, job training programs, apprenticeships, and a return to college or professional schools prepare women who previously pursued traditionally female jobs for sex-atypical occupations.

The link between education and training and occupational outcomes is better understood than is the one for childhood socialization. Premarket training or education is required for many occupations. Girls and boys are highly segregated in most vocational education programs, girls take fewer science and mathematics courses than boys in high school, and the sexes, on average, pursue different majors in college. In the past choices to pursue education and training have been subject to considerable constraint. Parents, teachers, and counselors may treat girls and boys differently and hold different goals for them. Tracking still occurs within the schools, as does sex stereotyping in educational materials. But these differences are declining. High school courses taken and college majors selected have changed for young women and men, and, during the past 10-15 years, admissions policies and people's perceptions have changed so that many women now apply to and are accepted at professional schools in numbers almost equal to men.

Family Responsibilities

Responsibility for the daily care of family members, which women bear more than men, also undoubtedly affects labor market outcomes in many ways, but its link specifically to sex-segregated occupations is less clear. One hypothesis, based on human capital theory, is that women choose female-dominated occupations because those occupations are more compatible with child-rearing (by penalizing work interruptions less than male-dominated occupations); this hypothesis has found equivocal empirical support. Nevertheless, it seems likely that some people, particularly women, do seek jobs

that they believe are compatible with raising families. Further research is warranted on connections between employment opportunities and family responsibilities for both women and men.

Opportunities

Sex-role socialization, education, training, and considerations about the compatibility of various jobs with domestic responsibilities all undoubtedly contribute to the employment decisions that female workers make, but a variety of evidence indicates that the occupational outcomes of most workers of both sexes largely reflect what jobs are available to them. Preferences change, stereotyping recedes in importance, and cultural beliefs are transformed as opportunities develop. A striking example is coal mining. When litigation and affirmative recruitment efforts opened jobs to women, large numbers of women sought work as miners. We believe the occupational opportunity structure that the labor market presents to workers is key to understanding the perpetuation of sex segregation. The collective, cumulative actions of employers create an opportunity structure that strongly influences workers' preferences, knowledge, and occupational outcomes. Employers also respond to changes in workers' behavior and alter their policies accordingly.

Of course, all of the factors we have discussed are interrelated. As beliefs have changed about the jobs that women might hold, young women's occupational aspirations have become less sex-typed. That their behavior follows suit is seen in the unprecedented numbers of women training for what were formerly almost wholly male professional occupations. Employers, too, have responded to women's changing attitudes and behaviors. Because broader opportunities and diminished barriers have been accompanied by changing cultural values and heightened consciousness regarding gender equity, it is difficult to judge their relative impact. Nevertheless, we place central importance on removing the remaining barriers that prevent women from exercising free occupational choice and enjoying equal employment opportunity in the labor market.

Reducing Sex Segregation

Laws and regulations instituted in the 1960s and 1970s prohibit sex discrimination in employment and apprenticeship programs and mandate sex equity in federally funded job training programs and vocational and general education. Although their implementation was often slow and enforcement sometimes inadequate, the evidence indicates that when leadership has been strong, employers and educators have had adequate incentives, and resources have been allocated to eliminate barriers, women have made substantial progress in entering some predominantly male occupations and training and educational programs.

Definitively establishing that women's gains were caused directly by interventions is quite difficult, however. On one hand, the very existence of antidiscrimination laws or regulations may contribute to change. According to one theory underlying law enforcement, most change occurs through voluntary compliance by establishments against which no action has been taken, either out of the desire to avoid sanctions or because laws help to reshape employers' opinions about acceptable behavior. At the same time, laws encourage women to believe that they will not face discrimination and hence to train for and pursue sex-atypical occupations. On the other hand, important changes—including women's heightened consciousness of their rights and possibilities, prompted by the feminist movement—occurred during the period in which most interventions were implemented and were an important force for their enactment. Obviously, disentangling such cultural changes is difficult. Some of the studies that attempt to demonstrate the impact of specific laws or regulations are imperfect. Taken to-

gether, however, the case studies and statistical research present a compelling case for the long-term effectiveness of legislative remedies.

The decreases in federal enforcement effort that have occurred since 1981 and recent changes in the philosophy of enforcement, including reversals of federal civil rights policy in some areas, are likely to affect women's future employment opportunities. It remains to be seen what the effects will be. The evidence in this report suggests that the remedies introduced in the preceding two decades have generally reduced segregation. The committee is concerned that decreased federal effort and changes in policy will have negative effects, particularly because perceptions of reduced effort are likely to affect voluntary efforts.

Interventions in the Workplace

Most interventions to reduce segregation that have been implemented over the past two decades have been directed at the workplace. Data that assess their impact are limited, since evaluation was not a high priority for enforcement agencies. Most accounts of the enforcement process agree that the regulations have a history of uneven and often limited enforcement. Nevertheless, the evidence from case studies and statistical analyses supports the conclusion that when commitment to enforcement was vigorous and resources adequate, interventions contributed to increasing women's access to occupations, industries, and jobs that men have dominated. In particular, women's participation increased in three industries targeted for special emphasis by the Office for Federal Contract Compliance (banking, insurance, and mining); contractors in a special program in another industry, construction, admit that increases would not have occurred without goals and timetables. Fully implemented goals and timetables also fostered women's participation in apprenticeship programs.

Large increases in women's participation

in several predominantly male professions can be attributed in part to affirmative action programs. Some professional training programs actively recruited women students, and women were more willing to invest in extensive training with the assurance that jobs in the profession would be open to them.

Studies of firms against whom suits were filed show increases in the number of workers in sex-atypical occupations. This does not mean that segregation has been eliminated in these firms or others covered by statutes and regulations, but progress is undeniable. At the same time, however, many occupations and establishments appear to be almost untouched by the law. Surveys of large establishments indicate that the awareness of federal enforcement by top management has been an important factor in expanding the opportunities available to female employees. Restructuring personnel practices was often necessary to ensure women's access to some jobs. The association between managerial commitment and awareness of the enforcement of federal regulations supports the importance of strong federal enforcement of antidiscrimination laws.

The interventions that were least effective lacked either incentives for compliance or the support of those charged with their implementation. The link between these two factors indicates the necessity of including incentives in regulations: sanctions against violators or rewards for those in compliance. Evidence from the construction industry and certain apprenticeship programs demonstrates that goals and timetables are important for women's entry into male-dominated occupations. Goals create a demand for women that in turn generates a supply of applicants seeking training and jobs.

Interventions in Job Training

Job training programs also have potential for reducing sex segregation in work. The Comprehensive Employment and Training Act (CETA) was enacted in 1973 to provide job training and public service employment for the economically disadvantaged, unemployed, and underemployed with a goal of maximizing their employment options. In 1978 an amendment to CETA stipulated that all programs must contribute to the elimination of sex stereotyping. Evaluations of CETA's effects on women prior to the 1978 amendment suggest that it did not facilitate desegregation. CETA did support a few very effective small programs designed to increase women's participation in nontraditional occupations. These programs demonstrate the potential of federally sponsored training programs to integrate male craft and technical jobs and indicate that such programs can be effective intervention strategies.

Interventions in Education

It is more difficult to assess the impact on employment segregation of federal laws passed during the 1970s to eliminate discrimination and promote sex equity in general education. Foremost among them was Title IX of the 1972 Educational Amendments. To the extent that the educational system contributes to sex segregation in the workplace, legislation aimed at achieving sex equity in education may ultimately promote women's integration into customarily male jobs. Although women's participation in several male fields of study during the past decade has increased substantially, no evidence exists that allows us to attribute these increases directly to the enforcement of Title IX.

Evidence regarding the effectiveness of the 1976 amendments to the Vocational Education Act is clearer. These amendments called for vocational education programs that received federal funds to eliminate sex bias and stereotyping in vocational education programs. The effectiveness of this amendment has varied widely by state, suggesting that state laws or federal monitoring are necessary for the federal law to reduce sex bias. Where strong commitment was present at the state level, female students' representation in mixed or traditionally male programs increased substantially. State programs that were most successful established a broad support base for these women students and fostered contacts with prospective employers, much like the successful programs funded under CETA or sponsored by community groups. In both vocational education and job training, large-scale interventions have been less likely to show measurable success than smaller, locally run programs, probably because of the difficulty of ensuring replication in implementation.

Conclusion

Because the causes of segregation—cultural values, socialization, sex bias and tracking in the educational system and in job training programs, discrimination, and institutionalized and informal barriers in the workplace—interact with each other and operate together to restrict access to education, training, and employment in sex-atypical occupations, remedies are most likely to be effective when they address multiple causes (e.g., training combined with placement programs). That social values have changed during the same decades as remedies have been established is, of course, no coincidence. Changes in values and people's increasing willingness to entertain non-stereotyped possibilities create a context in which implementing remedies can be particularly effective.

POLICY RECOMMENDATIONS

Our recommendations are neither new nor startling. They do not detail new programs. Although there is still considerable debate within the scientific community about the causes of sex segregation in employment, there is little disagreement that barriers and constraints play a significant role. Our review of the available evidence regarding the effectiveness of the various remedies that

have been used to address sex segregation convinces us that many work when implemented properly. Consequently, our recommendations concern improving the enforcement of equal opportunity laws and expanding voluntary efforts in employment and education. The evidence also clearly indicates that leadership is a critical component of efforts to bring about change in this area. Committed leadership, in the executive and legislative branches, in businesses and workplaces, in schools, and in the national media, all contribute to a climate that encourages voluntary change and enhances the credibility of enforcement efforts.

Sex segregation is a deeply rooted social and cultural phenomenon. It is perpetuated not only by barriers and constraints, but also by habit and perceptions. Everyone's attitudes and behaviors, including women's, are affected by existing occupational patterns; even if there were no obvious discriminatory practices, these patterns would tend to be perpetuated. Consequently, our recommendations are addressed to employers and educational institutions as well as to enforcement agencies, and they concern family responsibilities as well as employment conditions.

Recommendations for Enforcement Agencies Regarding Employment

During the past decade sex segregation has broken down in many occupations, and substantial change has occurred in many others. Those changes would have been far less likely without governmental enforcement and private litigation. In view of these considerations, any reductions in personnel and budget for important federal enforcement agencies may have a negative effect on women's employment opportunities. Strong enforcement of antidiscrimination laws in employment has been effective in reducing sex segregation in the workplace. If this goal is to be pursued, enforcement agencies such as the Equal Employment

Opportunity Commission and the Office of Federal Contract Compliance Programs should continue to play an important role, by sustaining and improving efforts that have been shown to work and by developing new effective approaches. These agencies require sufficient resources to carry out their mandate.

Compliance and Enforcement

The rate at which sex segregation will continue to decline will be influenced by the magnitude of the efforts and the determination of agencies charged with enforcing antidiscrimination laws and regulations. Enforcement agencies particularly need clear policy direction and committed leadership. Laws and regulations prohibiting discrimination must be vigorously enforced to eliminate remaining barriers to equal employment opportunity in the workplace. Although the selection of particular strategies will continue to depend on the outcomes of political and judicial processes, goals and timetables have been effective, especially in highly sex-segregated industries, and the committee believes the use of these important tools should continue. Identification of particular areas has been effective and should be continued, with specific occupations and industries selected on the basis of women's representation in them. While individual claims must be processed efficiently, enforcement agencies should also pursue larger, more visible cases, because of their impact on other employers, employees, and the public generally. Employers with whom conciliation agreements or consent decrees have been reached should be monitored and adequate funding should be provided for this purpose.

Continued progress in reducing sex segregation will depend on the development and implementation of new and more effective enforcement strategies, improved coordination between programs focused on different aspects of the problem, and the identification of new approaches to pay equity. A major objection to occupational segregation is that to the extent it results from discrimination, it produces wage inequity. Even if strategies to reduce segregation are fully implemented, because of the stability built into the occupational structure, sex segregation will continue for a very long time. For this reason, we recommend the exploration of efforts to redress wage inequity as well as to reduce segregation. We urge the Equal Employment Opportunity Commission and the Office of Federal Contract Compliance Programs to explore and develop enforcement strategies that would ensure equitable pay for female-dominated jobs whose wage rates have been depressed by discrimination.

Although we believe wage equity strategies should be explored, we stress that the traditional equal access and affirmative action approaches are also necessary to ensure equal opportunity in the labor market. The two strategies are related: higher wages for women's jobs may encourage more men to enter them, thus enhancing integration, and strategies focused on integration may contribute to wage equity.

Research and Evaluation

The enforcement agencies should develop much stronger programs of policy-relevant research on such issues as the sources of change in occupations and industries in which the most rapid change has occurred; newly identified problems, such as sexual harassment; techniques for evaluating jobs and other issues related to pay equity; and the extent and causes of resegregation of jobs. In addition, policy evaluation units of enforcement agencies should study ways to improve the effectiveness of enforcement activities, including identifying the features of the most successful compliance or voluntary activities carried out by employers or others, analyzing the applicability and transferability of successful programs and the need for changes in laws and regulations, evaluating and exploring alternative strategies to assist in the most effective targeting of enforcement resources, and developing enforcement and training programs for newly emerging issues.

Recommendations for Employers

Voluntary action by employers has contributed a great deal to desegregating certain occupations and workplaces. The most important factors in employer action have been found to be, first, top managerial commitment and, second, communicating that commitment to employees at all levels. To this end, incorporating the goal of nondiscrimination in statements of corporate missions and building equal opportunity into a business's public image are vitally important.

Compliance with antidiscrimination laws and regulations is essential, but employers can do considerably more to achieve greater sex integration. Employers can pursue a more systematic approach that includes informing recruiters, managers, supervisors, and employees of the detrimental effects of sex-typed jobs; setting targets; identifying potentially discriminatory mechanisms; establishing monitoring procedures; including responsibility for achieving equal employment objectives in job descriptions; and evaluating and rewarding line managers for fulfilling those objectives. Women applicants for and employees in stereotypically female positions should be informed about and offered training for opportunities in predominantly male jobs. At the same time, job requirements and policies regarding promotion and on-the-job training (including the organization of seniority systems and collective bargaining agreements) should be reviewed to ensure access. Access and performance are also facilitated by the availability of equipment that is comfortable for both women and men and facilities such as locker rooms and rest rooms that are conveniently located.

Employers should also evaluate job-related compensation criteria and current job evaluation systems for sex bias and revise them if necessary. Compensation equity should extend to benefits, such as pension accruals and parental leave.

Employers should also pay close attention to the environment in their workplaces, because it is critically important. Employers can support informal networks that contribute to career advancement and information sharing and attempt to ensure that information systems are open. Women in atypical positions serve as positive role models, and both formal and informal networks enhance their contribution in encouraging others to follow them. The replacement of sex-biased training materials or offensive decorations can also contribute to an improved work climate. Employers should take appropriate disciplinary action against supervisors and employees who practice or condone sexual or other forms of harassment against women. The business environment can also be affected by considerations beyond the workplace. Work-related meetings or company-supported social events that take place at discriminatory clubs can convey a lack of commitment to equal employment opportunity goals and should be avoided.

In addition, we recommend that employers explore ways to make work schedules more flexible, with attention to both the workday and the sequencing of career stages, in order to ensure that employees with family responsibilities have equal access to all occupations and promotion opportunities. We believe that such options should be provided for both men and women across all the occupations and sectors of the firm, and we urge employers to encourage their use by parents of both sexes. To ensure that such policies are effective, organizations should take special care not to penalize men and women who elect part-time, flexible time, or parental leave options.

We recognize that, as useful as these remedies may be in reducing sex segregation, many employers may be unlikely to pursue them because of the costs involved as well as the inertia of established practices, unless they are encouraged to do so by government policy or by public or employee pressure. This is why the social and political climate that national leaders help to create is so critical. National leaders can point out that the social benefits of remedial action are greater than the apparent private costs. A supportive, encouraging public environment encourages voluntary compliance with the laws as well as other remedial actions. Employers who take such actions often subsequently find that the benefits to the firm, in terms of improved use of human resources, greater job satisfaction, and lower job turnover, outweigh the costs of change.

Recommendations for Education and Employment Training

While enforcement of equal opportunity laws in the employment area has been a major catalyst in improving women's position in the labor market, women's experiences prior to employment have important effects as well. Primary among these are education and employment training. Education and educational policy cannot by themselves eliminate job segregation by sex, of course, but educational authorities and schools at all levels can take measures that will promote integration. Sex equity in the public schools is already a matter of federal law under Title IX of the 1972 Educational Amendment and the 1976 Amendments to the Vocational Education Act. Compliance with these laws is an important first step; the responsible federal agencies must increase their enforcement and monitoring efforts, which have been very small.

Elementary schools should provide girls and boys with nonstereotyped information about a broad range of occupations and encourage them—without regard to sex, race, or ethnicity—to begin thinking about the wide range of possibilities they might pursue. Schools should also eliminate sex-stereotyped teaching materials dealing with family and home responsibilities or personal interests. Secondary educational institutions should develop programs that heighten teachers', counselors', and students' awareness of the economic consequences of sex segregation. They should encourage female and minority students to consider the consequences of alternative curricula and especially encourage their enrollment in mathematics and science courses that will enable them to prepare for and pursue scientific, technical, and professional occupations. The expected growth of new computer-related occupations makes it imperative that girls be encouraged to become comfortable with computer learning at both the primary and secondary levels. All students should be encouraged to enroll in courses on a non-segregated basis, and social and academic support should be provided to students who select classes that are atypical for their sex. Schools should also try to involve parents by informing them of educational and employment opportunities for their children.

Many of these recommendations apply also to postsecondary educational institutions. In the past, college women's choice of majors and their occupational aspirations became more stereotypically female as they advanced in college. Special academic, vocational, and personal counseling can help women to realize sex-atypical aspirations and to encourage others to pursue fields in which women are underrepresented. Academic departments in which women are underrepresented should determine whether subtle biases tend to discourage them and take action to eliminate the biases.

In the area of formal vocational education and employment training, states and local school districts need to make much greater efforts to comply with the Vocational Education Equity Amendment's mandate to eliminate sex stereotyping. Federally assisted secondary and postsecondary vocational education programs should make sex-integrated vocational education an explicit goal, and programs should allocate resources among vocational education areas to maximize students' training in marketable skills. Vocational educators must inform themselves about changing patterns of female employment, including women's growing work-life expectancy, and about wage differences between stereotypically male and female occupations. Special efforts are necessary to make traditionally male curricula hospitable to women and to encourage women's enrollment in historically male courses that provide skills and information useful for many craft and technical jobs. Links with employers in the community that can provide placement opportunities for graduates are particularly important for sex-atypical programs.

Continuing education programs offer women a second chance to enhance their employment options. Such programs should be encouraged to inform returning students about the consequences of occupational segregation and to provide counseling regarding career moves across sex-typed occupations that would lead to higher earnings or better prospects for advancement.

Federal training and employment programs should be continued, with increased efforts to prepare women and men for sex-atypical employment. Training must be accompanied by placement facilities. Program evaluation should be based in part on numbers of persons trained for and placed in jobs that are not typical for their sex. Counseling and support should be continued after job placement because discouragement and harassment are often problems for women workers in sex-atypical jobs. In addition, women who support themselves and dependents should be targeted for training in well-paid nontraditional areas. Age restrictions should be eliminated from apprenticeship programs. Affirmative steps to recruit women should be employed when veterans' preference policies operate against them.

Recommendations Concerning Family Responsibilities

An important factor outside the labor market that affects women's labor market performance and opportunities is the way in which family life is typically organized in our society. Although we have not been able to quantify the degree to which the organization of family life affects sex segregation in the workplace, it is our judgment that both beliefs and practices concerning family care contribute to segregation, and that better and more flexible child care is critical for change. The care of children and family members still appears to be largely women's responsibility, and this responsibility undoubtedly conflicts with their entrance into and advancement in a number of occupations that routinely require overtime, job-related travel, or inflexible or irregular hours. Moreover, a widespread belief that women rather than men should be primarily responsible for children and family care probably contributes negatively to attitudes toward women workers and their treatment in nearly all occupations and work situations. It is critical that assumptions about women's responsibilities for children and families not be used as a basis for discrimination.

Because half of all mothers of preschool children and more than half of those of school-age children are in the labor force, and fathers are nearly universally so, opportunities for combining paid work and parenting that reduce the strain on parents and children are needed. Policies to encourage such opportunities also serve a broader public policy goal of facilitating the best use of available human resources by reducing constraints. Child care of good quality is the most critical service that needs to be provided. While most parents wish to play a major role in caring for their children, doing so is not incompatible with public or private child care assistance. Child care facilities should be sufficiently varied and flexible to accommodate both the different needs families experience at various stages in the domestic cycle and varying parental preferences. Establishing flexible alternatives may require an expansion of existing federal policies that involve an array of approaches, such as tax incentives to employers who set up work-site day care centers, small business loans for neighborhood centers, public support of such facilities for low-income families, and larger and more flexible child care income tax credits or deductions for parents. Local and state initiatives can include extending the services that schools provide.

While more equal sharing by men and women of child care and other home tasks may await change in gender ideology, policy can affect that process. Workplace policies that allow flexible scheduling of work time, part-time employment for both sexes across all occupations in a firm, and paternity as well as maternity leave will help to reduce sex segregation. Such inclusive policies will neutralize the inclination to view such arrangements as necessary only for women and may thereby encourage men to experiment with alternative allocations of their time and energy between home and the workplace. We also encourage the ongoing reexamination of the federal income tax and social security systems to attempt to bring about more equitable treatment of two-earner couples compared with single-earner families, because it would also facilitate the reallocation of paid and family time between husbands and wives. Policies that facilitate more equal sharing will enhance the ability of both sexes to combine parenting with paid work without undue hardship and will undoubtedly advance equal employment opportunity as well.

DATA AND RESEARCH RECOMMENDATIONS

Throughout this report we point to the need for further research, better data, and improved measurement techniques. Here we review and amplify these points.

Data Collection

Policies for reducing occupational segregation require accurate data on the extent, causes, and consequences of the phenomenon. The most pressing data needs are the collection of establishment-level data and longitudinal data on individuals; the improvement of data necessary to assess the effectiveness of statutes and regulations prohibiting employment discrimination; the improvement of data on the extent of occupational segregation, particularly by ethnicity; and the collection of observational data concerning the processes of discrimination and job segregation and the responses of individuals and organizations to change.

Establishment-Level Data

Although much research concludes that employer personnel policies are an important cause of occupational sex segregation, only a small portion of this research is based on establishment-level data. Establishment-level data can yield considerable additional information over census-based materials. For example, a study by Bielby and Baron (1984), based on a sample of California firms, revealed nearly total sex segregation when employer definitions of job categories were used, a degree of segregation much higher than that found in studies based on census job classifications. At the present time, no nationally representative sample of firms that contains information on job segregation or personnel policies or occupations more generally exists. Such a data base would not only allow one to determine the generalizability of Bielby and Baron's findings to the economy at large, but would also permit assessment of the impact of specific employer personnel policies on segregation. We recognize that a sample of firms is not easy to develop. Two important sources of difficulty are the lack of a sampling frame for firms in the American economy and the need to secure employer cooperation. The benefits of such a national sample for this and other issues suggest the value of developing this data base. Progress in determining the effects of job segregation on the earnings gap between the sexes will depend on developing sources of more detailed data than the census-detailed occupational classification provides. Data on jobs will necessarily be of limited generalizability, but the potential contribution of up-to-date firm- or establishment-level data outweighs this limitation. At the present time, some establishment-level job data are available as the result of disclosure during court cases resulting from complaints of discrimination. While some such disclosed information is later sealed, some of it remains available. An extremely useful service that could be provided by a research center or a public agency would be the gathering, editing, and documenting of this material (which is sometimes available on computer tape) to preserve confidentiality and make it accessible and usable by researchers.

Longitudinal Data on Individuals

Much recent job segregation research based on samples of individual workers has emphasized the importance of careers, job ladders, and job mobility. Several existing nationally representative longitudinal data bases—the University of Michigan Panel Study of Income Dynamics, the National Longitudinal Surveys at Ohio State University, the Continuous Work History Survey, and the National Longitudinal Study of the high school class of 1972—have been in-

valuable. These sample surveys generally contain 10-15 years' information on the same individuals, but, because such a time horizon captures only part of a worker's career mobility, these data bases must continue to be funded so that data for completed careers are available for some cohorts of workers. In addition, consideration should be given to developing a longitudinal sample that would include all job changes and full job event histories, not simply records of job status at year end or time of interview, as is the case with currently available samples.

Data to Assess the Effectiveness of Laws

Assessing the efficacy of statutes and regulations prohibiting employment discrimination is very difficult. In part this is due to the intrinsic difficulty of distinguishing among various causes of change in a complex society. The problem is exacerbated by the lack of adequate data on the activities of enforcement agencies and their results and by an even greater lack of data about individual litigation. No systematic data regarding complaints filed and their disposition are available. When individuals privately pursue their cases through the courts, little is known about settlements, in court or out. It may be possible to develop a sampling method for private cases and to compile data more systematically from state and federal enforcement agencies. More detailed data on patterns of job segregation in individual enterprises would facilitate research on changes that occur in these employment patterns as a consequence of intervention by enforcement agencies and would greatly improve our ability to assess the effectiveness of equal employment opportunity policies.

Data on Race and Ethnicity

In order to understand the patterns and effects of occupational segregation, data must be tabulated by race and ethnicity as well as sex. Currently, most tabulations are restricted to white-black distinctions. Yet for particular regions of the country the pattern of occupational sex segregation varies by other ethnic and racial groups as well. Although, even in the census and the Current Population Survey, problems of sample size sometimes preclude tabulating data for small population groups in small areas, efforts should be made to provide such tabulations whenever possible.

Data From Workplace Studies

The collection of observational and interview data from intensive studies of workplaces should be encouraged. We have very few detailed studies of power in workplaces, especially as it pertains to race, sex, and ethnic differences. By what processes do discrimination and job segregation occur? How are they maintained? Similarly, we have virtually no studies of the texture of change within organizations in response to equal employment opportunity policies. Who resists and how? Who gains? How meaningful and long-lasting are the gains? What is needed to answer this type of question is close observation of workplaces (and such related organizations as unions or families) and the collection of qualitative as well as quantitative data about people's experiences, their attitudes toward change, and their adjustment to new social arrangements.

Measurement

The census occupational classifications need considerable scrutiny. Almost all research on job segregation uses the census job definitions. Yet some job groups are covered in much greater detail than others. To the extent that such differences in coverage are correlated with the sex composition of the job categories, a biased picture of segregation is obtained. For example, if male-dominated occupations are categorized in more detail than female-dominated occu-

pations, men's occupational mobility relative to women's may very well be exaggerated. If, however, the census aggregates several different segregated jobs into a single category, then a census-based segregation index will necessarily understate the degree of segregation.

In the 1970 census classification, occupations that were at least 80 percent female were about three times as large as those at least 80 percent male (Treiman and Hartmann, 1981). Whether this reflects the crowding of women into a few jobs, as some have claimed, or finer census distinctions among jobs dominated by men than among those dominated by women remains an open question. This issue could be investigated by comparing job classifications from firms (of the kind we call for above) with the census detailed occupational classification. If the average number of job titles mapping onto each occupational category is larger for those census categories in which most incumbents are women than for those in which most incumbents are men, distortion in the creation of occupational categories, rather than crowding, would be suggested. The utility of making comparisons using disaggregated lists of job titles from other sources, such as the titles listed in the Census Classified Index of Occupations, the job titles offered by individuals in response to open-ended questions in sample surveys, and job titles used in help-wanted advertisements, should also be explored. Analysis of what jobs entail may also be warranted. It is not impossible, for example, that common usage results in many vastly different jobs being labeled "secretary." In such a case, titles that convey finer functional distinctions should be developed and adopted.

Research

Research is needed to assess several explanations that have been proposed to explain sex segregation. In particular, we recommend further study of how occupational aspirations are formed and how they may be linked to occupational outcomes. Although we know that the sexes differ from childhood in their occupational aspirations, our understanding of both the formation of these aspirations and any effect on occupational outcomes is quite limited. Prospective studies that follow individuals from before their entry into the labor force to well into their careers would clarify the ways that aspirations and prejudices contribute to segregation in the workplace. Of particular interest are the effects of adolescents' occupational aspirations, as well as their expectations, on their early and subsequent occupational outcomes. Although no studies have yet demonstrated a definite link between sex-typed preferences and sex-typed occupational outcomes, it is entirely possible that such a link exists. It would be important to know whether having traditional preferences tends to be correlated with being in sex-typical occupations.

Studies of both female and male workers that clarify the nature of any relationships between workers' personal characteristics, occupational values, education, and preemployment training, on one hand, and various occupational characteristics (e.g., skill requirements), on the other, would also reveal the extent of the match between workers' choices and their subsequent occupations.

The connections between workers' family responsibilities, their occupational choices, and their job outcomes also require further study. To date, the human capital explanation for occupational segregation has received at best mixed empirical support; direct investigation of whether women choose various occupations because they think they will accommodate family care responsibilities would contribute to a better understanding of this model. Family responsibilities may also affect men's work decisions, and their decision-making processes should also be studied. It would also be important to learn how and to what extent husbands and fathers influence women's decisions

about the work they pursue and the time they contribute to family care.

Our knowledge of how labor markets operate suggests the importance of occupational information for workers' access to jobs. Not enough is known, however, about how people acquire information about occupations, how the sexes differ in their knowledge of sex-typical and sex-atypical occupations, or how this knowledge is linked to their occupational outcomes. More generally, research on how both sexes make decisions about vocational training and job search strategies would also bear on the human capital explanations for occupational segregation.

Additional investigation is also necessary to determine what kinds of barriers exist in labor markets and within establishments to workers' movement into and their retention in sex-atypical jobs and how they might be improved. In many occupations job training represents the primary vehicle through which workers move up job ladders. Very little is known, however, about differences in the sexes' access to on-the-job training, the type of training available to workers in typically female and male occupations, and whether the benefits of training are similar for the sexes. We encourage in-depth studies of large firms to determine what features of firms' internal labor markets—including opportunities for on-the-job training—restrict or foster workers' access to sex-atypical jobs. Such in-depth studies, if extended to workers' and employers' behavior through observation and interview, could also increase our understanding of various more general phenomena related to discrimination and opportunity, such as group cohesion and informal information networks. One way to shed light on some of these issues would be to study belief systems concerning women and work, in order to understand the structure of beliefs that underlie employer decisions, career selection, and coworker response. Another important aspect of the problem of discrimination within workplaces is discrimination in work-related social life, particularly the conduct of business in single-sex environments, such as clubs and sports. The reasons for the perpetuation of these single-sex organizations and their importance for work life should be further explored.

Several studies that we reviewed revealed considerable mobility by workers of both sexes between sex-typical and sex-atypical occupations. The movement of workers out of occupations not customarily held by persons of their sex is consistent with the existence of structural and informal barriers to workers' success and retention in sex-atypical jobs. We recommend systematic case studies that compare the experiences of workers in sex-typical and sex-atypical jobs on several dimensions to determine the factors associated with retention in sex-atypical occupations. In general, during the 1970s, women's movement into occupations that men have dominated was not matched by men's movement into traditionally female nonprofessional occupations. Additional research is needed to determine whether employers resist employing men in these jobs or whether men avoid them because they lack the necessary training, seek higher wages, or fear that they will be stigmatized. It will also be interesting to see whether young women who have entered formerly male-dominated occupations have careers and age-earnings profiles similar to their male counterparts, or whether, like earlier female cohorts, their earnings and career prospects tend to fall off over time.

Some observers have speculated that occupational integration may be a temporary phenomenon; they suggest that the entry of substantial numbers of sex-atypical workers into an occupation may ultimately be followed by its becoming dominated by members of that sex. As evidence they typically offer historical examples; we found no systematic research on resegregation. Not enough time has elapsed since women's recent movement into some formerly male-dominated occupations to determine if those occupations will become predominantly female. It is important to learn whether integrating occupations tend to be unstable and if integration or resegregation is accompanied by change in real wages or occupational status or the development of new barriers to free occupational choices. If resegregation occurs, it may be because opportunities remain limited in yet other sectors of the labor market, so that women flock to the few newly available jobs. Whether resegregation is a "second generation" response to efforts at integration warrants investigation. If women's gains are subverted anew by new mechanisms, the prospects for lasting improvements require new understanding, regardless of the effectiveness of current strategies for desegregation.

Further research is also necessary to determine the conditions under which various interventions contribute to reduced sex segregation that is sustained in the long run. In particular, we recommend closer study of the channels through which the statistically observed effects of federal enforcement agencies, such as the Equal Employment Opportunity Commission and the Office of Federal Contract Compliance Programs, occur. Much of the evidence regarding the effectiveness of federal regulations against employment discrimination is based on comparisons of black and white men. Research that compares race and sex groups is needed to test whether race effects also hold for gender. We noted above the enormous need for policy-relevant research on such issues as the effectiveness of targeting and the replicability of remedies. We do not know how the intensity of effort is linked to the magnitude of change and which strategies are most cost-effective. Without such knowledge we cannot know whether greater enforcement efforts or different enforcement tools are necessary to further reduce sex segregation.

References

Aga, Synnøva
1984 "I'll never go back to women's work again!" Women's Studies International Forum 7 (6): 441-448.

Ahart, Gregory J.
1976 "A process evaluation of the contract compliance program in nonconstruction industry." Industrial and Labor Relations Review 29 (July):565-571.

Aigner, Dennis and Glen Cain
1977 "Statistical theories of discrimination in labor markets." Industrial and Labor Relations Review 30:175-187.

Allison, Elisabeth K.
1976 "Sex linked earning differentials in the beauty industry." Journal of Human Resources 11 (Summer):383-90.

Almquist, Elizabeth
1974 "Sex stereotypes in occupational choice: the case of college women." Journal of Vocational Behavior 5 (August):13-21.

Almquist, Elizabeth M. and Shirley S. Angrist
1970 "Career salience and atypicality of occupational choice among college women." Journal of Marriage and the Family 32:242-9.
1971 "Role model influences on college women's career aspirations." Merrill-Palmer Quarterly 17 (July):263-79.

Arrow, Kenneth
1972 "Models of job discrimination." Pp. 83-102 in Anthony H. Pascal (ed.), Racial Discrimination in Economic Life. Lexington, Mass.: D.C. Heath.

Ashenfelter, Orley and James Heckman
1976 "Measuring the effect of an antidiscrimination program." In Orley Ashenfelter and James Blum (eds.), Evaluating the Effects of Social Programs. Princeton, N.J.: Princeton University Press.

Astin, Alexander W. and R.J. Panos
1969 The Educational and Vocational Development of College Students. Washington, D.C.: American Council on Education.

Astin, Helen S.
1969 The Woman Doctorate in America: Origins, Career and Family. New York: Russell Sage Foundation.

Astin, Helen S. and Mary Beth Snyder
1982 "Affirmative action 1972-1982: a decade of response." Change 14 (July/August):26-31, 59.

Atkin, Charles K.
1975 Effects of Television Advertising on Children. Second Year Experimental Evidence. Michigan State University, Department of Communication.

Axelson, Leland J.
1970 "The Working Wife: Differences in Perception Among Negro and White Males." Journal of Marriage and the Family 32 (August):457-464.

Bachman, Jerald G., Lloyd D. Johnston, and Patrick M. O'Malley
1980 Monitoring the Future: Questionnaire Responses from the Nation's High School Seniors. Ann Arbor: University of Michigan, Institute for Social Research.

Baer, Judith A.
1978 The Chains of Protection: The Judicial Response to Women's Labor Legislation. Westport, Conn.: Greenwood Press.

Barrett, Nancy S.
1979 "Women in the job market: unemployment and work schedules." Pp. 63-98 in Ralph E. Smith (ed.), The Subtle Revolution: Women at Work. Washington, D.C.: The Urban Institute.

Barrett, Nancy S. and Richard D. Morgenstern
1974   "Why do blacks and women have high un-
        employment rates?" Journal of Human Re-
        sources 9 (Fall):452-64.
1977   The Determinants of Unemployment Among
        Blacks and Women: A Cross Sectional Analysis.
        Unpublished paper.

Barron, Deborah Durfee and Daniel Yankelovich
1980   Today's American Woman: How the Public Sees
        Her. Prepared for the President's Advisory
        Committee for Women by the Public Agenda
        Foundation (December).

Basow, Susan A. and Karen Glasser Howe
1979   "Model influence on career choices of college
        students." Vocational Guidance Quarterly
        27:239-43.

Bass, Bernard M., Judith Krussell, and Ralph A. Alexander
1971   "Male managers' attitudes toward working
        women." American Behavioral Scientist 15:221-
        36.

Beach, A.M.
1977   A Review of Literature Concerning Behaviors
        Which Inhibit or Reduce Sex Bias and Sex Role
        Stereotyping. Report to the U.S. Office of Ed-
        ucation. Washington, D.C.: U.S. Department
        of Health, Education, and Welfare.

Beardslee, D.C. and D.D. O'Dowd
1962   "Students and the occupational world." In N.
        Sanford (ed.), The American College. New York:
        Wiley.

Beattie, Muriel Yoshida and Leslie A. Diehl
1979   "Effects of social conditions on the expression
        of sex-role stereotypes." Psychology of Women
        Quarterly 4:241-55.

Beck, E.M., Patrick M. Horan, and Charles M. Tolbert
1980   "Industrial segmentation and labor market dis-
        crimination." Social Problems 28 (Decem-
        ber):113-30.

Becker, Gary S.
1957   The Economics of Discrimination. Second edi-
        tion, 1971. Chicago: University of Chicago
        Press.
1974   "A theory of marriage." Pp 299-344 in Theodore
        W. Schultz (ed.), Economics of the Family:
        Marriage, Children and Human Capital. A
        Conference Report of the National Bureau of
        Economic Research. Chicago: University of
        Chicago Press.

Bell, Carolyn
1979   "Implementing safety and health regulations
        for women in the workplace." Feminist Studies
        5 (Summer):286-301.

Beller, Andrea H.
1978   "The economics of enforcement of an antidis-
        crimination law: Title VII of the Civil Rights
        Act of 1964." Journal of Law and Economics
        21 (October):359-80.
1979   "The impact of equal employment opportunity
        laws on the male/female earnings differential."
        In Cynthia B. Lloyd, Emily S. Andrews, and
        Curtis L. Gilroy (eds.), Women in the Labor
        Market. New York: Columbia University Press.
1980   "The effect of economic conditions on the suc-
        cess of equal employment opportunity laws."
        Review of Economics and Statistics 62 (Au-
        gust):379-87.
1981   The Impact of Education on Entry into Non-
        traditional Occupations. Revision of paper pre-
        sented at the Econometric Society meetings,
        Denver, Colorado, September, 1980 (March).
1982a   "The impact of equal opportunity policy on sex
        differentials in earnings and occupations."
        American Economic Review (May):171-5.
1982b   "Occupational segregation by sex: determi-
        nants and changes." Journal of Human Re-
        sources 17 (Winter):371-2.
1984   "Trends in occupational segregation by sex,
        1960-1981." Pp. 11-26 in Barbara F. Reskin
        (ed.), Sex Segregation in the Workplace: Trends,
        Explanations, Remedies. Washington, D.C.:
        National Academy Press.

Beller, Andrea H. and Kee-ok Kim Han
1984   "Occupational sex segregation: prospects for the
        1980s." Pp. 91-114 in Barbara F. Reskin (ed.),
        Sex Segregation in the Workplace: Trends, Ex-
        planations, Remedies. Washington, D.C.: Na-
        tional Academy Press.

Beller, Daniel J.
1981   "Coverage patterns of full-time employees un-
        der private retirement plans." Social Security
        Bulletin 44 (July):3-29.

Bem, Sandra L. and Daryl J. Bem
1973   "Does sex-biased job advertising 'aid and abet'
        sex discrimination?" Journal of Applied Social
        Psychology 3:6-18.

Benbow, Pamilla P. and Julian C. Stanley
1983   "Sex differences in mathematical reasoning
        ability: more facts." Science 222:1029-31 (De-
        cember 2).

Bendix, Reinhard, Seymour M. Lipset, and F. Theodore Malm
1954   "Social origins and occupational career plans."
        Industrial and Labor Relations Review 7 (Jan-
        uary):246-61.

Benham, Lee
1975   Nonmarket returns to women's investment in
        education. In Cynthia B. Lloyd, ed., Sex Dis-
        crimination and the Division of Labor. New
        York: Columbia University Press.

Benson, Helene A.
1980   Women and Private Pension Plans. Paper pre-
        sented to the Advisory Council on Employee
        Welfare and Pension Benefit Plans (Novem-
        ber).

Bergmann, Barbara R.
1971   "The effect on white incomes of discrimination
        in employment." Journal of Political Economy
        79 (March/April):294-313.
1974   "Occupational segregation, wages and profits
        when employers discriminate by race or sex."
        Eastern Economic Journal 1 (April/July):103-
        10.

Bergmann, Barbara R. and William Darity
1981   "Social relations, productivity, and employer discrimination." Monthly Labor Review 104 (April):47-9.

Berk, Sarah Fenstermaker
1979   "Husbands at home: organization of the husband's household day." Pp. 125-58 in K.W. Feinstein (ed.), Working Women and Families. Beverly Hills: Sage.

Berryman, Sue E.
1983   Who Will Do Science?—Trends and Their Causes, in Minority and Female Representation among Holders of Advanced Degrees in Science and Mathematics. New York: The Rockefeller Foundation.

Berryman, Sue E. and Winston K. Chow
1981   "CETA: is it equitable for women?" Pp. 153-8 in Increasing the Earnings of Disadvantaged Women. Washington, D.C.: National Commission for Employment Policy.

Berryman, Sue E., Winston K. Chow, and Robert M. Bell
1981   "CETA: is it equitable for women?" Rand Note N-1683-NCEP. Santa Monica, Calif.: The Rand Corporation.

Bianchi, Suzanne M. and Nancy F. Rytina
1984   Occupational Change, 1970-1980. Paper prepared for the annual meeting of the Population Association of America, Minneapolis, May 4.

Bielby, Denise Del Vento
1978a   "Career sex-atypicality and career involvement of college educated women: baseline evidence from the 1960's." Sociology of Education 51:7-28.
1978b   "Maternal unemployment and socioeconomic status as factors in daughter's career salience: some substantive refinements." Sex Roles 4:249-65.

Bielby, William T. and James N. Baron
1984   "A woman's place is with other women: sex segregation within organizations." Pp. 27-55 in Barbara F. Reskin (ed.), Sex Segregation in the Workplace: Trends, Explanations, Remedies. Washington, D.C.: National Academy Press.
1986   "Men and women at work: sex segregation and statistical discrimination." American Journal of Sociology 91 (4): January.

Bingham, William C. and Elaine W. House
1973   "Counselors view women and work: accuracy of information." Vocational Guidance Quarterly 21:262-8.

Bird, Caroline
1979   The Two-Paycheck Marriage: How Women at Work are Changing Life in America. New York: Rowson, Wade.

Blakemore, Judith E.O., Asenath A. LaRue, and Antony B. Olejnik
1979   "Sex-appropriate toy preference and the ability to conceptualize toys as sex-role related." Developmental Psychology 15:339-40.

Blau, Francine D.
1977   Equal Pay in the Office. Lexington, Mass: Lexington Books.
1984a   "Discrimination against women: theory and evidence." Pp. 53-89 in William A. Darity (ed.), Labor Economics: Modern Views. Boston: Martinus Nijhoff.
1984b   "Occupational segregation and labor market discrimination." Pp. 117-143 in Barbara F. Reskin (ed.), Sex Segregation in the Workplace: Trends, Explanations, Remedies. Washington, D.C.: National Academy Press.

Blau, Francine D. and Wallace E. Hendricks
1979   "Occupational segregation by sex: trends and prospects." Journal of Human Resources 14 (2):197-210.

Blau, Francine D. and Carol L. Jusenius
1976   "Economists' approaches to sex segregation in the labor market: an appraisal." Pp. 181-99 in Martha Blaxall and Barbara Reagan (eds.), Women and the Workplace: The Implications of Occupational Segregation. Chicago: University of Chicago Press.

Blau, Francine D. and Lawrence M. Kahn
1981a   "Causes and consequences of layoffs." Economic Inquiry 19 (April):270-96.
1981b   "Race and sex differences in quits by young workers." Industrial and Labor Relations Review 34 (July):563-77.

Block, Jeanne H.
1976   "Issues, problems and pitfalls in assessing sex differences: a critical review of *The Psychology of Sex Differences*." Merrill-Palmer Quarterly 22:283-308.

Blumberg, Rae Lesser
1978   Stratification: Socioeconomic and Sexual Inequality. Dubuque, Iowa: William C. Brown.

Bose, Christine E. and Peter H. Rossi
1983   "Prestige standings of occupations as affected by gender." American Sociological Review 48 (June):316-30.

Boserup, Ester
1970   Woman's Role in Economic Development. New York: St. Martin's Press.

Bourne, Patricia and Norma Wikler
1978   "Commitment and the cultural mandate: women in medicine." Social Problems 25:430-9.

Brenner, O.C. and Joseph Tomkiewicz
1979   "Job orientation of males and females: are sex differences declining?" Personnel Psychology 32:741-50.

Brenner, Patricia
1981   "Sex equity in the schools." Pp. 41-85 in Increasing the Earnings of Disadvantaged Women. Report no. 11. Washington, D.C.: National Commission for Employment Policy.

Bridges, William P.
1980   "Industry marginality and female employment: a new appraisal." American Sociological Review 45 (February):58-75.

Bridges, William P. and Richard A. Berk
1978   "Sex, earnings, and the nature of work: a job-level analysis of male-female income differences." Social Science Quarterly 58 (March):553-65.

Brief, Arthur P. and L.J. Aldag
1975   "Male-female differences in occupational attitudes within minority groups." Journal of Vocational Behavior 6:305-14.

Briggs, Norma
1981   "Overcoming barriers to successful entry and retention of women in traditionally male skilled blue-collar trades in Wisconsin." Pp. 106-31 in Vernon M. Briggs, Jr. and Felician Foltman (eds.), Apprenticeship Research: Emerging Findings and Future Trends. Ithaca: New York State School of Industrial Relations.

Brito, Patricia K. and Carol L. Jusenius
1978   "Sex segregation in the labor market: an analysis of young college women's occupational preferences." Pp. 57-75 in Frank L. Mott (ed.), Women, Work, and Family: Dimensions of Change in American Society. Lexington, Mass.: Lexington Books.

Brown, Charles
1982   "The federal attack on labor market discrimination: the mouse that roared?" Pp. 33-58 in Ronald Ehrenberg, ed., Research in Labor Economics. Vol. V. Greenwich, Conn.: JAI Press.

Brown, Judith K.
1970   "A note on the division of labor by sex." American Anthropologist 72(5).

Brush, Lorelei R.
1979   Why Women Avoid the Study of Mathematics: A Longitudinal Study. Report to the National Institute of Education by Abt Associates Inc., Cambridge, Mass.

Buckley, John E.
1971   "Pay differences between men and women in the same job." Monthly Labor Review 94 (November):36-9.

Bumpass, Larry
1982   Employment Among Mothers of Young Children: Changing Behavior and Attitudes. Center for Demography and Ecology working paper no. 82-25. University of Wisconsin, Madison.

Burbridge, Lynn C.
1984   The Impact of Changes in Policy on the Federal Equal Employment Opportunity Effort. Washington, D.C.: Urban Institute.

Burlin, F.
1976   "Sex role stereotyping: occupational aspirations of female high school students." The School Counselor 24:102-8.

Burstein, Paul
1983   Some Intended, Unintended and Unnoticed Consequences of EEO Legislation. Unpublished paper.

Burton, Michael L., Lilyan A. Brudner, and Douglas R. White
1977   "A model of the sexual division of labor." American Ethnologist 4(2):227-251.

Butler, Richard and James J. Heckman
1977   "The impact of the government on the labor market status of black Americans: a critical review." In Industrial Relations Research Association, Equal Rights and Industrial Relations, Madison, Wis.

Byrne, E.
1983   "Women and mining—policies for opening up blue collar work." Equal Opportunities International 2:14-19.

Cabral, Robert, Marianne A. Ferber, and Carole A. Green
1981   "Men and women in fiduciary institutions: a study of sex differences in career development." Review of Economics and Statistics 63 (November):573-80.

Cain, Glen G.
1966   Married Women in the Labor Force. Chicago: University of Chicago Press.
1984   The Economic Analysis of Labor Market Discrimination: A Survey. Special Report Series SR 37. Institute for Research on Poverty, Madison, Wis.

Campbell, Margaret A.
1973   "Why would a girl go into medicine?" In Medical Education in the United States: A Guide for Women. Old Westbury, N.Y.: Feminist Press.

Caplette, Michele K.
1981   Women in Book Publishing: A Study of Careers and Organizations. Ph.D. dissertation, State University of New York, Stony Brook.

Caplow, Theodore
1954   The Sociology of Work. Minneapolis: University of Minnesota Press.

Carey, Max L.
1981   "Occupational employment growth through 1990." Monthly Labor Review 104 (August):42-55.

Carruthers, Sandy
1980   Don't Believe Those Pipe-lines! Getting Women into Skilled Trades. Paper presented at the Conference on the Experience of Women in Employment and Training Programs held by the National Commission for Employment Policy, Washington, D.C. (September).

Carter, D.B. and C.J. Patterson
1979   Sex Roles as Social Conventions: The Development of Children's Conceptions of Sex-Role Stereotypes. Unpublished manuscript, University of Michigan.

Cassell, Frank H. and Samuel L. Doctors
1972   A Three Company Study of the Intrafirm Mobility of Blue Collar and Lower Level White Collar Workers. Chicago: Northwestern University. (ETA-ORD-NTIS, PB226184).

Casserly, Patricia Lund
1979   Helping Able Young Women Take Math and Science Seriously in School. New York: The College Board.
1982   Encouraging Young Women to Persist and Achieve in Mathematics: What Works. Paper presented at the 1982 annual meetings of the American Psychological Association, Washington, D.C.

Cherlin, Andrew, and Pamela B. Walters
1981   "Trends in United States men's and women's sex-role attitudes: 1972 to 1978." American Sociological Review 46 (August):453-60.

Clauss, Carin
1982   Legal Factors Affecting Job Segregation by Sex: An Assessment of the Impact on Job Segregation of Barriers Imposed or Permitted by Law. Paper presented at the Workshop on Job Segregation by Sex, Committee on Women's Employment and Related Social Issues, National Research Council, Washington, D.C. (May).

Committee on Education and Employment of Women in Science and Engineering
1983   Climbing the Ladder: An Update on the Status of Doctoral Women Scientists and Engineers. National Research Council. Washington, D.C.: National Academy Press.

Condry, John and Sharon Condry
1976   "Sex differences: a study of the eye of the beholder." Child Development 47 (September):812-19.

Corcoran, Mary, Greg Duncan, and Michael Ponza
1984   "Work experience, job segregation, and wages." Pp. 171-191 in Barbara F. Reskin (ed.), Sex Segregation in the Workplace: Trends, Explanations, Remedies. Washington, D.C.: National Academy Press.

Cornfield, Daniel B.
1981   Job Loss, Layoffs, and the Sexes. Paper presented at annual meeting of American Sociological Association, Toronto (August).

Darland, M.G., S.M. Dawkins, J.L. Lovasich, E.L. Scott, M.E. Sherman, and J.Z. Whipple
1974   "Applications of multivariate regression to studies of salary differences between men and women faculty." In Proceedings of the Social Statistics Section of the American Statistical Association. Washington, D.C.: American Statistical Association.

Davidson, Emily S., Amy Yasuna, and Alan Tower
1979   "The effects of television cartoons on sex-role stereotyping in young girls." Child Development 50:597-600.

Davies, Margery W.
1975   "Woman's place is at the typewriter: the feminization of the clerical labor force." Pp. 279-96 in Richard Edwards, Michael Reich, and D. Gordon (eds.), Labor Market Segmentation. Lexington, Mass.: D.C. Heath.

1982   Woman's Place is at the Typewriter: Office Work and Office Workers, 1870-1930. Philadelphia: Temple University Press.

Davis, James A.
1965   Undergraduate Career Decisions. Chicago: Aldine.

Davis, Natalie Zemon
1975   "Women on top." Pp. 124-51 in Natalie Zemon Davis (ed.), Society and Culture in Early Modern France. Stanford, Calif.: Stanford University Press.

DeFleur, Melvin L.
1964   "Occupational roles as portrayed on television." Public Opinion Quarterly 28:57-74.

di Leonardo, Micaela
1982   Occupational Segregation and Cultural Analysis. Paper presented at the Workshop on Job Segregation by Sex, Committee on Women's Employment and Related Social Issues, National Research Council, Washington, D.C. (May).

Doeringer, Peter B. and Michael J. Piore
1971   Internal Labor Markets and Manpower Analysis. Lexington, Mass.: D.C. Heath.

Dolan, Eleanor F. and Margaret P. Davis
1960   "Anti-nepotism rules in colleges and universities: their effect on the faculty employment of women." Educational Record 41:285-91.

Douglas, Priscilla Harriet
1980   "Black working women: factors affecting labor market experience." Center for Research on Women working paper no. 39. Wellesley College, Wellesley, Mass.

Douvan, Elizabeth
1976   "The role of models in women's professional development." Psychology of Women Quarterly 1:5-20.

Dubeck, Paula J.
1979   "Sexism in recruiting management personnel for a manufacturing firm." Pp. 88-99 in Rodolfo Alvarez, Kenneth G. Lutterman, and Associates (eds.), Discrimination in Organizations. San Francisco: Jossey-Bass.

Dublin, Thomas
1979   Women at Work: The Transformation of Work and Community in Lowell, Massachusetts, 1826-1860. New York: Columbia University Press.

Duncan, Greg J. and Saul Hoffman
1978   "Training and earnings." Pp. 105-50 in Greg Duncan and James Morgan (eds.), Five Thousand American Families: Patterns of Economic Progress, Volume 6. Ann Arbor: University of Michigan, Institute for Social Research.
1979   "On-the-job training and earnings differences by race and sex." Review of Economics and Statistics 61(Nov.):594-603.

Duncan, Otis Dudley
1961   "A socio-economic index for all occupations." In Albert J. Reiss, Jr. et al. (eds.), Occupations and Social Status. New York: Free Press.

Duncan, Otis Dudley and Beverly Duncan
1955   "A methodological analysis of segregation in-
        dices." American Sociological Review 20:200-
        17.

Dwyer, C.A.
1973   "Sex differences in reading: an evaluation and
        a critique of current methods." Review of Ed-
        ucational Research 43:455-61.

Eastwood, Mary
1978   "Legal protection against sex discrimination."
        Pp. 108-23 in Ann H. Stromberg and Shirley
        Harkess (eds.), Women Working: Theories and
        Facts in Perspective. Palo Alto, Calif.: May-
        field Publishing Co.

Edelbrock, Craig and Alan I. Sugawara
1978   "Acquisition of sex-typed preferences in pre-
        school-aged children." Developmental Psy-
        chology 14:614-23.

Enarson, Elaine
1980   Sexual Relations of Production: Women in the
        U.S. Forest Service. Paper presented at the
        annual meetings of the Pacific Sociological As-
        sociation.

England, Paula
1979   "Women and occupational prestige: a case of
        vacuous sex equality." Signs 5 (2):252-65.
1982   "The failure of human capital theory to explain
        occupational sex segregation." Journal of Hu-
        man Resources 17 (Summer):358-370.
1984   "Wage appreciation and depreciation: a test of
        neoclassical economic explanations of occupa-
        tional sex segregation." Social Forces 62:726-
        749.

England, Paula and Teresa Gardner
1983   Sex differentiation in magazine advertising: a
        content analysis using log linear modeling. Pp.
        253-268 in Claude R. Martin (ed.), Current
        Issues and Research in Advertising. Vol. 1. Ann
        Arbor: University of Michigan Business School,
        Division of Research.

Entwisle, Doris R. and Ellen Greenberger
1972   "Adolescents' views of women's work role."
        American Journal of Orthopsychiatry 42
        (July):648-56.

Epstein, Cynthia Fuchs
1970a   Woman's Place: Options and Limits in Profes-
        sional Careers. Berkeley: University of Cali-
        fornia Press.
1970b   "Encountering the male establishment: sex-
        status limits on women's careers in the profes-
        sions." American Journal of Sociology 75 (2):965-
        82.
1976   "Sex role stereotyping, occupations and social
        exchange." Women's Studies 3:185-95.
1981   Women in Law. New York: Basic Books.

Equal Employment Opportunity Commission
1984   Eighteenth Annual Report. Washington, D.C.:
        Equal Employment Opportunity Commission.

Ernest, John
1976   Mathematics and Sex. Santa Barbara: Univer-
        sity of California.

Evans, Gaynelle and Cheryl M. Fields
1985   "Equal-employment agency to focus its probes
        on individual victims of bias." Chronicle of
        Higher Education, February 20.

Evenson, Jill S. and Mary L. O'Neill
1978   Current Perspectives on the Role of Career
        Education Combatting Occupational Sex-Role
        Stereotyping. Washington, D.C.: National In-
        stitute of Education.

Farley, Lin
1978   Sexual Harassment of Women on the Job. New
        York: McGraw Hill.

Faulkender, Patricia J.
1980   "Categorical habituation with sex-typed toy
        stimuli in older and younger preschoolers."
        Child Development 51:515-19.

Federal Government Service Task Force
1981   RIF Report—Analysis of Impact on Women
        and Minorities. Washington, D.C.: Federal
        Government Service Task Force.

Feldberg, Roslyn L. and Evelyn N. Glenn
1979   "Male and female: Job vs. gender models in
        the sociology of work." Social Problems
        26(5):524-538.
1980   Technology and Work Degradation: Reexam-
        ining the Impacts of Office Automation. Un-
        published paper.

Fennema, Elizabeth
1983   "Sex differences in precollege mathematics and
        science preparation." Pp. 4-11 in Recent Stud-
        ies and New Directions in Research Concern-
        ing Women in Science and Engineering.
        Proceedings of a conference convened by the
        National Research Council and sponsored by
        the Ford Foundation. Washington, D.C.: Na-
        tional Academy Press.

Fennema, Elizabeth and Julia Sherman
1977   "Sex related differences in mathematics
        achievements, spatial visualization, and affec-
        tive factors." American Educational Research
        Journal 14:51-71.

Ferber, Marianne, Joan Huber, and Glenna Spitze
1979   "Preference for men as bosses and profession-
        als." Social Forces 58 (December):466-76.

Ferree, Myra Marx
1980   Women's Work and Employment Attitudes: A
        Longitudinal Causal Model. Paper presented
        at the annual meeting of the American Soci-
        ology Association (August).

Fidell, Linda S.
1970   "Empirical verification of sex discrimination in
        hiring practices in psychology." American Psy-
        chologist 25:1094-98.

Flanagan, Robert J.
1976   "Actual versus potential impact of government
        antidiscrimination programs." Industrial and
        Labor Relations Review 29 (July):486-503.

Flerx, Vicki C., Dorothy S. Fidler, and Ronald W.
Rogers
1976   "Sex role stereotypes: developmental aspects
        and early intervention." Child Development
        47:998-1007.

Folbre, Nancy
1982   "Exploitation comes home: a critique of the Marxian theory of family labour." Cambridge Journal of Economics 6:317-329.

Folk, Hugh
1968   "The problem of youth unemployment." Pp. 78-107 in The Transition from School to Work. A report based on the Princeton Manpower Symposium conducted by the Industrial Relations Section (May). Princeton, N.J.: Princeton University.

Fox, Greer Litton
1974   "Some observations and data on the availability of same-sex role models as a factor in undergraduate career choice." Sociological Focus 7:15-30.

Fox, Lynn H.
1981   The Problem of Women and Mathematics. New York: Ford Foundation.

Fox, Lynn H., Diane E. Tobin, and Linda Brody
1979   "Sex-role socialization and achievement in mathematics." Pp. 303-32 in Michele Andrisin Wittig and Anne C. Peterson (eds.), Sex-Related Differences in Cognitive Functioning. New York: Academic Press.

Fox, Mary Frank and Sharon Hesse-Biber
1984   Women at Work. Palo Alto, Calif.: Mayfield.

Freeman, Jo
1971   "The legal basis of the sexual caste system." Valparaiso University Law Review 5:203-56.

Freeman, Richard B.
1973   "Changes in the labor market for black Americans, 1948-1972." Pp. 67-131 in Brookings Papers on Economic Activity. Washington, D.C.: Brookings Institution.
1977   Black Elite. New York: McGraw-Hill.
1981   "Black economic progress after 1964: who has gained and why?" Pp. 247-94 in Sherwin Rosen (ed.), Studies in Labor Markets. Chicago: University of Chicago Press.

Friedl, Ernestine
1975   Women and Men: An Anthropologist's View. New York: Holt, Rinehart & Winston.

Frieze, Irene H., Jacquelynne E. Parsons, Paula B. Johnson, Diane N. Ruble, and Gail L. Zellman
1978   Women and Sex Roles: A Social Psychological Perspective. New York: W.W. Norton.

Frueh, Terry and Paul E. McGhee
1975   "Traditional sex-role developments and amount of time spent watching television." Developmental Psychology 11:109.

Garrett, C.S., P.L. Ein, and L. Tremaine
1977   "The development of gender stereotyping of adult occupations in elementary school children." Child Development 48:507-12.

Garrison, Howard H.
1979   "Gender differences in the career aspirations of recent cohorts of high school seniors." Social Problems 27 (December):170-85.

Gaskell, Jane
1985   "Course enrollments in the high school: the perspective of working-class females." Sociology and Education 58 (January):48-59.

Gates, Margaret
1976   "Occupational segregation and the law." Signs 1:3 (Part 2, Spring):335-41.

Gera, Surendra and Abrar Hasan
1982   "More on returns to job search: a test of two models." Review of Economics and Statistics 64 (February):151-6.

Gilbert, Susan
1980   Barriers to Effectively Using Employment and Training Programs to get Women into Nontraditionally Female Jobs. Paper presented at Conference on the Experience of Women in Employment and Training Programs held by the National Commission for Employment Policy, Washington, D.C. (September).

Ginsburg, Allan and Wayne Vroman
1976   Black Men's Relative Earnings in Major SMSA's: 1957-1972. Paper presented at meeting of the Econometric Society (September).

Goldstein, Elyse
1979   "Effect on same-sex and cross-sex role models on the subsequent academic productivity of scholars." American Psychologist 34:407-10.

Goldstein, Morris and Robert S. Smith
1976   "The estimated impact of the antidiscrimination program aimed at federal contracts." Industrial and Labor Relations Review 29:523-43.

Golladay, Mary A. and Rolf M. Wulfsberg
1981   The Condition of Vocational Education. Washington, D.C.: U.S. Department of Education. National Center for Education Statistics.

Gordon, Nancy M.
1979a   "The federal income tax system." Pp. 201-222 in Ralph E. Smith (ed.), The Subtle Revolution: Women at Work. Washington, D.C.: The Urban Institute.
1979b   "Institutional responses: the social security system." Pp. 223-256 in Ralph E. Smith (ed.), The Subtle Revolution: Women at Work. Washington, D.C.: The Urban Institute.

Gottfredson, Linda S.
1978   Race and Sex Differences in Occupational Aspirations: Their Development and Consequences for Occupational Segregation. Center for Social Organization of Schools, report no. 254 (July). Baltimore, Md.: The Johns Hopkins University.

Granovetter, Mark
1981   "Toward a sociological theory of income differences." Pp. 11-47 in Ivar Berg (ed.), Sociological Perspectives on Labor Markets. New York: Academic Press.

Grasso, John T.
1980   "The effects of school curriculum on young women." Pp. 79-114 in Education, Sex Equity and Occupational Stereotyping. Washington,

D.C.: National Commission for Employment Policy.

Grasso, John T., and John R. Shea
1979   Vocational Education and Training: Impact on Youth. Berkeley, Calif.: Carnegie Council on Policy Studies in Higher Education.

Greenbaum, Joan
1976   "Division of labor in the computer field." Monthly Review 28:19-39.
1979   In the Name of Efficiency: Management Theory and Shopfloor Practice in Data Processing Work. Philadelphia: Temple University Press.

Greenberger, Marcia D.
1978   "The effectiveness of federal laws prohibiting sex discrimination in employment in the United States." Pp. 108-28 in Ronnie Steinberg Ratner (ed.), Equal Employment Policy for Women. Philadelphia: Temple University Press.

Grimm, James W. and Robert N. Stern
1974   "Sex roles and internal labor market structures: the 'female' semi-professions." Social Problems 21:690-705.

Grinder, Charles E.
1961   "Factor of sex in office employment." Office Executive 36:10-13.

Grinker, William J., Donald D. Cooke, and Arthur W. Kirsch
1970   Climbing the Job Ladder. Prepared for American Foundation on Automation and Employment. New York: E.F. Shelley and Co.

Gross, Edward
1968   "Plus ça change. . .? The sexual structure of occupations over time." Social Problems 16:198-208.

Gruber, James E. and Lars Bjorn
1982   "Blue-collar blues: the sexual harassment of women autoworkers." Work and Occupations 9 (August):271-98.

Gurwitz, Sharon B. and Kenneth A. Dodge
1975   "Adults' evaluations of a child as a function of sex of adult and sex of child." Journal of Personality and Social Psychology 32 (November):322-28.

Guttman, Robert
1983   "Job Training Partnership Act: new help for the unemployed." Monthly Labor Review 106 (March):3-10.

Haber, Sheldon E., Enrique J. Lamas, and Gordon Green
1983   "A new method for estimating job separations by sex and race." Monthly Labor Review 106 (June):20-33.

Hacker, Sally L.
1979   "Sex stratification, technology and organizational change: a longitudinal analysis." Social Problems 26:539-57.

Haignere, Lois V., Cynthia H. Chertos, and Ronnie J. Steinberg
1981   Managerial Promotions in the Public Sector: The Impact of Eligibility Requirements on Women and Minorities. Center for Women in Government, State University of New York, Albany (November).

Halaby, Charles N.
1979a   "Sexual inequality in the work place: an employer-specific analysis of pay differences." Social Science Research 8 (March):79-104.
1979b   "Job-specific sex differences in organizational reward attainment: wage discrimination vs. rank segregation." Social Forces 58 (September):108-27.

Hall, Betty Jean
1981   Comments of Director, Coal Employment Project, addressed to Office of Federal Contract Compliance Program on the Labor Department's advance notice of proposed rulemaking, 46 FR 36213 (July 14, 1981), as amended 46 FR 42490 (August 21, 1981) regarding affirmative action requirements for government contractors.

Hall, Robert E. and Richard A. Kasten
1976   "Occupational mobility and the distribution of occupational success among young men." American Economic Review 66:309-15.

Hammond, Dorothy and Alta Jablow
1976   Women in Cultures of the World. Menlo Park, Calif.: Cummings.

Harkess, Shirley
1980   Hiring Women and Blacks in Entry-Level Manufacturing Jobs in a Southern City: Particularism and Affirmative Action. Paper presented at the annual meetings of the Society for the Study of Social Problems, New York.

Harlan, Anne and Carol Weiss
1981   Moving Up: Women in Managerial Careers: A Final Report. Center for Research on Women working paper no. 86. Wellesley College, Wellesley, Mass.

Harlan, Sharon L.
1979   Participation of Disadvantaged Groups in Employment and Training Programs (CETA) in New York and Pennsylvania. Unpublished Ph.D. dissertation, Cornell University.
1980   Sex Differences in Access to Federal Employment and Training Resources Under CETA: An Overview. Center for Research on Women working paper no. 58. Wellesley College, Wellesley, Mass.

Harlan, Sharon L. and Brigid O'Farrell
1981   "The social context of employment choice: women in CETA." New England Sociologist 3:32-45.
1982   "After the pioneers: prospects for women in nontraditional blue-collar jobs." Work and Occupations 9 (August):363-86.

Harnischfeger, Annegret and David Wiley
1980   "High school tracking and vocational stereotyping: means of socioeconomic placement." Pp. 137-62 in Education, Sex Equity and Occupational Stereotyping (Conference Report). Washington, D.C.: National Commission for Employment Policy.

Harrison, Bennett and Andrew Sum
1979   "The theory of 'dual' or segmented labor markets." Journal of Economic Issues 13 (September):687-706.

Harrison, Laurie R.
1980   "The American Institutes for Research study of sex equity in vocational education: efforts of states and local education agencies." Pp. 179-97 in Education, Sex Equity and Occupational Stereotyping. Washington, D.C.: National Commission for Employment Policy.

Harrison, Laurie R., Peter Dahl, Marian F. Shaycoft, and Beverly J. Parks
1979   Primary Data of the Vocational Education Equity Study. Final Report. Volume 1. Palo Alto, Calif.: American Institutes for Research.

Hartley, Ruth E.
1966   "A developmental view of female sex-role identification." In Bruce Jeffrey Biddle and Edwin John Thomas (eds.), Role Theory: Concepts and Research. New York: Wiley.

Hartmann, Heidi I.
1976   "Capitalism, patriarchy, and job segregation by sex." Signs 1 (Spring, Part 2):137-69.
1981   "The family as the locus of gender, class and political struggle: the example of housework." Signs 6 (Spring):366-94.

Hartmann, Heidi I. and Barbara F. Reskin
1983   "Job segregation: trends and prospects." Appendix C in Cynthia H. Chertos, Lois Haignere, and Ronnie J. Steinberg (eds.), Occupational Segregation and Its Impact on Working Women. Report of a Conference held at the Ford Foundation, June 1982. Albany: State University of New York, Center for Women in Government.

Hayes, Cheryl D. and Sheila B. Kamerman (eds.)
1983   Children of Working Parents: Experiences and Outcomes. National Research Council. Washington, D.C.: National Academy Press.

Hayghe, Howard
1984   "Working mothers reach record number in 1984." Monthly Labor Review 107 (December):31-34.

Haynes, Suzanne G. and Manning Feinleib
1980   "Women, work and coronary heart disease: prospective findings from the Framingham Heart Study." American Journal of Public Health 70 (February):133-40.

Heckman, James and Kenneth Wolpin
1976   "Does contract compliance work? An analysis of Chicago data." Industrial and Labor Relations Review 29:544-64.

Heilman, Madeline E.
1979   "High school students' occupational interest as a function of projected sex ratios in male dominated occupations." Journal of Applied Psychology 64:275-79.

Herzog, A.R.
1982   "High school seniors' occupational plans and values: trends in sex differences 1976 through 1980." Sociology of Education 55:1-13.

Heyns, Barbara and Joyce Adair Bird
1982   "Recent trends in the higher education of women." Pp. 43-68 in Pamela J. Perun (ed.), The Undergraduate Woman: Issues in Educational Equity. Lexington, Mass.: Lexington Books.

Hind, Robert R. and Timothy E. Wirth
1969   "The effect of university experience on occupational choice among undergraduates." Sociology of Education 42:50-70.

Hochschild, Arlie R.
1975   "Inside the clockwork of male careers." Pp. 47-80 in Florence Howe (ed.), Women and the Power to Change. New York: McGraw Hill.

Hofferth, Sandra L.
1979   "The implications for child care." In Ralph Smith (ed.), Women in the Labor Force in 1990. Washington, D.C.: The Urban Institute.
1980a   High School Experience in the Attainment Process of Non-College Boys and Girls: When and Why do Their Paths Diverge? Working paper 1303-01. Washington, D.C.: The Urban Institute.
1980b   "Long-term labor market effects of vocational education on young women." Pp. 115-36 in Education, Sex Equity and Occupational Stereotyping. Washington, D.C.: National Commission for Employment Policy.

Hofferth, Sandra L. and Kirstin A. Moore
1979   "Women's employment and marriage." Pp. 99-124 in Ralph E. Smith (ed.), The Subtle Revolution: Women at Work. Washington, D.C.: The Urban Institute.

Hoffman, Lois W.
1977   "Changes in family roles, socialization, and sex differences." American Psychologist 32:644-57.

Hornig, Lilli S.
1980   The Missing Scientists. Women in Science and Engineering. Unpublished paper prepared for the National Research Council (March).

Huston, Aletha C.
1983   "Sex-typing." In Carmichael's Manual of Child Psychology. Fourth Edition. New York: John Wiley.

Hutchins, Edwin
1980   Culture and Inference: A Trobriand Case Study. Cambridge, Mass.: Harvard University Press.

Illinois Unemployment and Job Training Research Project
1985   Civil Rights, the New Federalism, and the Job Training Partnership Act. Report to the Subcommittee on Employment Opportunities, Committee on Education and Labor, U.S. House of Representatives, June 26.

Jacobs, Jerry A.
1983   The Sex Segregation of Occupations and Women's Career Patterns. Unpublished doctoral dissertation, Department of Sociology, Harvard University.

Jacobs, Jerry and Brian Powell
1983   Occupational Prestige and Sex Segregation: Further Evidence. Paper presented at the

Southern Sociological Society meetings, Atlanta.

Jacobus, Betsey
1980   Barriers to Effectively Using Employment and Training Programs to get Women into Non-traditionally Female Jobs. Paper presented at the Conference on the Experience of Women in Employment and Training Programs held by the National Commission for Employment Policy, Washington, D.C. (September).

Johnson, George E. and Frank P. Stafford
1974   "The earnings and promotion of women faculty." American Economic Review 64 (December):888-903.

Jordanova, L.J.
1980   "Natural facts: a historical perspective on science and sexuality." Pp. 42-69 in C. MacCormack and M. Strathern (eds.), Nature, Culture and Gender. Cambridge: Cambridge University Press.

Kahn, Lawrence M.
1978   "The returns to job search: a test of two models." Review of Economics and Statistics 15 (November):496-503.
1980   "Wage growth and endogenous experience." Industrial Relations 19(Winter):50-63.
1981   "Sex discrimination in professional employment: a case study." Industrial and Labor Relations Review 34 (January):273-76.

Kamerman, Sheila B. and Cheryl D. Hayes (eds.)
1982   Families That Work: Children in a Changing World. National Research Council. Washington, D.C.: National Academy Press.

Kamerman, Sheila B. and Paul W. Kingston
1982   "Employer responses to the family responsibilities of employees." Pp. 144-208 in Sheila B. Kamerman and Cheryl D. Hayes (eds.), Families That Work: Children in a Changing World. National Research Council. Washington, D.C.: National Academy Press.

Kane, Roslyn and Pamela Frazee
1978   Women in Non-Traditional Vocational Education in Secondary Schools. Final Report to the Office of Education, U.S. Department of Health, Education and Welfare.
1979   Adult Women in Vocational Education: Reentrants and Career Changers. Final report to Office of Education, U.S. Department of Health, Education, and Welfare.

Kane, Roslyn and Jill Miller
1981   "Women and apprenticeship: a study of programs designed to facilitate women's participation in the skilled trades." Pp. 83-105 in Vernon M. Briggs, Jr. and Felician Foltman (eds.), Apprenticeship Research: Emerging Findings and Future Trends. Ithaca, N.Y.: New York State School of Industrial Relations.

Kane, Roslyn D., Elizabeth Dee, and Jill Miller
1977   Problems of Women in Apprenticeship. Arlington, Va.: RJ Associates.

Kane, Roslyn, Pamela Frazee, and Elizabeth Dee
1976   A Study of the Factors Influencing the Participation of Women in Non-traditional Occupations in Postsecondary Area Vocational Training Schools. Final report to Office of Education, U.S. Department of Health, Education, and Welfare.

Kaniuga, Nance, Thomas Scott, and Eldon Gade
1974   "Working women portrayed on evening television programs." Vocational Guidance Quarterly 23:134-37.

Kanter, Rosabeth M.
1976   "The impact of hierarchical structures on the work behavior of men and women." Social Problems 23:415-430.
1977   Men and Women of the Corporation. New York: Harper and Row.

Karpicke, Susan
1980   "Perceived and real sex differences in college students' career planning." Journal of Counseling Psychology 27:240-45.

Kaufman, Debra
1977   "Women and the professions: can what's preached be practiced?" Soundings 60 (Winter):410-27.

Kelley, Maryellen R.
1982   "Discrimination in seniority systems: a case study." Industrial and Labor Relations Review 36 (1):40-55(October).

Kessler-Harris, Alice
1975   "Where are all the organized women workers?" Feminist Studies 3(1-2 Fall):92-110.
1982   Out to Work. New York: Oxford University Press.

Kimmel, E.
1970   "Can children's books change children's values?" Educational Leadership 28:209-14.

Klemmack, David L. and John N. Edwards
1973   "Women's acquisition of stereotyped occupational aspirations." Sociology and Social Research 57 (July):510-25.

Knight-Ridder News Service
1985   "Reynolds sees end to hiring favor for minorities." Washington Post, February 9:A6.

Kohen, Andrew I.
1975   Women and the Economy: A Bibliography and Review of the Literature on Sex Differentiation in the Labor Market. Columbus: Ohio State University, Center for Human Resources Research.

Kohen, Andrew I. and Susan C. Breinich
1975   "Knowledge of the world of work: a test of occupational information for young men." Journal of Vocational Behavior 6:133-44.

Kohn, Melvin L. and Carmi Schooler, with the collaboration of Joanne Miller, Carrie Schoenbach, and Ronald Schoenberg
1983   Work and Personality: An Inquiry Into the Impact of Social Stratification. Norwood, N.J.: Ablex.

Kohout, Vernon A. and John W.M. Rothney
1964 "A longitudinal study of vocational preferences." American Educational Research Journal 1:10-21.

Konda, Suresh L. and Shelby Stewman
1980 "An opportunity labor demand model." American Sociological Review 45 (April):276-301.

Krause, Neal, Arne Kalleberg, and Lowell L. Hargens
1982 The Impact of Work on Psychological and Physical Well-Being of Male and Female Workers: A Longitudinal Assessment. Unpublished paper.

Krucoff, Carol
1981 "Careers: opening new doors on alternative work schedules." Washington Post (Oct. 7):B-5.

Kuvlesky, William P. and Robert C. Bealer
1967 "The relevance of adolescents' occupational aspirations for subsequent job attainments." Rural Sociology 32:290-301.

Lantz, Alma E., Con Carlberg, and Vicki Eaton
1982 Women's Choice of Science as a Career. Unpublished paper, E.S.R. Associates, Inc., Denver, Colorado.

Lantz, Alma E. with Marna C. Whittington, M. Louise Fox, Linda Elliott, and Karen Sackett
1980 Reentry Programs for Female Scientists. New York: Praeger.

Lapidus, Gail Warshofsky
1978 Women in Soviet Society. Berkeley: University of California Press.

Laws, Judith Long
1976 "The Bell Telephone System: a case study." Pp. 155-69 in Phyllis A. Wallace (ed.), Equal Employment Opportunity and the AT&T Case. Cambridge, Mass.: MIT Press.

League of Women Voters Education Fund
1982 Achieving Sex Equity in Vocational Education: A Crack in the Wall. Washington, D.C.: League of Women Voters.

Lembright, Muriel Faltz and Jeffrey W. Riemer
1982 "Women truckers' problems and the impact of sponsorship." Sociology of Work and Occupations 9(Nov.):457-74.

Leon, Carol Boyd and Phillip L. Rones
1980 Employment and Unemployment During 1979: An Analysis. Special Labor Force Report 234. Washington, D.C.: U.S. Department of Labor, Bureau of Labor Statistics.

Leonard, Jonathan S.
1984a "Antidiscrimination or reverse discrimination: the impact of changing demographics, Title VII, and affirmative action on productivity." Journal of Human Resources 19(2):145-174.
1984b "Employment and occupational advance under affirmative action." Review of Economics and Statistics 66(3 Aug.):377-385.
1984c "The impact of affirmative action on employment." Journal of Labor Economics 2(4):439-463.

Levine, M.
1976 Identification of Reasons Why Qualified Women Do Not Pursue Mathematical Careers. Report to the National Science Foundation. Grant No. GY-11411 (August).

Levinson, Richard
1975 "Sex discrimination and employment practices: an experiment with unconventional job inquiries." Social Problems 22:533-43.

Lewin, Arie and Linda Duchan
1971 "Women in academia." Science 173 (Sep. 3):892-95.

Lewis, M.V. and L.W. Kaltreider
1976 Attempts to Overcome Sex Stereotyping in Vocational Education. University Park, Penn.: Institute for Research on Human Resources.

Liben, Lynn S.
1978 "Performance on Piagetian spatial tasks as a function of sex, field dependence, and training." Merrill-Palmer Quarterly 24:97-110.

Lloyd, Cynthia B. and Beth T. Niemi
1979 The Economics of Sex Differentials. New York: Columbia University Press.

Lorber, Judith
1981 "The limits of sponsorship of women physicians." Journal of the American Medical Women's Association 36:11.

Luchins, Edith H. and Abraham S. Luchins
1980 "Female mathematicians: a contemporary appraisal." Pp. 7-22 in Lynn H. Fox, Linda Brody, and Diane Tobin (eds.), Women and the Mathematical Mystique. Baltimore: Johns Hopkins University Press.

Lueptow, Lloyd B.
1980 "Social change and sex-role change in adolescent orientations toward life, work, and achievement: 1964-1975." Social Psychology Quarterly 43 (1):48-59.
1981 "Sex typing and change in the occupational choices of high school seniors: 1964-1975." Sociology of Education 54 (January):16-24.

Maccoby, Eleanor E. and Carol Nagy Jacklin
1974 The Psychology of Sex Differences. Stanford, Calif.: Stanford University Press.

MacDonald, C.T.
1980 "An experiment in mathematics education at the college level." Pp. 115-137 in Lynn H. Fox, L. Brody, and D. Tobin, eds., Women and the Mathematical Mystique. Baltimore: Johns Hopkins University Press.

MacKinnon, Catherine A.
1979 Sexual Harassment of Working Women. New Haven: Yale University Press.

Madden, Janice F.
1975 "Discrimination—a manifestation of male market power?" Pp. 146-74 in Cynthia B. Lloyd (ed.), Sex, Discrimination, and the Division of Labor. New York: Columbia University Press.
1978 "An empirical analysis of spatial elasticity of labor supply." Papers of Regional Science Association 39:157-71.

1981   "Why women work closer to home." Urban Studies:181-194.

Maeroff, Gene I.
1982   "Sex barriers to vocations fall." Education Section. New York Times, July 25.

Malkiel, B.G. and J.A. Malkiel
1973   "Male-female pay differentials in professional employment." American Economic Review 63:693-705.

Malveaux, Julianne
1982a   "Moving forward, standing still: women in white collar jobs." Chapter 5 in Phyllis A. Wallace (ed.), Women in the Workplace. Boston: Auburn House.
1982b   Recent Trends in Occupational Segregation by Race and Sex. Paper presented at the Workshop on Job Segregation by Sex, Committee on Women's Employment and Related Social Issues, National Research Council, Washington, D.C. (May, revised Oct.).

Marini, Margaret Mooney
1978   "Sex differences in the determination of adolescent aspirations: a review of research." Sex Roles 4(5):723-753.
1980   "Sex differences in the process of occupational attainment: a closer look." Social Science Research 9:307-61.

Marini, Margaret Mooney and Mary Brinton
1984   "Sex typing in occupational socialization." Pp. 192-232 in Barbara F. Reskin (ed.), Sex Segregation in the Workplace: Trends, Explanations, Remedies. Washington, D.C.: National Academy Press.

Marini, Margaret Mooney and Ellen Greenberger
1978   "Sex differences in occupational aspirations and expectations." Sociology of Work and Occupations 5 (May):147-78.

Martin, Susan E.
1978   "Sexual politics in the workplace: the interactional world of policewomen." Symbolic Interaction 1 (Spring):44-60.
1980   Breaking and Entering: Policewomen on Patrol. Berkeley: University of California Press.

Marwell, Gerald, Rachel Rosenfeld, and Seymour Spilerman
1979   "Geographic constraints on women's careers in academia." Science 205(Sept. 21):1225-1231.

Mason, Karen Oppenheim, John L. Czajka, and Sara Arber
1976   "Change in U.S. women's sex role attitudes, 1964-1974." American Sociological Review 41:573-96.

McCrate, Elaine
1984   The Growth of Non Marriage Among U.S. Women: 1957-1980. Unpublished paper, University of Massachusetts, Amherst.

McDonald, Gerald W.
1980   "Family power: the assessment of a decade of theory and research, 1970-1979." Journal of Marriage and the Family 42 (November):841-54.

McLane, Helen J.
1980   Selecting, Developing and Retaining Women Executives: A Corporate Strategy for the Eighties. New York: Van Nostrand Reinhold.

McNulty, D.
1967   "Difference in pay between men and women workers." Monthly Labor Review 90 (December):40-43.

McPherson, J. Miller and Lynn Smith-Lovin
1982   "Women and weak ties: differences by sex in the size of voluntary organizations." American Journal of Sociology 87:883-904.

Medvene, Arnold M. and Anne M. Collins
1976   "Occupational prestige and appropriateness: the views of mental health specialists." Journal of Vocational Behavior 9:63-71.

Meissner, M., E.W. Humphreys, S.M. Meiss, and W.J. Scheu
1975   "No exit for wives: sexual division of labour and the cumulation of household demands." Canadian Review of Sociology and Anthropology 12 (November):424-43.

Mennerick, Lewis A.
1975   "Organizational structuring of sex roles in a nonstereotyped industry." Administrative Science Quarterly 20 (December):570-86.

Mertens, Donna M. and John A. Gardner
1981   Vocational Education and the Younger Adult Worker. Columbus: National Center for Research in Vocational Education, Ohio State University.

Meyer, John W. and Barbara Sobiezek
1972   "Effect of a child's sex on adult interpretations of its behavior." Developmental Psychology 6:42-48.

Milkman, Ruth
1980   "Organizing the sexual division of labor: historical perspectives on 'women's work' and the American labor movement." Socialist Review 49:95-150.

Miller, Ann R., Donald J. Treiman, Pamela S. Cain, and Patricia A. Roos, eds.
1980   Work, Jobs, and Occupations: A Critical Review of the Dictionary of Occupational Titles. Committee on Occupational Classification and Analysis. Washington, D.C.: National Academy Press.

Miller, Joanne and Howard H. Garrison
1982   "Sex roles: the division of labor at home and in the workplace." Annual Review of Sociology 8:237-262.

Miller, Joanne, Carmi Schooler, Melvin L. Kohn, and Karen A. Miller
1979   "Women and work: the psychological effects of occupational conditions." American Journal of Sociology 85:66-94.

Miller, Jon, James Lincoln, and Jan Olson
1981   "Rationality and equity in professional networks: gender and race as factors in the stratification of interorganizational systems." American Journal of Sociology 87:309-35.

Mincer, Jacob
1962a "Labor force participation of married women."
Pp. 63-97 in Committee for Economic Research, Aspects of Labor Economics. Princeton, N.J.: Princeton University Press for the
National Bureau of Economic Research.
1962b "On-the-job training: costs, returns and some
implications." Journal of Political Economy 70
(October):550-79.

Mincer, Jacob and Haim Ofek
1982 "Interrupted work careers." Journal of Human
Resources 17 (Winter):3-24.

Mincer, Jacob and Solomon Polachek
1974 "Family investments in human capital: earnings of women." Journal of Political Economy
82 (March/April, Part II):S76-S108.
1978 "Women's earnings reexamined." Journal of
Human Resources 13 (Winter):118-34.

Moore, Kristin A. and Isabel V. Sawhill
1976 "Implications of women's employment for home
and family life." Pp. 102-22 in Juanita M. Kreps
(ed.), Women and the American Economy: A
Look to the 1980s. Englewood Cliffs, N.J.:
Prentice-Hall.
1978 "The implications of occupational segregation."
Pp. 201-25 in Ann H. Stromberg and Shirley
Harkess (eds.), Women Working. Palo Alto,
Calif.: Mayfield.

Mortimer, J.T.
1976 "Social class, work and the family: some implications of the father's occupation for familial
relationships and son's career decisions." Journal of Marriage and the Family 38:241-256.

Moss, Ann
1983 "Social insecurity: pension plans shortchange
women." Women's Political Times 8(Feb.):2.

Mott, Frank L. and Sylvia F. Moore
1976 The Determinants and Consequences of Occupational Information for Young Women.
Center for Human Resources, Ohio State University.

National Advisory Council on Vocational Education and
National Advisory Council on Women's Educational
Programs
1980 Increasing Sex Equity: The Impact of the 1976
Education Amendments on Sex Equity in Vo-
cational Education. Washington, D.C.: U.S.
Department of Education.

National Advisory Council on Women's Educational
Programs
1981 Title IX: The Half Full-Half Empty Glass.
Washington, D.C.: U.S. Government Printing
Office.
1982 Increasing Sex Equity: 1980 Update. Washington, D.C.: U.S. Department of Education.

National Center for Education Statistics
1981 Degree Awards to Women: A 1979 Update.
Washington, D.C.: U.S. Department of Education.

National Commission for Employment Policy
1980 Education, Sex Equity and Occupational Stereotyping. Special Report no. 38. Washington,
D.C.: National Commission for Employment
Policy.
1981 The Experience of Women in Federally Sponsored Employment and Training Programs.
Special Report no. 39. Washington, D.C.: National Commission for Employment Policy.

National Commission on Working Women
1979 National Survey of Working Women: Perceptions, Problems and Prospects. Washington,
D.C.: National Manpower Institute.

Nemerowicz, Gloria Morris
1979 Children's Perceptions of Gender and Work
Roles. New York: Praeger.

Nerlove, Sara B.
1974 "Women's work load and infant feeding practices: a relationship with demographic implications." Ethnology 13:207-214.

New York State Commission on Management and Productivity in the Public Sector
1977 Job Promotion under New York State's Civil
Service System: A Case Study of the Office of
General Services.

Newman, Winn
1976 "Combatting occupational segregation: pres-
entation iii" Pp. 265-272 in Martha Blaxall and
Barbara Reagan, eds., Women and the Workplace: The Implications of Occupational Segregation. Chicago: University of Chicago Press.

Newman, Winn and Carole W. Wilson
1981 "The union role in affirmative action." Labor
Law Journal (June):323-42.

Newson, John and Elizabeth Newson
1976 Seven Years Old in the Home Environment.
London: Allen & Unwin.

Niemi, Beth T.
1974 "The male-female differential in unemployment rates." Industrial and Labor Relations Review 27 (April):331-50.

Nieva, Veronica and Barbara Gutek
1981 Women in Work: A Psychological Perspective.
New York: Praeger Press.

Nilsen, Alleen Pace
1977 "Sexism in children's books and elementary
teaching materials." Pp. 161-80 in Alleen Pace
Nilsen, Haig Bosmajian, H. Lee Gershuny,
and Julia P. Stanley (eds.), Sexism and Language. Urbana, Ill.: National Council of Teachers of English.

Nilson, Linda Burzotta
1976 "The occupational and sex-related components
of social standing." Sociology and Social Research 60:328-36.

Northrup, Herbert R. and John A. Larson
1979 The Impact of the AT&T-EEO Consent Decrees. University of Pennsylvania, Industrial
Research Unit, Labor Relations and Public Policy Series no. 20 (November).

Norwood, Janet L.
1982 "The female-male earnings gap: a review of
employment and earnings issues." Report 673.

Bureau of Labor Statistics. Washington, D.C.: U.S. Department of Labor.

O'Farrell, Brigid
1980   "Women and nontraditional blue-collar jobs: a case study of Local I." Report prepared for the Employment and Training Administration, U.S. Department of Labor (August).
1981   "Response." Pp. 150-54 in Vernon M. Briggs, Jr. and Felician Foltman (eds.), Apprenticeship Research: Emerging Findings and Future Trends. Ithaca, N.Y.: New York State School of Industrial Relations.
1982   "Women and nontraditional blue collar jobs in the 1980s: an overview." Pp. 135-65 in Phyllis A. Wallace (ed.), Women in the Workplace: The Management of Human Resources. Boston: Auburn Press.

O'Farrell, Brigid and Sharon Harlan
1982   "Craftworkers and clerks: the effect of male co-worker hostility on women's satisfaction with non-traditional blue-collar jobs." Social Problems 29 (February):252-64.
1984   "Job integration strategies: today's programs and tomorrow's needs." Pp. 267-291 in Barbara F. Reskin (ed.), Sex Segregation in the Workplace: Trends, Explanations, Remedies. Washington, D.C.: National Academy Press.

O'Hara, Robert P.
1962   "The roots of careers." Elementary School Journal 62:277-80.

Olson, Craig, and Brian E. Becker
1983   "Sex discrimination in the promotion process." Industrial and Labor Relations Review 36(July):624-641.

O'Neill, June and Ralph Smith
1976   The 1974-1975 Recession and the Employment of Women. Washington, D.C.: The Urban Institute.

Oppenheimer, Valerie Kincaid
1970   The Female Labor Force in the United States: Demographic and Economic Factors Governing Its Growth and Changing Composition. Population Monograph Series, Number 5. Westport, Conn.: Greenwood Press.

Ortiz, Florence and Janice Covel
1978   "Women in school administration: a case analysis." Urban Education 13:213-36.

Osterman, Paul
1978   Sex, Marriage, Children, and Statistical Discrimination. Unpublished paper, Department of Economics, Boston University.
1979   "Sex discrimination in professional employment: a case study." Industrial and Labor Relations Review 32 (July):451-64.
1982   "Affirmative action and opportunity: a study of female quit rates." Review of Economics and Statistics. 64 (4):604-612.

Parnes, Herbert S. and Andrew I. Kohen
1975   "Occupational information and labor market status: the case of young men." Journal of Human Resources 10:44-55.

Peng, Samuel S., W.B. Fetters, and A.J. Kolstad
1981   High School and Beyond, a National Longitudinal Study for the 1980's: A Capsule Description of High School Students. Washington, D.C.: National Center for Education Statistics.

Peterson, Bill
1985a   "Reynolds opposes bill to counter bias ruling." Washington Post, March 8:A2.
1985b   "Civil Rights Commission boycotted by groups." Washington Post, March 7:A7.

Peterson-Hardt, Sandra and Nancy D. Perlman
1979   Sex-Segregated Career Ladders in New York State Government: A Structural Analysis of Inequality in Employment. Working Paper no. 1. Center for Women in Government, State University of New York at Albany (October).

Phelps, Edmund S.
1972   "The statistical theory of racism and sexism." American Economic Review 62 (September):659-66.

Pleck, Joseph H., with M. Rustad
1981   Wives' Employment, Role Demands, and Adjustment: Final Report. Wellesley College Center for Research on Women, Wellesley, Mass.

Polachek, Solomon
1976   "Occupational segregation: an alternative hypothesis." Journal of Contemporary Business 5 (Winter):1-12.
1978   "Sex differences in education: an analysis of the determinants of college major." Industrial and Labor Relations Review 31:498-508.
1979   "Occupational segregation among women: theory, evidence, and a prognosis." Pp. 137-57 in Cynthia B. Lloyd, Emily S. Andrews and Curtis L. Gilroy (eds.), Women in the Labor Market. New York: Columbia University Press.
1981a   "Occupational self-selection: a human capital approach to sex difference-occupational structure." Review of Economics and Statistics (February):60-69.
1981b   A Supply Side Approach to Occupational Segregation. Paper presented at the annual meetings of the American Sociological Association, Toronto (August).

Poll, Carol
1978   No Room at the Top: A Study of the Social Processes that Contribute to Underrepresentation of Women in the Administrative Levels of the New York City School System. Ph.D. dissertation, City University of New York.

Porter, Richard
1954   "Predicting vocational plans of high school senior boys." Personnel and Guidance Journal 33:215-18.

Powell, Brian and Jerry Jacobs
1984   "The prestige gap: differential evaluations of male and female workers." Work and Occupations 11 (Aug.):283-308.

Presser, Harriet
1980   Working Women and Child Care. Paper presented at Research Conference on Women: A

Developmental Perspective, National Institute of Child Health and Human Development, National Institute on Mental Health, and National Institute on Aging, Washington, D.C. (November).

Presser, Harriet B. and Wendy Baldwin
1980 "Child care as a constraint on employment: prevalence, correlates, and bearing on the work and fertility nexus." American Journal of Sociology 85 (5):1202-13.

Project on Equal Education Rights
1978 Stalled at the Start: Government Action on Sex Bias in the Schools. Washington, D.C.: NOW Legal Defense and Education Fund.

Project on the Status and Education of Women
1981 On Campus with Women 30 (Spring):8.

Quadagno, Jill
1976 "Occupational sex-typing and internal labor market distributions: an assessment of medical specialties." Social Problems 23:442-53.

Rainwater, Lee
1979 "Mothers' contribution to the family money economy in Europe and the United States." Journal of Family History 4(2):198-211.

Rapp, Rayna, Ellen Ross, and Renate Bridenthal
1979 "Examining family history." Feminist Studies 5(1):174-200.

Ratner, Ronnie Steinberg
1981 Barriers to Advancement: Promotion of Women and Minorities into Managerial Positions in New York State Government. Center for Women in Government, State University of New York at Albany (March).

Reich, Michael
1981 Racial Inequality: A Political Economic Analysis. Princeton, N.J.: Princeton University Press.

Remick, Helen
1982 Oral remarks. Working Conference on Women's Employment and Economic Status, National Academy of Sciences, Washington, D.C., May 6 and 7, 1982. Cosponsored by the Women's Research and Educational Institute of the Congressional Caucus for Women's Issues and the Committee on Women's Employment and Related Social Issues of the National Academy of Sciences/National Research Council.

Reskin, Barbara F.
1978 "Sex differentiation and the social organization of science." Sociological Inquiry 48(3-4):6-37.

Reubens, Beatrice G. and Edwin P. Reubens
1979 "Women workers, nontraditional occupations and full employment." Pp. 103-26 in Ann Foote Cahn (ed.), Women in the U.S. Labor Force. New York: Praeger.

Reynolds, Lloyd
1951 The Structure of Labor Markets: Wages and Labor Mobility in Theory and Practice. New York: Harper and Row.

Richmond, P.G.
1980 "A limited sex difference in spatial test scores with a preadolescent sample." Child Development 51:601-602.

Rieder, Corrine H.
1977 "Work, women and vocational education." American Education (June):27-32.

Robinson, Joan
1936 The Economics of Imperfect Competition. London: Macmillan.

Roche, G. R.
1979 "Probing opinions." Harvard Business Review 57:14-28.

Roe, Ann
1966 "Women in science." Personnel and Guidance Journal 54:784-87.

Roos, Patricia A.
1981 "Sex stratification in the workplace: male-female differences in economic returns to occupations." Social Science Research 10 (3):195-223.
1983 "Marriage and women's occupational attainment in cross-cultural perspective." American Sociological Review 48(Dec.):852-864.
1985 Work, Jobs, and Gender: A Comparative Analysis of Industrial Societies. Albany, N.Y.: SUNY Press.

Roos, Patricia A. and Barbara F. Reskin
1984 "Institutional factors affecting job access and mobility for women: a review of institutional explanations for occupational sex segregation." Pp. 235-260 in Barbara F. Reskin (ed.), Sex Segregation in the Workplace: Trends, Explanations, Remedies. Washington, D.C.: National Academy Press.

Rosenfeld, Carl
1979 "Occupational mobility during 1977." Monthly Labor Review 102 (December):44-48.

Rosenfeld, Rachel
1980 "Race and sex differences in career dynamics." American Sociological Review 45 (August):583-609.
1982 Job Shifts, the Lifecycle, and Economic Segmentation. Unpublished paper, Department of Sociology, University of North Carolina (July).
1984 "Job-changing and occupational sex-segregation: sex and race comparisons." Pp. 56-86 in Barbara F. Reskin (ed.), Sex Segregation in the Workplace: Trends, Explanations, Remedies. Washington, D.C.: National Academy Press.

Rosenfeld, Rachel A. and Aage B. Sorensen
1979 "Sex differences in patterns of career mobility." Demography 16:89-101.

Rossi, Alice S.
1965 "Barriers to career choice of engineering, medicine, or science among American women." Pp. 51-127 in Jacquelyn A. Mattfeld and Carol G. Van Aken (eds.), Women and the Scientific Professions. Cambridge, Mass.: MIT Press.

Rossiter, Margaret W.
1982 Women Scientists in America. Baltimore: Johns Hopkins University Press.

Rotella, Elyce J.
1981   "The transformation of the American office: changes in employment and technology." Journal of Economic History 41 (March):51-7.

Ruble, Diane N. and Thomas L. Ruble
1980   "Sex stereotypes." Pp. 188-252 in Arthur G. Miller (ed.), In the Eye of the Beholder: Contemporary Issues in Stereotyping. New York: Holt, Rinehart and Winston.

Rytina, Nancy
1981   "Occupational segregation and earnings differences by sex." Monthly Labor Review 104 (January):49-52.
1982   "Earnings of men and women: a look at specific occupations." Monthly Labor Review 105 (April):25-31.

Rytina, Nancy F. and Suzanne M. Bianchi
1984   "Occupational reclassification and changes in distribution by gender." Monthly Labor Review 107 (March):11-17.

Sandell, Steven H.
1980   "Is the unemployment rate of women too low? A direct test of the theory of job search." Review of Economics and Statistics 62 (November):634-8.

Sandell, Steven H. and David Shapiro
1978   "The theory of human capital and the earnings of women: a reexamination of the evidence." Journal of Human Resources 13:103-17.

Saperstein, Saundra
1985   "U.S. sues D.C. on hiring plan." Washington Post, March 12:H1.

Saxonhouse, Gary and Gavin Wright
1982   Two Forms of Cheap Labor in Textile History. Unpublished paper, Economics Department, University of Michigan.

Schafran, Lynn Hecht
1981   Removing Financial Support From Private Clubs That Discriminate Against Women. New York: Women and Foundations Corporate Philanthropy (April).

Schau, Candace Garrett, Lynne Kahn, John H. Diepold, and Frances Cherry
1980   "The relationships of parental expectations and preschool children's verbal sex typing to their sex-typed toy play behavior." Child Development 51:266-70.

Schmidt, John L. and John W.M. Rothney
1955   "Variability of vocational choices of high school students." Personnel and Guidance Journal 34:142-6.

Schreiber, Carol Tropp
1979   Changing Places: Men and Women in Transitional Occupations. Cambridge, Mass.: MIT Press.

Scott, Richard Ira, and Moshe Semyonov
1983   Long-Term Trends in Occupational Differentiation by Sex: A Reexamination. Unpublished paper.

Sells, Lucy W.
1973   "High school mathematics as the critical filter in the job market." Pp. 37-9 in Developing Opportunities for Minorities in Graduate Education, Proceedings of the Conference on Minority Graduate Education at the University of California, Berkeley (May).
1979   "Counseling the young." Science 203 (January 19):231.

Sewell, William H., Robert M. Hauser, and Wendy C. Wolf
1980   "Sex, schooling and occupational status." American Journal of Sociology 86:551-83.

Shaeffer, Ruth Gilbert and Helen Axel
1978   Improving Job Opportunities for Women: A Chartbook Focusing on the Progress in Business. Report no. 744. New York: The Conference Board.

Shaeffer, Ruth Gilbert and Edith F. Lynton
1979   Corporate Experiences in Improving Women's Job Opportunities. Report no. 755. New York: The Conference Board.

Shapiro, Ellen, Florence Haseltine, and Mary Rowe
1978   "Moving up: role models, mentors, and the 'patron system'." Sloan Management Review 19:51-8.

Sherman, J. and Elizabeth Fennema
1977   "The study of mathematics by high school girls and boys: related variables." American Educational Research Journal 14:159-68.

Shortlidge, Richard L.
1977   The Hypothetical Labor Market Response of Black and White Women to a National Program of Free Day Care Centers. Columbus: Ohio State University, Center for Human Resources Research.

Shuchat, Jo with Genii Guinier and Aileen Douglas
1981   The Nuts and Bolts of NTO: A Handbook for Recruitment, Training, Support Services, and Placement of Women in Nontraditional Occupations. Cambridge, Mass.: The Women's Outreach Project, Technical Education Research Centers.

Simmons, Adele, Ann Freedman, Margaret Dunkle, and Francine Blau
1975   Exploitation from 9 to 5. Report of the 20th Century Fund Task Force on Women and Employment. Lexington, Mass.: Lexington Books.

Simon, Rita James, Shirley M. Clark, and Larry L. Tifft
1966   "Of nepotism, marriage and the pursuit of an academic career." Sociology of Education 39 (Fall):344-58.

Singer, Stanley L. and Buford Stefflre
1954   "Sex differences in job values and desires." Personnel and Guidance Journal 32:483-4.

Smith, A.
1976   New Pioneers Project. Raleigh: North Carolina State Department of Education.

Smith, Catherine Begnoche
1979   "Influence of internal opportunity structure and sex of worker on turnover patterns." Administrative Science Quarterly 24:362-81.

Smith, Georgina M.
1964   Help Wanted—Female. A Study of Demand
        and Supply in a Local Job Market for Women.
        New Brunswick, N.J.: Institute of Manage-
        ment and Labor Relations, Rutgers University.

Smith, Judith
1974   The "New Woman" Knows How to Type: Some
        Connections Between Sexual Ideology and
        Clerical Work, 1900-1930. Paper presented at
        the Berkshire Conference on Women's His-
        tory.

Smith, Ralph E.
1977   The Impact of Macroeconomic Conditions on
        Employment Opportunities for Women. Paper
        no. 6, prepared for the U.S. Congress, Joint
        Economic Committee.

Smith, Shirley J.
1982   "New worklife estimates reflect changing pro-
        file of labor force." Monthly Labor Review 105
        (March):15-20.
1985   "Revised worklife tables reflect 1979-80 ex-
        perience." Monthly Labor Review 108(Au-
        gust):23-30.

Sommers, Dixie and Alan Eck
1977   "Occupational mobility in the American labor
        force." Monthly Labor Force 100 (January):3-
        19.

Sorensen, Aage B.
1975   "The structure of intragenerational mobility."
        American Sociological Review 40 (August):456-
        71.
1977   "The structure of inequality and the process of
        attainment." American Sociological Review 42
        (December):965-78.

Sorkin, Alan
1973   "On the occupational status of women, 1870-
        1970." American Journal of Economics and Sta-
        tistics 32 (July):235-43.

Spangler, Eve, Marsha A. Gordon, and Ronald M.
Pipkin
1978   "Token women: an empirical test of Kanter's
        hypothesis." American Journal of Sociology
        84:160-70.

Speizer, Jeanne
1981   "Role models, mentors and sponsors: the elu-
        sive concepts." Signs 6:692-712.

Spilerman, Seymour
1977   "Careers, labor market structure and socioec-
        onomic achievement." American Journal of So-
        ciology 83 (November):551-93.

Spitze, Glenna and John Huber
1980   "Changing attitudes towards women's nonfam-
        ily roles: 1938-1978." Sociology of Work and
        Occupations 7:317-35.

Spitze, Glenna and Linda Waite
1980   "Labor force and work attitudes." Sociology of
        Work and Occupations 7 (February):3-32.

Stafford, Frank P. and Greg J. Duncan
1979   The Use of Time and Technology by House-
        holds in the United States. Survey Research

Center, Institute for Social Research, University of Michigan, Ann Arbor.

Steiger, JoAnn, Arlene Fink, and Jacqueline Kosecoff
1979   Literature and Secondary Data Review of the
        Vocational Education Equity Study. Final Re-
        port. Volume 2. Palo Alto, Calif.: American
        Institutes for Research.

Stein, Aletha Huston
1971   "The effects of sex-role standards for achieve-
        ment and sex-role preference on three deter-
        minants of achievement motivation." Devel-
        opmental Psychology 4:219-31.

Steinberg, Ronnie
1982   Wages and Hours: Labor and Reform in Twen-
        tieth Century America. New Brunswick, N.J.:
        Rutgers University Press.

Steinberg, Ronnie and Alice Cook
1981   Women, Unions, and Equal Employment Op-
        portunity. Working Paper no. 3. Center for
        Women in Government, State University of
        New York at Albany (January).

Stevenson, Mary H.
1977   Internal Labor Markets and the Employment
        of Women in Complex Organizations. Working
        paper, Center for Research on Women,
        Wellesley College.
1978   "Wage differences between men and women:
        economic theories." Pp. 89-107 in Ann H.
        Stromberg and Shirley Harkess (eds.), Women
        Working. Palo Alto, Calif.: Mayfield.

Stolzenberg, Ross
1982   Industrial Profits and the Propensity to Employ
        Women Workers. Paper presented at the
        Workshop on Job Segregation by Sex, Com-
        mittee on Women's Employment and Related
        Social Issues, National Research Council,
        Washington, D.C. (May).

Strober, Myra
1982   "The MBA: same passport to success for women
        and men?" Pp. 25-44 in Phyllis A. Wallace (ed.),
        Women in the Workplace: The Management
        of Human Resources. Boston: Auburn House.
1984   "Toward a general theory of occupational sex
        segregation: the case of public school teaching.
        Pp. 144-156 in Barbara F. Reskin (ed.), Sex
        Segregation in the Workplace: Trends, Expla-
        nations, Remedies. Washington, D.C.: Na-
        tional Academy Press.

Strober, Myra H. and Audri Gordon Lanford
1981   The Percentage of Women in Public School
        Teaching: A Cross-Section Analysis, 1850-80.
        Paper presented at the annual meetings of the
        Social Science History Association (October).

Sweet, James A.
1973   Women in the Labor Force. New York: Aca-
        demic Press.

Talbert, Joan and Christine E. Bose
1977   "Wage attainment processes: the retail clerk
        case." American Journal of Sociology 33 (Sep-
        tember):403-24.

Tangri, Sandra Schwartz
1972   "Determinants of occupational role innovation among college women." Journal of Social Issues 28:177-99.

Taylor, M.G. and S.F. Hartley
1975   "The two-person career: a classic example." Sociology of Work and Occupation 2:354-372.

Taylor, Patricia A.
1985   "Institutional job training and inequality." Social Science Quarterly 66(March):67-78.

Terman, Louis M. and L.E. Tyler
1954   "Psychological sex differences." Pp. 1064-114 in L. Carmichael (ed.), Manual of Child Psychology. Second edition. New York: Wiley.

Terry, Sylvia Lazos
1982   "Unemployment and its effect on family income in 1980." Monthly Labor Review 105 (April):35-43.

Thomas, Arthur H. and Norman R. Stewart
1971   "Counselor response to female clients with deviate and conforming career goals." Journal of Counseling Psychology 18:352-7.

Thomas, Hoben and Wesley Jamison
1975   "On the acquisition of understanding that still water is horizontal." Merrill-Palmer Quarterly 21:31-44.

Thornton, Arland, Duane F. Alwin, and Donald Camburn
1983   "Causes and consequences of sex-role attitude change." American Sociological Review 48 (April):211-27.

Thurow, Lester
1975   Generating Inequality. New York: Basic Books.

Tibbetts, S.L.
1975   "Sex-role stereotyping in the lower grades: part of the solution." Journal of Vocational Behavior 6:255-61.

Tilly, Louise A.
1979   "The family wage economy of a French textile city: Robaix, 1872-1906." Journal of Family History 4 (Winter):381-94.

1982   Rich and Poor in a French Textile City. Walter Prescott Webb Lecture, University of Texas, Arlington.

Tittle, Carol K.
1981   Careers and Family: Sex Roles and Adolescent Life Plans. Beverly Hills, Calif.: Sage.

Tolbert, Charles, III
1982   "Industrial segmentation and men's career mobility." American Sociological Review 47 (August):457-77.

Touhey, John C.
1974   "Effects of additional women professionals on ratings of occupational prestige and desirability." Journal of Personality and Social Psychology 29:86-9.

Treiman, Donald J. and Heidi I. Hartmann (eds.)
1981   Women, Work, and Wages: Equal Pay for Jobs of Equal Value. Report of the Committee on Occupational Classification and Analysis. Washington, D.C.: National Academy Press.

Treiman, Donald J. and Kermit Terrell
1975a   "Sex and the process of status attainment: a comparison of working women and men." American Sociological Review 40 (April):174-200.

1975b   "Women, work, and wages—trends in the female occupational structure since 1940." Pp. 157-200 in Kenneth C. Land and Seymour Spilerman (eds.), Social Indicator Models. New York: Russell Sage Foundation.

Tuchman, Gaye, Arlene K. Daniels, and James Benet
1978   Hearth and Home: Images of Women in the Mass Media. New York: Oxford University Press.

Tyack, David B. and Myra H. Strober
1981   "Jobs and gender: a history of the structuring of educational employment by sex." Pp. 131-52 in Patricia Schmuck and W.W. Charters (eds.), Educational Policy and Management: Sex Differentials. New York: Academic Press.

Ullman, Joseph C. and Kay K. Deaux
1981   "Recent efforts to increase female participation in apprenticeship in the basic steel industry in the Midwest." In Vernon M. Briggs, Jr., and Felician Foltman (eds.), Apprenticeship Research: Emerging Findings and Future Trends. Ithaca, N.Y.: New York State School of Industrial Relations.

Underwood, Lorraine A.
1979   Women in Federal Employment Programs. Washington, D.C.: The Urban Institute.

1980   The Contribution of the Work Incentive (WIN) Program to the Self-Sufficiency of Women. Paper presented at the Conference on the Experience of Women in Employment and Training Programs held by the National Commission for Employment Policy, Washington, D.C. (September).

Urquhart, Michael A. and Marilyn A. Hewson
1983   "Unemployment continued to rise in 1982 as recession deepened." Monthly Labor Review 106 (February):3-12.

U.S. Commission on Civil Rights
1975   The Federal Civil Rights Enforcement Effort—1974. Volume 5. To Eliminate Employment Discrimination (July). Washington, D.C.: U.S. Commission on Civil Rights.

1980   Enforcing Title IX. Washington, D.C.: U.S. Commission on Civil Rights.

1981a   The Voting Rights Act: Unfulfilled Goals. Washington, D.C.: U.S. Commission on Civil Rights.

1981b   Child Care and Equal Opportunity for Women. Clearinghouse Publication No. 67. Washington, D.C.: U.S. Commission on Civil Rights.

U.S. Comptroller General of the United States
1976   Report to the Congress: The Equal Employment Opportunity Commission Has Made Limited Progress in Eliminating Employment Discrimination. September 28. HRD-76-147.

Washington, D.C.: U.S. Government Printing Office.

1984   Distribution of Male and Female Employees in Four Federal Classification Systems. November 27. GAO/GGD-85-20. Washington, D.C.:U.S. General Accounting Office.

U.S. Congress, House
1982   Committee on Education and Labor. Hearings on Reauthorization of the Vocational Education Act of 1963. Part II: Sex Equity in Vocational Education. December 16 and 17, 1981. Washington, D.C.: U.S. Government Printing Office.

1984   Pay Equity: EEOC's Handling of Sex Based Wage Discrimination Complaints. May 22. House Report 98-796. Washington, D.C.: U.S. Government Printing Office.

U.S. Department of Commerce
1981   Statistical Abstract of the United States. Available from the U.S. Government Printing Office. Washington, D.C.: U.S. Department of Commerce.

U.S. Department of Commerce, Bureau of the Census
1972   Census of Population: 1970. Occupation by Industry. Final report PC(2)-7C. Available from the U.S. Government Printing Office. Washington, D.C.: U.S. Department of Commerce.

1973a   Census of Population: 1970. Detailed Characteristics. Final Report PC(1)-D1, U.S. Summary. Available from the U.S. Government Printing Office. Washington, D.C.: U.S. Department of Commerce.

1973b   Census of Population: 1970. Occupational Characteristics. Final Report PC(2)-7A. Available from the U.S. Government Printing Office. Washington, D.C.: U.S. Department of Commerce.

1982   Trends in Child Care Arrangements of Working Mothers. Current Population Reports, Special Studies P-23, No. 117. Available from the U.S. Government Printing Office. Washington, D.C.: U.S. Department of Commerce.

1983a   Money Income and Poverty Status of Families and Persons in the United States. Current Population Reports, Series P-60, No. 145. Available from the U.S. Government Printing Office. Washington, D.C.: U.S. Department of Commerce.

1983b   Detailed Occupation and Years of School Completed by Age, for the Civilian Labor Force by Sex, Race, and Spanish Origin: 1980. Supplementary Report PC80-S1-8. Available from the U.S. Government Printing Office. Washington, D.C.: U.S. Department of Commerce.

1983c   "Wives who earn more than their husbands." Special demographic analysis prepared by Suzanne M. Bianchi. Available from the U.S. Government Printing Office. Washington, D.C.: U.S. Department of Commerce.

1984a   Census of Population: 1980. Detailed Occupation of the Experienced Civilian Labor Force by Sex for the United States and Regions: 1980 and 1970. Supplemental Report PC80-S1-15.

Available from the U.S. Government Printing Office. Washington, D.C.: U.S. Department of Commerce.

1984b   "Households, families, marital status, and living arrangements: March 1984." Advance report. Current Population Reports, Series P-20, No. 391. Available from the U.S. Government Printing Office. Washington, D.C.: U.S. Department of Commerce.

U.S. Department of Education, National Center for Education Statistics
1981   Earned Degrees Conferred. Washington, D.C.: U.S. Department of Education.

U.S. Department of Labor
1977   Dictionary of Occupational Titles. Fourth edition. Washington, D.C.: U.S. Department of Labor.

U.S. Department of Labor, Bureau of Labor Statistics
1980   Perspectives on Working Women: A Databook. Bulletin 2080. Washington, D.C.: U.S. Department of Labor.

1981a   Employment and Earnings, 28 (January).
1981b   Employment and Earnings, 28 (August).
1981c   Employment and Unemployment: A Report on 1980. Special Labor Force Report 244. April. Washington, D.C.: U.S. Department of Labor.
1982a   Employment and Earnings, 29 (January).
1982b   Employment and Earnings, 29 (March).
1985a   Employment and Earnings, 32 (January).
1985b   Employment and Earnings, 32 (February).

U.S. Department of Labor, Employment Standards Administration
1981   Participation of Females in the Construction Trades. Report prepared by Office of Federal Contract Compliance Programs (September 4).

U.S. Department of Labor, Employment and Training Administration
1975   State and National Apprenticeship System Report. Bureau of Apprenticeship and Training. Washington, D.C.: U.S. Department of Labor.

1977   Women and Work. R&D Monograph 46 prepared by Patricia Cayo Sexton. Washington, D.C.: U.S. Department of Labor.

1978   Women in Traditionally Male Jobs: The Experiences of Ten Public Utility Companies. R&D Monograph 65. Washington, D.C.: U.S. Department of Labor.

1979a   Bureau of Apprenticeship and Training Bulletin 80-5. Washington, D.C.: U.S. Department of Labor.

1979b   State and National Apprenticeship System Report. Bureau of Apprenticeship and Training. Washington, D.C.: U.S. Department of Labor.

1979c   Work Attitudes and Work Experience. The Impact of Attitudes on Behavior. R&D Monograph 60. Washington, D.C.: U.S. Department of Labor.

1982   Women and Apprenticeship: A Study of Programs Designed to Facilitate Women's Participation in the Skilled Trades. Prepared for the Division of Apprenticeship Research and Development by Roslyn D. Kane. Washington, D.C.: U.S. Department of Labor.

U.S. Department of Labor, Labor-Management Services Administration
1980   Women and Private Pension Plans. Washington, D.C.: U.S. Department of Labor.

U.S. Department of Labor, Manpower Administration
1975   Dual Careers. A Longitudinal Study of Labor Market Experience of Women. Volume 3. Manpower Research Monograph No. 21. Washington, D.C.: U.S. Department of Labor.

U.S. Department of Labor, Women's Bureau
1975   1975 Handbook on Women Workers. Bulletin 297. Washington, D.C.: U.S. Department of Labor.
1978   A Working Woman's Guide to Her Rights. Leaflet 55. Washington, D.C.: U.S. Department of Labor.
1980a   A Woman's Guide to Apprenticeship. Pamphlet 17. Washington, D.C.: U.S. Department of Labor.
1980b   Most Women Work Because of Economic Need. Chart. October.
1980c   CETA Journey: A Walk on the Woman's Side. Pamphlet 19. Washington, D.C.: U.S. Department of Labor.
1982a   Equal Employment Opportunity for Women: U.S. Policies. Washington, D.C.: U.S. Department of Labor.
1982b   Employers and Child Care: Establishing Services Through the Workplace. Pamphlet 23. Washington, D.C.: U.S. Department of Labor.
1983   Handbook on Women Workers. Bulletin 298. Washington, D.C.: U.S. Department of Labor.

U.S. Systems Protection Board, Office of Merit Systems Review and Studies
1981   Sexual Harassment in the Federal Workplace: Is It a Problem? Washington, D.C.: U.S. Department of Labor.

Vanek, Joann
1980   "Household work, wage work, and sexual equality." Pp. 275-91 in Sarah F. Berk (ed.), Women and Household Labor. Beverly Hills, Calif.: Sage.

Vetter, Betty M. and Eleanor L. Babco
1984   Professional Women and Minorities—A Manpower Data Resource Service. 5th ed. Washington, D.C.: Scientific Manpower Commission.

Viscusi, W. Kip
1980   "Sex differences in quitting." Review of Economics and Statistics 62(Aug.):388-398.

Vroman, Wayne
1975   "Changes in the labor market position of black men since 1964." Pp. 294-301 in the Proceedings of the Twenty-Seventh Annual Winter Meeting, Industrial Relations Research Association.

Waite, Linda J.
1981   U.S. Women at Work. Population Bulletin 36 (May):1-44.

Waite, Linda J. and Sue Berryman
1984   "Occupational desegregation in CETA programs." Pp. 292-307 in Barbara F. Reskin (ed.),

Sex Segregation in the Workplace: Trends, Explanations, Remedies. Washington, D.C.: National Academy Press.

Waite, Linda J. and Paula M. Hudis
1981   The Development and Maintenance of a Segregated Labor Force: Review, Synthesis, Critique of Recent Research. Unpublished paper prepared for the National Commission for Employment Policy.

Walker, K. and M. Woods
1976   Time Use: A Measure of Household Production of Family Goods and Services. Washington, D.C.: American Home Economics Association.

Wallace, Phyllis A.
1979   "Comment." Pp. 356-61 in Cynthia B. Lloyd, Emily S. Andrews, and Curtis L. Gilroy (eds.), Women in the Labor Market. New York: Columbia University Press.
1982   Women in the Workplace. Boston: Auburn House.

Walsh, Mary Roth
1977   Doctors Wanted: No Women Need Apply. Sexual Barriers in the Medical Profession, 1835-1975. New Haven, Conn.: Yale University Press.

Walshok, Mary Lindenstein
1981a   Blue-Collar Women. Garden City, N.Y.: Anchor Books.
1981b   "Some innovations in industrial apprenticeship at General Motors: introductory comments." Pp. 173-82 in Vernon M. Briggs, Jr. and Felician Foltman (eds.), Apprenticeship Research: Emerging Findings and Future Trends. Ithaca, N.Y.: New York State School of Industrial Relations.

Weil, Mildred W.
1961   "An analysis of the factors influencing married women's actual or planned work participation." American Sociological Review 26(Feb.):91-96.

Welch, Michael and Stephen Lewis
1980   "A mid-decade assessment of sex biases in placement of sociology Ph.D.'s: evidence for contextual variation." American Sociologist 15:120-7.

Westley, Laurie A.
1982   A Territorial Issue: A Study of Women in the Construction Trades. Washington, D.C.: Wider Opportunities for Women.

White, Harrison
1970   Chains of Opportunity. Cambridge, Mass.: Harvard University Press.

White, Kinnard
1967   "Social background variables related to career commitment of women teachers." Personnel and Guidance Journal 45:649-52.

Williams, Gregory
1979   "The changing U.S. labor force and occupational differentiation by sex." Demography 16:73-88.

Williams, Juan
1985a   "EEOC shifting its anti-bias policy." Washington Post, February 13:A1.

1985b   "Rights panel in new uproar." Washington Post, February 26:A15.

1985c   "EEOC rejects comparable worth case." Washington Post, June 18:A1.

Wilms, Welford W.
1974   Public and Proprietary Vocational Training. Berkeley, Calif.: Center for Research and Development in Higher Education.

Wise, L.L., L. Steel, and C. MacDonald
1979   Origins and Career Consequences of Sex Differences in Mathematics Achievement. Report to the National Institute of Education. Palo Alto, Calif.: American Institute for Research.

Witty, Paul A. and Harvey C. Lehman
1930   "Some factors which influence the child's choice of occupations." Elementary School Journal 31:285-91.

Wolf, Wendy C.
1981   "The experience of women in federally sponsored employment and training programs." Pp. 87-130 in National Commission for Employment Policy (ed.), Increasing the Earnings of Disadvantaged Women. Washington, D.C.: National Commission for Employment Policy.

Wolf, Wendy C. and Neil D. Fligstein
1979a   "Sex and authority in the workplace." American Sociological Review 44 (April):235-52.

1979b   "Sexual stratification: differences in power in the work setting." Social Forces 58:94-107.

Wolf, Wendy C. and Rachel Rosenfeld
1978   "Sex structure of occupations and job mobility." Social Forces 56:823-44.

Women Employed
1980   The Status of Equal Employment Opportunity Enforcement: An Assessment of Federal Agency Enforcement Performance—OFCCP and EEOC. Chicago (October).

1982   Damage Report: The Decline of Equal Employment Opportunity Enforcement Under the Reagan Administration. Chicago (November).

Women on Words and Images
1975   Channeling Children: Sex Stereotyping in Prime-Time T.V. Princeton, N.J.

Working Women
1981   In Defense of Affirmative Action: Taking the Profit Out of Discrimination. Cleveland.

Working Women Education Fund
1981   Warning: Health Hazards for Office Workers. Cleveland.

Wright, Michael J.
1979   "Reproduction hazards and 'protective' discrimination." Feminist Studies 5 (Summer):274-85.

Zellner, Harriet
1975   "The determinants of occupational segregation." Pp. 125-45 in Cynthia B. Lloyd (ed.), Sex, Discrimination and the Division of Labor. New York: Columbia University Press.

Zornitsky, Jeffrey and Margaret McNally
1980   Measuring the Effects of CETA on Women: Issues in Assessing Local Program Performance. Paper presented at the Conference on the Experience of Women in Employment and Training Programs held by the National Commission for Employment Policy, Washington, D.C. (September).

Zuckerman, Harriet
1977   Scientific Elite: Nobel Laureates in the United States. New York: Free Press.

APPENDIX A
Contents, *Sex Segregation in the Workplace*

163

APPENDIX B
Biographical Sketches of Committee Members and Staff

ALICE STONE ILCHMAN is president of Sarah Lawrence College. Previously, she was assistant secretary of state for educational and cultural affairs and associate director of the U.S. International Communication Agency. Prior to her government service, she was dean of Wellesley College and a founder of the Wellesley College Center on the Research of Women. Ilchman has a B.A. from Mount Holyoke College and a Ph.D. from the London School of Economics. Her scholarly interests include the economics of education and political and economic development in South Asia. She is chair of the panel on parents and work of the Economic Policy Council at the UN Association, a member of the Smithsonian Council, and on the board of directors of the Markle Foundation.

CECILIA PRECIADO BURCIAGA is associate dean for graduate studies and research at Stanford University. She served previously as assistant provost and also as assistant to the president and adviser to the provost for Chicano affairs. She serves a wide variety of organizations concerned with higher education, the status of women, and the interests of minorities. For example, she has served as a commissioner of the California State Commission on Civil Rights, as cochair of the National Network of Hispanic Women, as a commissioner with the Ford Foundation Study on the Status of Minorities in Higher Education, and as a member of the board of trustees of the Educational Testing Service. She has also consulted for a wide variety of agencies and foundations, as well as taught and conducted research in the field of education. She has a B.A. from California State University at Fullerton and an M.A. in sociology and policy studies from the University of California.

CYNTHIA FUCHS EPSTEIN is professor of sociology at the Graduate Center of the City University of New York and a resident scholar at the Russell Sage Foundation. She has been codirector of a National Institute of Mental Health training grant on the sociology and economics of women and work at the Graduate Center and was codirector of the program in sex roles and social change at Columbia University. She has a B.A. in political science from Antioch College, an M.A. from the New School for Social Research, and a Ph.D. in sociology from Columbia University. She is a member of the American Sociological Association and the Eastern Sociological Society (serving as president in 1984). She was a White House appointee to the Committee on the Economic Roles of Women, advising the Council of Economic Advisers. Her research and writing have centered on women in the professions, business, and politics; on the salience of gender in the maintenance of the social order; and on the impact of social change on men and women in the workplace.

HEIDI I. HARTMANN is study director of both the Committee on Women's Employment and Related Social Issues and the Panel on Technology and Women's Employment at the National Research Council. She previously served as associate executive director of the Commission on Behavioral and Social Sciences and Education and as research associate to the Committee on Occupational Classification and Analysis. In that capacity she coedited (with Donald J. Treiman) the committee's final report on comparable worth. Her research has concentrated on employment issues related to women and minorities, particularly discrimination and internal labor markets, and on political economy and feminist theory. She is the author of several articles on women's economic status; she lectures frequently on that and other topics and has testified in congressional hearings on comparable worth. She has a B.A. from Swarthmore College and M.Ph. and Ph.D. degrees from Yale University, all in economics.

LAWRENCE M. KAHN is professor of economics and labor and industrial relations at the University of Illinois, Urbana-Champaign. His research has encompassed the economics of trade unionism, job search, unemployment and turnover, statistical issues in assessing the extent of labor market discrimination by employers, and issues relating to age discrimination. He received a B.S. in mathematics from the University of Michigan and a Ph.D. in economics from the University of California, Berkeley.

GENE E. KOFKE was director of human resources at American Telephone and Telegraph Company in New York. After a long managerial career in both line and staff roles in an operating subsidiary, he has since 1974 had corporate responsibilities in many major areas of human resources, including management training and development; equal employment and affirmative action; planning and policies; and employee attitudes, motivation, and quality of work life. Most recently he was instrumental in sponsoring nationwide union-management worker participation efforts. He retired from AT&T on December 1, 1984, and is now an independent personnel consultant.

ROBERT E. KRAUT is a social psychologist on the technical staff at Bell Communications Research and an adjunct faculty member in the department of psychology at Princeton University. He has previously held positions at Bell Laboratories, Cornell University, and the University of Pennsylvania. His research has been on the way people judge themselves and others, on interpersonal interaction, and on the social impact of new information technologies. He has a B.A. from Lehigh University and a Ph.D. from Yale University.

JEAN BAKER MILLER is clinical professor of psychiatry at Boston University School of Medicine, a lecturer at Harvard Medical School, and scholar-in-residence at the Stone Center for Developmental Services and Studies at Wellesley College. She has been a lecturer at the London School of Economics at the University of London and an associate at Tavistock Institute and Clinic in London. A psychoanalyst, she is a graduate of Sarah Lawrence College and has an M.D. from Columbia University Medical School. Her professional activities have included membership on the board of trustees of the American Academy of Psychoanalysis, the American Orthopsychiatric Association, and the Elizabeth Stone House; she was principal faculty of the NIMH Staff College course on mental health needs of women. Her publications include books on the psychology of women and numerous professional papers.

ELEANOR HOLMES NORTON is a professor of law at Georgetown University School of Law. She served as the chair of the U.S. Equal Employment Opportunity Commission from 1977 to 1981. Prior to that time she was executive assistant to the mayor of New York City and chair of the Commission on Human Rights (1970-1976); she served as the assistant legal director of the American Civil Liberties Union from 1965 to 1970. A constitutional and civil rights lawyer, she received a B.A. from Antioch College and an M.A. in American studies and an LL.B. from Yale University. She has written numerous journal articles, coauthored a legal text on sex discrimination, and received numerous awards and honors, including the Louise Waterman Wise award.

GARY ORFIELD is professor of political science, public policy, and education at the University of Chicago. He has held positions at the Brookings Institution, Princeton University, the University of Illinois, the University of Virginia, and the U.S. Civil Rights Commission. His work deals primarily with minority rights, Congress, education, and urban policy. He has participated in many civil rights lawsuits and been appointed to advise the courts hearing school desegregation cases in Los Angeles, St. Louis, and San Francisco. He has served as a consultant to numerous federal, state, and local agencies on civil rights issues. He has a B.A. degree from the University of Minnesota and M.A. and Ph.D. degrees from the University of Chicago.

NAOMI QUINN is associate professor of anthropology at Duke University. Her research is on cultural models and their role in the organization of knowledge. Her current work focuses on Americans' cultural model of marriage. She has also taught and written on women's position cross-culturally and has carried out field research in West Africa as well as in the United States. She has a B.A. from Radcliffe College and a Ph.D. from Stanford University, both in anthropology.

BARBARA F. RESKIN is a professor of sociology at the University of Illinois. During the period in which she served as study director for the Committee on Women's Employment and Related Social Issues, she was on leave from the Department of Sociology at Indiana University. Subsequently she was professor of sociology and women's studies at the University of Michigan. Her research focuses on sex stratification, and she has published extensively on sex differences in scientists' careers and, more generally, the operation of scientific reward systems. She has also investigated statistical methods for assessing discrimination, how the courts use statistical evidence of discrimination, and jury decisions in sexual assault cases. Recently she has been studying the concomitants of women's entry in male-dominated occupations. She received B.A., M.A., and Ph.D. degrees in sociology from the University of Washington.

ISABEL V. SAWHILL is a senior fellow at the Urban Institute. She previously served as the Institute's program director for women and family policy (1975-1977) and later as program director for employment policy (1980-1981). Between 1977 and 1980, she was director of the National Commission for Employment Policy—an independent agency responsible for advising the President and Congress on employment and training issues. She has lectured and written extensively on such topics as employment, inflation, income transfers, the changing status of the family, and the role of women in the labor market. She is currently codirecting a large three-year project to assess the social and economic policies of the Reagan administration and their implications for the future. She attended Wellesley College and received B.A. and Ph.D. degrees in economics from New York University.

ROBERT M. SOLOW is institute professor in the Department of Economics at the Massachusetts Institute of Technology, where he has taught since 1949. He has B.A. and Ph.D. degrees from Harvard University. He is an economic theorist whose research and experience have been primarily in macroeconomics. He was senior economist on the Council of Economic Advisers in 1961-1962, and a director of the Boston Federal Reserve Bank from 1976 to 1982 (chairman, 1980-1982). He has also worked on the economics of unemployment and is a member of the board of directors of Manpower Demonstration Research Corporation, which has operated and analyzed federal and state experiments with supported work, youth employment schemes, and work-welfare linkages. He is a member of the National Academy of Sciences and past president of the American Economic Association and the Econometric Society.

LOUISE A. TILLY is professor of history and sociology on the graduate faculty of the New School for Social Research and chair of its Committee on Historical Studies. Previously she taught at the University of Michigan, Michigan State University, and at the École des Hautes Études en Sciences Sociales, Paris. She received an A.B. from Douglass College, an M.A. from Boston University, and a Ph.D. from the University of Toronto. She is treasurer of the Social Science Research Council, a member of the Council of the American Historical Association, and chair of the Panel on Technology and Women's Employment of the National Research Council's Committee on Women's Employment and Related Social Issues. Her current research includes a comparative historical study of the state, class, and the family in French cities; she is completing a monograph on the labor force and the working class in late nineteenth century Milan.

DONALD J. TREIMAN is professor of sociology at the University of California at Los Angeles. His research interests center on the comparative study of social stratification and social mobility. He has written extensively on problems of occupational classification and measurement, including a book analyzing occupational prestige data from 60 countries. Previously he served as study director of the Committee on Occupational Classification and Analysis at the National Research Council, which produced reports on job evaluation, comparable worth, and the *Dictionary of Occupational Titles*; he was also study director of the Committee on Basic Research in the Behavioral and Social Sciences, which produced two volumes on the value and usefulness of basic research. He has a B.A. from Reed College and M.A. and Ph.D. degrees from the University of Chicago, all in sociology.

Index

860023506